Lecture Notes in Computer Science 9306

Commenced Publication in 1973
Founding and Former Series Editors:
Gerhard Goos, Juris Hartmanis, and Jan van Leeuwen

More information about this series at http://www.springer.com/series/7408

Schahram Dustdar · Frank Leymann
Massimo Villari (Eds.)

Service Oriented and Cloud Computing

4th European Conference, ESOCC 2015
Taormina, Italy, September 15–17, 2015
Proceedings

 Springer

Editors
Schahram Dustdar
Distributed Systems Group
TU Wien
Austria

Frank Leymann
Institute of Architecture of Application
    Systems
University of Stuttgart
Baden-Württemberg
Germany

Massimo Villari
Faculty of Engineering
University of Messina
Messina
Italy

ISSN 0302-9743   ISSN 1611-3349   (electronic)
Lecture Notes in Computer Science
ISBN 978-3-319-24071-8   ISBN 978-3-319-24072-5   (eBook)
DOI 10.1007/978-3-319-24072-5

Library of Congress Control Number: 2015948156

LNCS Sublibrary: SL2 - Programming and Software Engineering

Springer Cham Heidelberg New York Dordrecht London

Printed on acid-free paper

Springer International Publishing AG Switzerland is part of Springer Science+Business Media
(www.springer.com)

Preface

Service-oriented computing – together with web services as its major implementation platform – has become the most important paradigm for distributed software development and application for a number of years now. The former ECOWS (European Conference on Web Services) conference series addressed key issues of service-oriented computing, in particular web services, in nine successful conferences until 2011. In the meantime, as services are increasingly used remotely, i.e., in the "cloud", the focus of the conference series has shifted slightly. Accordingly, ECOWS was re-launched in 2012 as the "European Conference on Service-Oriented and Cloud Computing" (ESOCC) in Bertinoro, Italy, addressing the state of the art and practice of service-oriented computing and cloud computing. The second European Conference on Service-Oriented and Cloud Computing, ESOCC 2013, was held in Málaga, Spain, in September 2013. Following the third conference of the series in Manchester, UK, on September 2–4, 2014, this fourth iteration took place in Taormina (Messina), Italy, on September 15–17, 2015.

This volume contains the technical papers presented at the conference. The conference consisted of multiple tracks: Research Track, Industrial Track, and Work-in-Progress (WIP) Track. There were a total of 48 submissions from which 13 papers were selected for the research track (yielding an acceptance rate of 27 %), together with 2 short papers for the WIP track, and 3 papers accepted for the industrial track. The review and selection process was performed rigorously, with each paper being reviewed by at least three PC members (sometimes with the help of additional reviewers).

There were 2 excellent invited talks at the conference, given by Marco Aiello (Professor of Distributed Systems at the University of Groningen) and Eliot Salant (Manager, Virtualization and Systems Management at IBM Haifa Research).

Six workshops were co-located with the conference: the 3rd International Workshop on CLoud for IoT (CLIoT 2015), the 5th International Workshop on Adaptive Services for the Future Internet (WAS4FI 2015), the 2nd Workshop on Seamless Adaptive Multi-cloud Management of Service-based Applications (SeaClouds), the 1st International Workshop on Cloud Adoption and Migration (CloudWay 2015), the 1st Workshop on Federated Cloud Networking (FedCloudNet), and the 1st International Workshop on Digital Enterprise Architecture and Engineering (IDEA). A PhD symposium was held on the same day as the workshops.

All in all, ESOCC 2015 was a successful conference, and we owe its success to many people: all the authors who submitted papers, and those who presented papers at the conference; all the PC members who took part in the review and selection process, as well as the additional reviewers they called on for help; all the invited speakers; the members of the Organizing Committee who chaired the industrial track, work-in-progress track, EU-projects track, workshops, and the PhD symposium, as well as the people who helped organize these events. Last but not least, we are grateful to the Local Organizing Committee for their efficient organization and warm hospitality. To all of you: we say a heart-felt 'Thank you'!

July 2015

Schahram Dustdar
Frank Leymann
Massimo Villari

Organization

ESOCC 2015 was organized by the MDSLab of the University of Messina.

Organizing Committee

General Chair

Massimo Villari — University of Messina, Italy

Program Chairs

Schahram Dustdar — TU Wien, Austria
Frank Leymann — University of Stuttgart, Germany

Industrial Track Chairs

Andreas Roth — SAP, Germany
Stefano De Panfilis — Engineering Ingegneria Informatica S.p.A., Italy

Work-in-Progress Track Chair

Orazio Tomarchio — University of Catania, Italy

EU-Project Track Chairs

Antonio Brogi — University of Pisa, Italy
Silvana Muscella — CloudWATCH Coordinator, Italy

Workshop Chairs

Antonio Celesti — University of Messina, Italy
Philipp Leitner — University of Zurich, Switzerland

Publicity Chair

Cesare Pautasso — University of Lugano, Switzerland

PhD Symposium Chairs

Gianluigi Zavattaro — University of Bologna, Italy
Wolf Zimmermann — University of Halle, Germany

Program Committee

Marco Aiello — University of Groningen, The Netherlands
Farhad Arbab — CWI, The Netherlands
Luciano Baresi — Politecnico di Milano, Italy
Mario Bravetti — University of Bologna, Italy

Antonio Brogi	University of Pisa, Italy
Christoph Bussler	Xtime, Inc., USA
Antonio Celesti	University of Messina, Italy
Javier Cubo	University of Malaga, Spain
Stefano De Panfilis	Engineering Ingegneria Informatica S.p.A., Italy
Flavio De Paoli	University of Milano-Bicocca, Italy
Eric Dubois	CRP Henri Tudor Service Science and Innovation (SSI), Luxembourg
Juergen Dunkel	FH Hannover, Germany
Schahram Dustdar	TU Wien, Austria
Rik Eshuis	Eindhoven Univ. of Technology, The Netherlands
David Eyers	University of Otago, New Zealand
Maria Fazio	University of Messina, Italy
George Feuerlicht	Prague University of Economics, Czech Republic
Claude Godart	Université de Lorraine, France
Michael Goedicke	University of Duisburg-Essen, Germany
Paul Grefen	Eindhoven University of Technology, The Netherlands
Thomas Gschwind	IBM Zurich Research Lab, Switzerland
Martin Henkel	Stockholm University, Sweden
Dionisis Kehagias	CERTH-ITI, Greece
Friederike Klan	Friedrich-Schiller-University Jena, Germany
Ernö Kovacs	NEC Europe Network Labs, Germany
Akhil Kumar	Pennsylvania State University, USA
Birgitta König-Ries	Universität Jena, Germany
Peep Küngas	University of Tartu, Estonia
Patricia Lago	VU University Amsterdam, The Netherlands
Winfried Lamersdorf	University of Hamburg, Germany
Kung-Kiu Lau	University of Manchester, UK
Philipp Leitner	University of Zurich, Switzerland
Frank Leymann	Institute of Architecture of Application Systems, Germany
Heiko Ludwig	IBM Research, USA
Welf Löwe	Linnaeus University, Sweden
Ingo Melzer	DaimlerChrysler Research, Germany
Silvana Muscella	CloudWATCH Coordinator, Italy
Roy Oberhauser	Aalen University, Germany
Guadalupe Ortiz	University of Cádiz, Spain
Claus Pahl	Dublin City University, Ireland
George Papadopoulos	University of Cyprus, Cyprus
Cesare Pautasso	University of Lugano, Switzerland
Willy Picard	Poznań University of Economics, Poland
Ernesto Pimentel	University of Malaga, Spain
Wolfgang Reisig	Humboldt-Universität zu Berlin, Germany
Andreas Roth	SAP, Germany
Ulf Schreier	University of Applied Sciences Furtwangen, Germany
Orazio Tomarchio	University of Catania, Italy

Emilio Tuosto	University of Leicester, UK
Rainer Unland	University of Duisburg-Essen, Germany
Massimo Villari	University of Messina, Italy
Erik Wilde	UC Berkeley, USA
Gianluigi Zavattaro	University of Bologna, Italy
Olaf Zimmermann	HSR FHO Rapperswil, Switzerland
Wolf Zimmermann	University of Halle, Germany
Christian Zirpins	KIT/Seeburger AG, Germany

Local Organization Committee

Dario Bruneo	University of Messina, Italy
Maria Fazio	University of Messina, Italy
Antonio Puliafito	University of Messina, Italy
Marco Scarpa	University of Messina, Italy

Additional Reviewers

Achilleos, Achlleas

Alizadeh Moghaddam, Fahimeh

Arshad, Rehman

Cavallo, Marco

Damiani, Ferruccio

Di Cola, Simone

Di Modica, Giuseppe

Fahmideh, Mehdi

Georgievski, Ilche

Haubeck, Christopher

Ibrahim, Ahmad

Kalinowski, Julian

Me, Gianantonio

Moelle, Andre

Nizamic, Faris

Orsini, Gabriel

Pallis, George

Panarello, Alfonso

Polito, Carmelo

Pourmirza, Shaya

Prüfer, Robert

Qian, Chen

Razavian, Maryam

Soldani, Jacopo

Sürmeli, Jan

Abstracts of Invited Talks

Coordinating the Internet of Things by Service Composition

Marco Aiello

Abstract. Since its emergence, one of the most advertised opportunities offered by service oriented computing has been the possibility of composing loosely coupled services on a per need basis. Services, like Lego pieces, act as modular building blocks which are assembled when a given articulated user request comes and are ready to be reused for other requests. Over the years, the promise has been of reducing recoding and refactoring efforts while achieving scalability, run-time adaptability, and infinite reuse. After reviewing 12 years of personal experiences and research in dynamic service composition, going from initial work on composing trips based on a number of independent travel service operations to the more recent research in home and building automation where services often represent interconnected things in a defined physical space, I will introduce our current efforts in building dynamic service composition frameworks. In particular, I will present the RuG-planner which is able to defer composition decisions to run-time and to seamlessly make revisions in response to a constantly evolving execution environments.

Challenges in Developing an Efficient Cloud Management Framework

Eliot Salant

Abstract. Cloud Computing has developed rapidly over the last ten years with world-wide spending on public and private cloud hosting passing the $32bn. mark this year, and savings to businesses using the cloud are typically stated as better than 30 % due to the clouds ability to better take advantage of economies of scale. Yet, in actuality, in commercial data centres the utilization of resources still remain low. In this talk we will introduce the challenges in managing both the cloud infrastructure and the application more effectively to obtain better utilization of cloud ecosystem, including the challenges involved in multi-tenancy issues in placement of an application, sizing an application, adaptation of the infrastructure to improve workload performance and monitoring analytics of the ecosystem.

Contents

Industry Track

Work-In-Progress Track

Research Track

Decentralized Stream Processing Over Web-Enabled Devices

Masiar Babazadeh[(✉)], Andrea Gallidabino, and Cesare Pautasso

Faculty of Informatics, University of Lugano (USI), Lugano, Switzerland
{masiar.babazadeh,andrea.gallidabino,cesare.pautasso}@usi.ch

Abstract. Thanks to the recent introduction of peer-to-peer communication between browsers with WebRTC, real time processing of streams can now be deployed on browsers in addition to traditional server-side execution environments. In this paper we present the Web Liquid Streams framework for building and executing stream processing topologies capable of gathering data from Web-enabled sensors and process it through JavaScript operators scattered across a peer-to-peer Cloud of computing peers. i) support for arbitrary topologies and data streams, ii) deployment on heterogeneous Web-enabled devices, iii) transparent stream delivery across the WebRTC, WebSockets and ZeroMQ protocols, iv) stateful and stateless operators. WLS takes care of the deployment of the topology on the available resources, while users are only required to implement the operators and describe the topology graph using JSON. The structure of the topology can be dynamically adapted without stopping the stream flowing through it. We present the platform and its programming interface, showing a first evaluation of the system.

1 Introduction

As more and more sensors and smart devices are getting connected to the Internet, an interest has grown in exploring the use of the World Wide Web as platform for such devices. We have witnessed frameworks (i.e., EVRYTHNG [9]) and protocols (i.e., CoAP [13]) proposed to bridge the gap between the real-world and the Web. Some streaming applications have also started to appear [12], but there is still a lack of abstraction and flexibility for building complex stream processing pipelines [8] connecting smart devices to the Web.

To further raise the abstraction level at which stream processing and complex event processing topologies can be built across the Web of Things, in this paper we present a novel peer-to-peer streaming system that makes use of WebRTC and WebSockets to spread stream processing on both Web servers and Web browsers. The Web Liquid Streams (WLS) framework lets developers implement distributed stream processing topologies composed of operators written in JavaScript, the lingua franca of the Web. Thus, it becomes possible to deploy and run stream processing pipelines on any Web-enabled device, from small embedded microprocessors, or mobile smartphones, all the way to large virtualized Cloud computing clusters. The framework can be seen as a way to aggregate

© IFIP International Federation for Information Processing 2015
S. Dustdar et al. (Eds.): ESOCC 2015, LNCS 9306, pp. 3–18, 2015.
DOI: 10.1007/978-3-319-24072-5_1

volunteer computing resources and delivering them as a Platform as a Service (PaaS) Cloud, where stream processing applications built using JavaScript operators can be deployed and executed.

Exploiting such heterogeneous and dynamic execution environment introduces challenges in implementing and organizing the deployment of the stream processing operators. While differences in hardware platforms can be abstracted thanks to JavaScript used to implement the operators, dealing with the deployment constraints of streaming topologies, dynamic changes in the execution environment and fluctuations in the load of the streaming application can become difficult without a solid infrastructure. The WLS framework is able to guarantee the deployment of Topologies taking into account placement constraints on their operators. It also automatically deals with temporary and permanent disconnection errors by performing operator migration and recovery. Additionally, WLS also offers the possibility to alter the structure of the Topology without the need to stop it by offering an interface to add or remove streaming operators or modify their bindings at run time. This helps to adapt the topology semantics to, for example, new sensor/actuator devices that become available.

In [7] we described the RESTful API of the first version of WLS, which supported distributed stream processing only over Web server clusters, while in [6] we have shown a preliminary implementation of a controller infrastructure for the system which deals with the churn of connecting and disconnection Web browsers. In this paper we present the architecture and interface of the second version of WLS, which makes the following novel contributions: First, we show how WLS integrates heterogeneous devices and execution environments (such as Web browsers and Web servers, which may run on Web-enabled microcontrollers, mobile devices and Cloud virtual machines) in a homogeneous environment thanks to the choice of JavaScript as the operator programming language. Second, we discuss how the abstract streaming topology model is mapped to a deployment configuration taking into account multiple types of deployment constraints. Third, we demonstrate the feasibility and expressiveness of the approach through a preliminary set of experiments and case study applications.

The rest of this paper is structured as follows. Section 2 introduces the WLS framework from the developer's perspective, Section 3 is focused on its runtime operation and internal architecture. Section 4 discusses the evaluation of the system. Section 5 presents related work while Section 6 draws our conclusions and illustrates our plans for future work.

2   The WLS Stream Processing Framework

The Web Liquid Streams framework helps developers create stream processing topologies and run them across a peer-to-peer Cloud of connected devices, where they share and make use of shared resources. Developers must install the framework on their servers or microcontrollers and run a server instance of WLS, or they can connect with browsers to an existing WLS instance running to deploy operators and run them on their browsers. This Section describes the

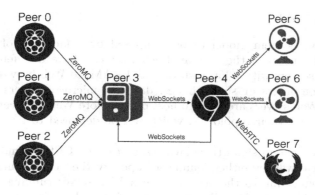

Fig. 1. Example stream deployed across Web servers and Web browsers.

main abstractions provided by WLS and how they can be used to set up arbitrary Topologies of stream Operators written in JavaScript. The basic building blocks to set up and execute a Topology are Peers and Operators.

- Peers are physical hosts where the computation happens. Any Web-enabled device that can run a Web server or a Web browser can become a Peer in the Web Liquid Streams. A Peer can host more than one Operator and stateless Operators can be redundantly deployed on multiple Peers for increased scalability and reliability.
- Operators receive incoming data stream, process its elements one at a time, and forward the results downstream. Each Operator is associated to a JavaScript file, which contains the stream element processing logic.
- The Topology describes how Operators are interconnected in the data stream. It defines an arbitrary graph of operators (nodes) using data flow bindings (edges). The structure of the topology can dynamically change while the stream is running.

The example of figure 1 shows three Peers being running data producer Operators, gathering measurements through sensors. They forward the data to an Operator running on a Web server (Peer 3), which stores the temperature fluctuations over time and forwards them to another Operator running on Peer 4, which decides which actuators have to be started (Peer 5 or Peer 6) and notifies the Operator in Peer 3 about its decision. The data is also forwarded to a visualization Operator (Peer 7) which graphically shows the current status of the running actuators.

Communication links use different protocols (WebSockets, ZeroMQ, WebRTC) which are used to transfer the data stream elements. The developer of the Operators does not need to worry about the actual protocol. Based on the Topology description, it is the Web Liquid Streams runtime's task to physically deploy it on the available resources and take care of abstracting the complexity and heterogeneity of the communication channels.

2.1 System Model

We consider our system model to be composed by a large set of networked Peers owned by users of the system. Each Peer can have a different nature: from big Web servers with a lot of storage and RAM, to Web browsers running on personal computers or smartphones, down to microcontrollers and smart devices. Like Web servers are used to host one or more Web applications, Peers are responsible for their topologies, which can be deployed to be managed on different Peers.

Users of the system share their own resources (i.e., CPU, memory, sensors) in a cooperative way by either joining a Topology (i.e., connecting to a Web address) or connecting to the system from a Web server running on a smart device. WLS takes care of handling the churn of Peers by informing other Peers of new arrivals [10]. In the same way, if a Peer has to leave the network, it will notify all the Peers it knows. If a Topology is making use of the Peer about to leave, the operators running on it are automatically migrated on another available Peer.

Users of the system can take advantage of shared resources by deploying and executing their Topologies on the set of available Peers. By uploading the description of the Topology or manually creating it through the user interface (both command line and graphical interactive monitoring tool), users can start a data stream Topology execution on the shared resources. The system checks if the request to run a Topology can be satisfied with the known resources. If that is the case, it will allocate Operators on the available Peers. More than one Topology can coexist within the peer-to-peer Cloud at the same time, even at the Peer level: a Peer may host different Operators that are part of different Topologies. These slices are dynamic as they can grow or shrink depending on user needs without the need to stop the data stream. Topologies may also be modified at runtime by, for example, adding/removing one or more Operators, resulting in a structural change of semantics of the Topology itself, which will thus affect its end result.

Operators are implemented and managed by the users themselves, thus no QoS guarantee is provided. Application failures resulting from Operators crashing during the execution of the Topology should be handled by the users running the Topology. What WLS ensures is cohesion among the heterogeneous set of resources that become a stream processing platform. As a liquid adapts its shape to the one of its container, the WLS adapts the stream computation to the pool of available resources. When the stream rate or in general the stream resource demand increases, new resources are allocated. These will be de-allocated and consolidated once the stream resource demand decreases.

2.2 Topology Description

The topology structure can be built on the fly by adding or removing Operators to an already executing stream. For convenience, it is possible to capture the configuration of a topology and represent it using JSON. The Topology description includes information about all Operators and how they are bound together. Operators can be associated with optional deployment constraints, which are used by the runtime to select a suitable Peer for running them.

Topologies must have an `id` that identifies them, a list of `operators` and a list of `bindings`. The Operators must have an `id` attribute and a link with the URL of the corresponding implementation `script`, and an optional `deploy` field which imposes deployment constraints. For example, it can specify a Peer where the Operator has to be deployed or a list of sensors that a Peer must have in order to host the Operator. If the `deploy` field is not specified, the Operator can run in any available Peer.

The list of bindings instead describes how operators are connected and which sending algorithm (Round Robin vs. Broadcast) is used when multiple operators are bound to the same upstream producer. Round Robin is used for sharding the stream across multiple operators, while Broadcast is intended to be used with multiple consumer operators that receive their copy of the stream.

2.3   Operator Script API

Operators are written in plain JavaScript and define the data processing logic. In the following example we demonstrate how to use the WLS API to write scripts which are then executed by the Operators in a simple home automation system application. The streaming application is composed by four Operators: the first one runs on microcontrollers that have access to a temperature sensor, the second one runs on servers, the third one Web browsers, while the fourth one runs on actuators that can modify the temperature in the house.

```javascript
var k = require('wls.js');
setInterval(function(){
    getTemperature(function(temp, sensor_id){
        k.send({
        "temperature"  : temp,
        "id"           : sensor_id,
        "timestamp"    : new Date()
        });
    });
}, 1000);
```

Listing 1.1. Example producer script

Listing 1.1 shows a producer script that forwards every second temperature sensor readings from the `getTemperature` function. The function reads the last measured temperature from the sensor API. The callback of the function wraps the data received into an object carrying the current timestamp and the sensor identifier and forwards it downstream using the `k.send()` function.

```
var k = require('wls.js');

//initialize operator state
k.createOperator(function(temp_data) {
    //store the received data: temperature, id, timestamp
    k.db_store("temperatures", temp_data);

    //get the last 1000 temperatures stored for that sensor
        id
    var average_temperature = avg( k.db_get("temperatures",
        temp_data.id, 1000) );

    //forwards the average
    k.send({
        "average" : average_temperature,
        "room_id" : temp_data.id
    });

}).start();
```

Listing 1.2. Example filter script

Listing 1.2 shows what the Web server does upon receiving the data from the sensors. First, it stores the observed temperature, computes an average over the last seen data for the room and forwards the average and the room id to the following Operator.

```
var k = require('wls.js');

k.createOperator(function(variation) {
    //get the temperature setpoint for a given room
    var setpoint = k.db_get("setpoint", temp_data.id);
    var threshold = k.db_get("threshold", temp_data.id);

    //if the temperature has to be changed, forward commands
        downstream
    if(abs(variation.average - setpoint) > threshold){
        k.send({
        "start"   : true,
        "room_id" : temp_data.id
        });
    }
    else //[...]
}).start();
```

Listing 1.3. Decision making Operator

Listing 1.3 shows a simple decision making Operator that receives objects containing an average of the last measured temperatures for a given room id. The Operator compares the received average to the setpoint and forwards a message to the actuator, which will either start or stop to reach the desired temperature.

The example can be further extended by adding sensors that notify human presence and describing new setpoints for rooms with or without people at which time of the day or night. Moreover, operators featuring machine learning could be used to detect and predict inhabitants behavior patterns (e.g., heat the bathroom before a shower event).

There is no constraint on the data structure of the messages exchanged along a Topology, as long as they can be serialized into JSON strings. The callback function and the `send` function handle deserialization and serialization automatically, allowing the developer of the Operator script to work directly with JavaScript objects.

3 The WLS Runtime: Usage and Architecture

3.1 Starting and Handling a Topology

Before starting a Topology, the user has to upload the Topology description file and the corresponding Operator scripts to the runtime using its API. The Web Liquid Streams framework runtime is able to spread the Operators across the available Peers following the instructions of the JSON topology description file. From the command line interface, it is sufficient to type `exec topology.js` where `topology.js` is the Topology description file. This will deploy and initialize each Operator and start the flow of the data stream.

A Topology may also be built on the fly by running operators with the command `run script.js peer_id` that runs a script on an appointed Peer (if no Peer is specified, it will be run on the most suited one [6]). To bind the Operators it is sufficient to write `bind op_from op_to` where `op_from` and `op_to` are the IDs of the two Operators to be bound.

Operations that can be executed on the Topology through the command line interface include stopping an Operator (`stop op_id`), unbind two Operators (`unbind op_from op_to`) and migrate an Operator on another Peer (`migrate op_id peer_id`).

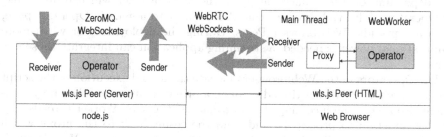

Fig. 2. Web Liquid Streams Runtime Architecture

3.2   Runtime Architecture

The WLS architecture presents two main components: one runs on servers (i.e., smart devices), while the other runs on Web browsers (i.e., smart mobile phones).

Node.JS Peer Architecture. Operators on the Node.JS Peer architecture spawn Node.JS processes to handle the incoming work. This process helps parallelizing the execution of the Operator's work, by spreading it on child processes. These child process are provided with an address and a port, thus they are directly connected to each other through ZeroMQ sockets according to the Topology bindings. The Operator takes care of adding or removing child processes in order to solve bottlenecks or free resources when possible. If the Peer hosting the Operator reaches a full CPU usage, the Peer will find another one to run an extra parallel instance of the Operator, thus solving the bottleneck.

Figure 2 (left) describes the Node.JS Peer. The grey arrows represent incoming and outgoing data streams. The Peer may host more than one Operator, for which multiple parallel instances can be started as needed. Hosted Operators may belong to different Topologies. Each parallel operator runs in its independent Node.JS process and is directly connected through the appropriate stream channel to the upstream and downstream operators. For what concerns communication to or from a Web browser, we use an adapter that can transparently perform the WebSocket-ZeroMQ (and vice-versa) protocol conversion.

Browser Peer Architecture. The architecture of the client-side WLS has been implemented using plain JavaScript with WebSockets and WebRTC. The Peer and Operator code had to be adapted to run in Web browsers. To run an Operator, a Web browser has to connect to a specific path (that is, performs a GET request) in a Web server which is running an instance of WLS. The Web server Peer updates the list of known Peers and updates the known Peers in the network, making the Web browser a new available Peer in the peer-to-peer Cloud. The path to which the Web browser has to connect is defined on the Topology description file. This path is also associated with a given Operator, thus depending on the connection path, the Web browser will execute different Operators. The Web browser can also connect to a generic Operator page, which accepts idle Web browser Peers. During the deployment or when more computational power is needed, a streaming application can integrate those idle Peers.

The Operators in the Web browser delegate the actual execution of the script to a dedicated Web Worker thread through a proxy component. The proxy component dispatches the incoming stream elements, the Web Worker threads execute the function to process it, and send the result back to the proxy which is in charge of forwarding it downstream. The number of active Web Workers can increase or decrease depending on the load fluctuations of the data stream. Figure 2 (right) graphically shows the process including the receiver and the sender components, which are WebRTC sockets that handle communication.

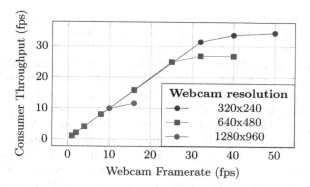

Fig. 3. Webcam resolution and framerate

Some Web browsers do not implement WebRTC yet, thus they would not be able to run an instance of the WLS Operator on them. We implemented a fallback system which is able to switch protocol to WebSockets and make the communication pass through the Web server in order to still being able to use the connected Web browser.

4 Evaluation

We executed many experiments with WLS with different use case scenarios and deployment configurations. The current status of the implementation supports Google Chrome and Mozilla Firefox as Web browsers and Raspberry Pi as microcontroller. We also tested a deployment on Arduino through Noduino. A more lightweight version for the Tessel.IO microcontroller is being developed as we are writing this paper. In this section, we first present the results of an experiment involving Web browsers, sensors and servers in two different deployment with a variable workload scenario. The experiment shows the throughput achieved by the Topology in terms of messages per second. Then, we compare the performance of a Topology when executed on a centralized deployment on a multi-core server vs. a decentralized deployment on Web Browsers running on laptops.

4.1 Variable Workload Use Case Scenario

In this use case scenario we show how the system performs when the data throughput of the stream changes. In the first example, by increasing the throughput at the producer Operator, we increase the computational effort on the Topology and show how the system performs by parallelising on a set of finite resources. On the second example, we increase and decrease the throughput of the produces to stress the Topology constantly.

The first experiment features a linear Topology composed by three Operators. The first Operator has a deployment constraint and has to be run on a machine with a webcam. It forwards the webcam feed to a filter Operator, which applies a negative filter on the video feed and forwards the result to the final Operator which has a Web browser deployment constraint and shows the aggregated feeds of the Webcams. For simplicity, we run the Topology on three machines only, one for each Operator. The first Operator runs on a Raspberry Pi with a webcam connected. The second Operator runs on MacBook Pros i7 (2.3GHz, 4 cores) with 16GB RAM on Google Chrome (OSX) version 37, while the last one on an iPhone 5S running Chrome (iOS) version 40. Data passes through WiFi with 30mb/s of maximum bandwidth. The WiFi is public, so external interference may be present. To increase the effort on the Topology, we increase the framerate of the webcam feed, thus increasing the workload on the filter Operator. We performed this evaluation with three different Webcam resolutions: 320x240, 640x480 and 1280x960 pixels.

The results (Figure 3) show that for a small webcam feed (320x240) we can reach a throughput of around 35 to 40 frames per seconds. By further increasing the frame rate, the system saturates the filter Operator (that is, Web Workers spawned to parallelise the execution saturated the CPU of the MacBook Pro). By doubling the resolution of the images, as expected, we see that the maximum performance that can be reached degrades in both cases (640x480 and 1280x960). It is important to notice that the parallelisation is executed only on the filter Operator, the system considers the Raspberry Pi and the smartphone too thin to be able to sustain the filter execution as well.

In the second experiment, the Topology again makes use CPU-intensive Operators that can be parallelized to process an incoming data stream with a variable data rate. This will require to use more or less of the available computing resources, depending on the actual workload. More concretely, the Topology takes as input a stream of tweets (producer), encrypts them using triple DES, and stores the encrypted result on a server (consumer). The deployment is as follows: the producer runs on the MacBook Pro i7, running the server (Node.JS) version of WLS, the encryption operator runs on a single server with twenty-four Intel Xeon 2 GHz cores running Ubuntu 12.04 with Node.JS version 0.10.15, while the consumer runs on a machine with four Intel Core 2 Quad 3GHz processors, running the same versions of Ubuntu and Node.JS.

We focused on two different workloads: the slow workload sending 40 messages per second and the fast workload sending 500 messages per second. These two workloads are alternated in a transition frequency passing from the slow workload to the fast workload every 5000 messages.We expect to see the Topology throughput to follow the fluctuating input rate of the tweets by parallelizing the work on the big machine where the bottleneck is (encryption operator).

Figure 4 shows the topology throughput of the experiment.We can see (top graph) that the fluctuating input rate (Producer) is well sustained by the system, which adapts the operator deployment configuration to deal with the increasing rate of messages. We can see in the bottom graph, how WLS parallelised the execution by allocating more Node.JS processes on the machine and de-allocating them as the load decreased.

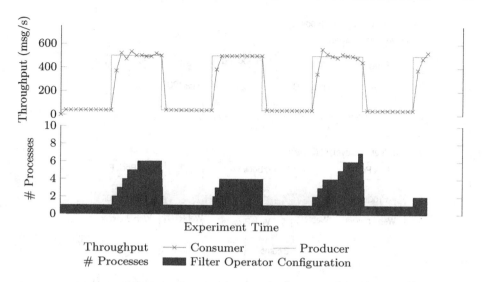

Fig. 4. Throughput and Topology deployment configuration dynamics during the workload transition experiment.

4.2 Centralized vs. Peer-to-Peer

In this evaluation we show two different deployments of the same Topology, one on a single, big machine, and one distributed on different smaller machines (Web browsers). This evaluation shows that even deploying a Topology on a very powerful machine, by using enough weak machines we can achieve a better performance. This claim turns out to be useful when trying to minimize the costs of deployment over Cloud servers (lower CPU usage means lower costs) in favour of a sub-Cloud of volunteer machines.

In this experiment we assess the overall throughput of the stream, i.e., the time taken to exchange a fixed number of stream items sent through the same Topology, deployed in two configurations. We have chosen to analyse the simplest Topology with a toy example in order to reduce complexity and obtain repeatable results about the deployment differences of a single Operator.

The Topology is a very simple pipeline composed by three Operators. The first Producer Operator generates a finite list of numbers which are sent one at a time downstream with a fixed data rate of 10 messages per second. The second Operator (CPU-bound filter) computes the number of prime numbers between 0 and the received number, then forwards the result to the third Consumer Operator which stores the result together with some performance metrics. The amount of data exchanged along the stream is minimal (one integer) thus reducing the impact of the network communication. The number sent by the Producer determines the time taken by the filter in computing the solution, a CPU-intensive operation. The stream begins with a relatively small number (easy work for the filter) and then switches it progressively to a bigger number (hard work for the

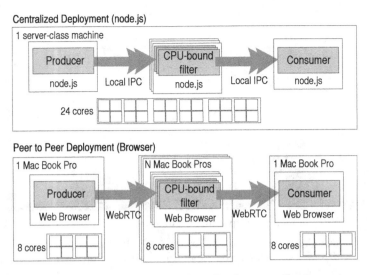

Fig. 5. Centralized vs. Peer-to-Peer Deployment Configurations

filter). This will force the elastic parallelisation of the execution of the filter Operator up to the limit of the server machine or the peer-to-peer Cloud of available machines. We keep track of the time taken to complete the processing of the entire stream of messages as well as of the delay incurred when processing each message through the entire pipeline.

Figure 5 shows the two deployment approaches compared in this evaluation. The centralized approach is deployed on a single server with twenty-four Intel Xeon 2 GHz cores running Ubuntu 12.04 with Node.JS version 0.10.15. The peer-to-peer approach instead is deployed only on Web browsers: we used Google Chrome v37 on MacBook Pros i7 (2.3GHz, 8 cores) with 16GB RAM.

Figure 6b shows the average delay of 10000 messages passing through the Topology. We compare the performance of the Node.JS server-side deployment on a single server-class machine vs. the behavior of the Browser only config-uration on the Mac Book Pros. We can see that by increasing the number of Peers the system can increase the number of parallel filter operators and further reduce the message processing delay. This shows that the WLS framework can effectively take advantage of additional resources as they appear to improve the performance of the pipeline, whose workload can be shared among multiple peers according to their processing power.

Figure 6a shows a comparison of the throughput of the two deployments (Web browser and Node.JS) for a different number of parallel filter operators, that are distributed on all available machines. The throughput is measured at the consumer and is shown relative to the throughput of the producer operator, to indicate how well can the Topology keep up with the incoming stream data rate. The results indicate that given the same degree of parallelism, the deployment on Web browsers obtains a slightly better performance by almost reaching the

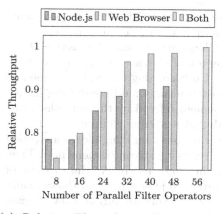

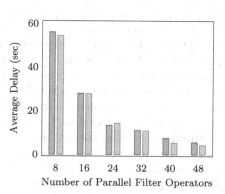

(a) Relative Throughput obtained with different deployment configurations having a larger pool of peers

(b) Average delay obtained with different deployment configurations having a larger pool of peers

same throughput of the producer. The best result was obtained for 56 parallel filters, where the Topology was deployed on both browsers and Node.JS servers. This gives a good indication of the value of the peer-to-peer Cloud concept, whereby the WLS framework can scale out a stream processing computation using opportunistic resources provided through Web browsers as well as relying on more stable foundation of server-side resources. Given an adequate amount of resources, deployment can happen on browsers only without performance loss, thus avoiding incurring in related costs of renting the corresponding amount of Cloud computing infrastructure to run the Web servers.

5   Related Work

Since the introduction of WebRTC, many browser-to-browser streaming applications have emerged. It has become possible to videoconference without the need of a central server [14], share content as in a peer-to-peer application [15] while interacting with a Web server by the means of WebSocket [16]. Still, there is a gap between the low-level messaging abstraction provided by WebSockets, the data channel of WebRTC and what is needed to conveniently build peer-to-peer streaming applications that can be deployed on a Cloud of Web-enabled devices.

Peer-to-peer, decentralized Cloud architectures have recently been recognized as an effective alternative to centralized Cloud computing infrastructures. In [4,5], the authors proposed the design and implementation of a general-purpose framework to support distributed applications running over a very large and unreliable set of networked computing devices. We also adopted the concepts of application suite description and slicing. Like our Topologies and their constraints, the application suite describes the constraints a subcloud must have in order to be spread across the peer-to-peer Cloud. The slicing idea is embedded in the middleware component responsible for assigning the right portion of the available Cloud to the application, taking care of satisfying its requirements without using too many unnecessary resources.

A streaming processing system for the Cloud making use of sensors is Curracurrong Cloud [12] which was developed on top of Curracurrong [11], a streaming platform for Wireless Sensor Networks. Curracurrong Cloud is designed to be deployed in large distributed clusters hosted using Cloud computing infrastructure, while maintaining the WSN deployment offered by the core platform.

Storm [1] (2011), an open source distributed real-time computational environment originally developed by Twitter. Storm's basic building blocks are called spouts (producing a data stream) and bolts (receiving streamed elements). They are used to produce and manipulate streaming data much like the concept of Operator in WLS. They can be seen as MapReduce jobs which can theoretically run forever. Spouts and bolts are executed inside Workers, physical JVMs executing a subset of the topology. Another similar approach is Discretized Streams (D-Streams) [17] (2012), a stream programming model that provides a set of transformations which treat the stream as a series of batch computations of small time intervals (reducing the latency of the jobs as much as possible).

MillWheel [2] (2013) is a Google framework that helps user build low-latency data-processing applications at large-scale without the need to think about how to deploy it in a distributed execution environment. The WLS runtime works at the same level of abstraction, but targets a more diverse, volunteer computing-style set of execution resources.

6   Conclusions

Stream processing is an important technology that is found in many real-time data processing scenarios. Its importance is likely to grow with the rise of the Web of Things, making it easy to process a wide variety of sensor data streams. These are typically uploaded to the Cloud for processing and storage, while the results are then downloaded to Web browsers for visualization that need to be updated in real-time.

In this paper we presented the Web Liquid Streams (WLS) framework. Developers can use it to create Topologies of connected Operators through which a data stream passes, going from data producers to data consumers. Thanks to the widespread adoption of the lingua franca of the Web, JavaScript, WLS is able to deploy operators across many heterogeneous devices, abstracting the complexity of implementing Operators and connecting them as they are deployed on Web-enabled execution environments (Web servers and Web browsers). These range from small devices (such as Arduino and Raspberry Pi), mobile phones and tablets (which run powerful mobile Web browsers), as well as traditional desktop and server class machines (which run both Web browsers and Web servers).

In this way, on the one hand we contribute an stream-centric abstraction for Web developers, while on the other we offer the capability of running a stream processing application on almost any kind of Web-enabled device without the need of installing additional software on them and without depending on a centralized Cloud infrastructure. We showed through a preliminary evaluation how the throughput of WLS Operators deals with increasing stream rate and message size. We also demonstrated that WLS can use the most appropriate communication protocol to stream data between peers and compared the corresponding overhead.

We are currently working at improving the parallelism of Operators and integrating more types of Web-enabled smart devices in the framework. We are also studying how to optimize the decision whether Operators should be deployed on Web browsers vs. Web servers and how to take into account the network latency between different Peers to determine the best possible location for an Operator. We plan to further studying the robustness, scalability and performance of WLS by porting some stream processing benchmarks to JavaScript [3], and by using WLS to build more complex Topologies in real-world use case scenarios.

References

1. Storm: distributed and fault-tolerant realtime computation (2011). http://storm-project.net/
2. Akidau, T., et al.: Millwheel: Fault-tolerant stream processing at internet scale. Proc. VLDB Endow. **6**(11), 1033–1044 (2013)
3. Arasu, A., et al: Linear road: a stream data management benchmark. In: Proc. of the Thirteenth International Conference on Very Large Data Bases, VLDB 2004, vol. 30, pp. 480–491. VLDB Endowment (2004)
4. Babaoglu, O., et al: Design and implementation of a p2p cloud system. In: Proc. of SAC 2012
5. Babaoglu, O., Jelasity, M., Kermarrec, A.-M., Montresor, A., van Steen, M.: Managing clouds: A case for a fresh look at large unreliable dynamic networks. SIGOPS Oper. Syst. Rev. **40**(3), 9–13 (2006)
6. Babazadeh, M., Gallidabino, A., Pautasso, C.: Liquid stream processing across web browsers and web servers. In: Cimiano, P., Frasincar, F., Houben, G.-J., Schwabe, D. (eds.) ICWE 2015. LNCS, vol. 9114, pp. 24–33. Springer, Heidelberg (2015)
7. Babazadeh, M., Pautasso, C.: A RESTful API for controlling dynamic streaming topologies. In: 5th International Workshop on Web APIs and RESTful Design (WS-REST 2014), Seoul, Korea, April 2014
8. Cugola, G., Margara, A.: Processing flows of information: From data stream to complex event processing. ACM Comput. Surv. **44**(3), 15:1–15:62 (2012)
9. Guinard, D.: A Web of Things Application Architecture - Integrating the Real-World into the Web. PhD thesis, ETH Zurich, Zurich, Switzerland, August 2011
10. Jelasity, M., Montresor, A., Babaoglu, O.: Gossip-based aggregation in large dynamic networks. ACM Trans. Comput. Syst. **23**(3), 219–252 (2005)
11. Kakkad, V., Attar, S., Santosa, A.E., Fekete, A., Scholz, B.: Curracurrong: a stream programming environment for wireless sensor networks. Softw. Pract. Exper. **44**(2), 175–199 (2014)
12. Kakkad, V., et al: Curracurrong cloud: Stream processing in the cloud. In: Proc. of ICDEW, pp. 207–214, March 2014

13. Kovatsch, M.: CoAP for the web of things: from tiny resource-constrained devices to the web browser. In: Adj. Proc. of UbiComp, pp. 1495–1504 (2013)
14. Rodríguez, P., et al: Advanced videoconferencing services based on WebRTC. In: Proc. of ICWBC, pp. 180–184, July 2012
15. Vogt, C., et al: Content-centric user networks: WebRTC as a path to name-based publishing. In: Proc. of ICNP, October 2013
16. Vogt, C., Werner, M.J., Schmidt, T.C.: Leveraging webRTC for P2P content distribution in web browsers. In: Proc. of ICNP, October 2013
17. Zaharia, M., et al: Discretized streams: an efficient and fault-tolerant model for stream processing on large clusters. In: Proc. of USENIX HotCloud 2012

Modelling and Analysing
Cloud Application Management

Antonio Brogi, Andrea Canciani, and Jacopo Soldani$^{(\boxtimes)}$

Department of Computer Science, University of Pisa, Pisa, Italy
soldani@di.unipi.it

Abstract. Managing complex applications over heterogeneous clouds is one of the emerging problems in the cloud era. The OASIS Topology and Orchestration Specification for Cloud Applications (TOSCA) aims at solving this problem by providing a language to describe and manage complex cloud applications in a portable and vendor-agnostic way. TOSCA permits to define an application as an orchestration of components, whose types can specify states, requirements, capabilities and management operations — but not how they interact with each other.

In this paper we propose a simple extension of TOSCA that permits to specify the behaviour of management operations and their relations with states, requirements, and capabilities. We show how such an extension permits to automate various useful analyses, like determining the validity of a management plan, which are its effects, or which plans reach certain system configurations. Finally, we illustrate a proof-of-concept graphical interface that permits to edit and analyse management protocols in TOSCA applications.

1 Introduction

Cloud computing has revolutionized IT, by allowing to run on-demand distributed software systems at a fraction of the cost of just a few years ago. However, due to the lack of standardization, how to flexibly manage applications over heterogeneous clouds is still an open issue.

In this scenario, OASIS released TOSCA (*Topology and Orchestration Specification for Cloud Applications* [15,17]), a standard to support the automated management of complex cloud-based applications. TOSCA provides a modelling language to describe, in a portable and vendor-agnostic way, a cloud application and its management. An application is defined by instantiating component types, and by connecting a component's requirements to the capabilities of other components. Its management can then be described by orchestrating the operations of its components (like *configure*, *install*, *start*, etc.) into workflow plans.

Unfortunately, the current version of TOSCA [15] does not permit to specify the behaviour of a cloud application's management operations. More precisely, it is not possible to describe the order in which the management operations of

---

Work partly supported by the European project SeaClouds (EU-FP7-ICT-610531).

S. Dustdar et al. (Eds.): ESOCC 2015, LNCS 9306, pp. 19–33, 2015.
DOI: 10.1007/978-3-319-24072-5_2

a component must be invoked, nor how those operations depend on the requirements or how they affect the capabilities of that component (and hence the requirements of other components they are connected to). This implies that the verification of whether a management plan is valid can only be performed manually, with a time-consuming and error-prone process.

In this paper we first propose a simple extension of TOSCA that permits to specify the behaviour of management operations and their relations with states, requirements, and capabilities. We define how to describe the management protocols of TOSCA components by means of finite state machines whose states and transitions are associated with conditions on the component's requirements and capabilities. Intuitively speaking, the objective of those conditions is to define the consistency of component's states and to constrain the executability of component's operations to the satisfaction of their requirements.

We then show how to the proposed extension of TOSCA permits to automate various analyses of management protocols, like determining whether management plans are valid, which are their effects, or which plans permit to reach certain system configurations.

Finally, we illustrate the feasibility of our approach by describing a proof-of-concept web-based application that permits to edit the management protocols of TOSCA application components, and to analyse plans describing the management of a whole application.

The rest of the paper is organized as follows. Sect. 2 introduces TOSCA, while Sect. 3 illustrates a scenario motivating the need for an explicit, machine-readable representation of management protocols. Sect. 4 describes how TOSCA can be extended to model the behaviour of management operations, and how the proposed modelling permits to automate different types of analysis. Sect. 5 illustrates our proof-of-concept. Related work is discussed in Sect. 6, while some concluding remarks are drawn in Sect. 7.

2   Background: TOSCA

TOSCA [15] is an emerging standard aimed at enabling the specification of portable cloud applications and the automation of their management. To do so, TOSCA provides a modelling language to describe the structure of a cloud application as a typed topology graph, and its tasks as plans. More precisely, each cloud application is represented as a `ServiceTemplate` (Fig. 1), consisting of a mandatory `TopologyTemplate` and of optional management `Plans`. Generic type definitions are also contained in the document defining the `ServiceTemplate` as they are referred to by the elements in its topology.

The `TopologyTemplate` is a typed directed graph describing the structure of the composite cloud application. Its nodes (`NodeTemplates`) model the application components, while its edges (`RelationshipTemplates`) model the relations among those components. `NodeTemplates` and `RelationshipTemplates` are typed by means of `NodeTypes` and `RelationshipTypes`, respectively. A `NodeType` defines (i) the observable properties of an application component, (ii)

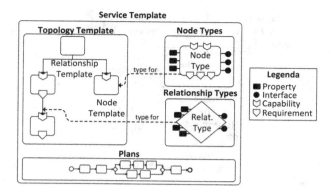

Fig. 1. TOSCA `ServiceTemplate`.

the possible states of its instances, (iii) its requirements, (iv) the capabilities it offers to satisfy other components' requirements, and (v) its management operations. `RelationshipTypes` describe the properties of relationships occurring among components. Syntactically, properties are described by `PropertiesDefinition`, states by `InstanceStates`, requirements by `RequirementDefinitions` (of certain `RequirementTypes`), capabilities by `CapabilityDefinitions` (of certain `CapabilityTypes`), and operations by `Interfaces` and `Operations`.

Plans instead allow to describe the management aspects of a `ServiceTemplate`. More precisely, each `Plan` is a workflow orchestrating the management `Operations` offered by the application components to address (part of) the management of the whole cloud application[1].

3   Motivating Scenario

Consider two utility web services, *Translator* and *Convertor*, and suppose that we want to manage them on a TOSCA-compliant cloud platform. After describing the services in TOSCA, we have to specify the third-party application components needed to properly host them. For instance, we may indicate that they have to run on an *Apache* server installed on a *Debian* operating system, which in turn runs on an *VMWare* virtual machine. Fig. 2 illustrates the resulting `Topology-Template`, according to the graphical notation introduced by Winery [14]. For the sake of readability, we focus only on the lifecycle interfaces [8] of each `Node-Type` instantiated in the topology (i.e., the interfaces containing the operations to install, configure, start, stop, and uninstall a component).

Suppose now that we want to specify the deployment of the *Translator* and *Convertor* services by writing a TOSCA `Plan`. It is worth noting that, since TOSCA does not include any representation of the management protocols of (third-party) `NodeTypes`, one may produce invalid `Plans`. For instance, while Fig. 3 illustrates three seemingly valid BPMN `Plans`, only (c) is a valid `Plan`.

---

[1] A more detailed and self-contained introduction to TOSCA can be found in [8].

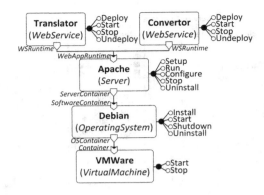

Fig. 2. Motivating scenario.

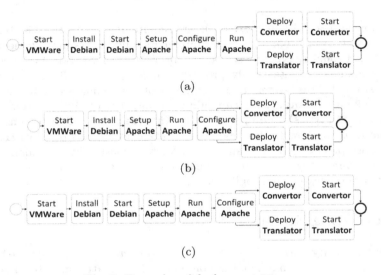

Fig. 3. Examples of deployment `Plans`.

`Plan` (a) is not valid since *Apache*'s `Configure` operation cannot be executed before *Apache* itself is running, while `Plan` (b) is not valid since *Apache* cannot be installed if the *Debian* operating system is not running.

While the validity of `Plans` can be manually verified, this is a time-consuming and error-prone process. In order to enable the automated verification of the validity of `Plans`, TOSCA needs to be extended with an explicit, machine-readable representation of `NodeTypes`' management protocols.

4   Management Protocols for Cloud Applications

TOSCA `NodeTypes` can be described by means of their states, requirements, capabilities, and management operations, but there is currently no way to specify how management operations affect states, how operations or states depend on requirements, or which capabilities are concretely provided in a certain state.

In this section we propose an extension of TOSCA that permits to specify the behaviour of management operations and their relations with states, requirements, and capabilities.

4.1 Definition of Management Protocols

Let N be a TOSCA NodeType, and let us denote its states, requirements, capabilities, and management operations with S_N, R_N, C_N, and O_N, respectively.

We want to describe whether and how the management operations of N depend on (i) other operations of the same node and/or on (ii) operations of other nodes providing the capabilities that satisfy the requirements of N.

(i) The first kind of dependencies can be easily described by specifying the relationship between states and management operations of N. More precisely, to describe the order with which the operations of N can be executed, we introduce a transition relation τ specifying whether an operation o can be executed in a state s, and which state is reached by executing o in s.

(ii) The second kind of dependencies can be described by associating transitions and states with (possibly empty) sets of requirements to indicate that the corresponding capabilities are assumed to be provided. More precisely, the requirements associated with a transition t specify which are the capabilities that must be offered to allow the execution of t. The requirements associated with a state of a NodeType N specify which are the capabilities that must (continue to) be offered by other nodes in order for N to (continue to) work properly.

To complete the description, we also associate to each state s of a NodeType N the capabilities provided by N in s.

Definition 1. *Let $N = \langle S_N, R_N, C_N, O_N, \mathcal{M}_N \rangle$ be a* NodeType, *where S_N, R_N, C_N, and O_N are the finite sets of its states, requirements, capabilities, and management operations. $\mathcal{M}_N = \langle \overline{s}_N, \rho_N, \chi_N, \tau_N \rangle$ is the* management protocol *of N, where*

- *$\overline{s}_N \in S_N$ is the initial state,*
- *ρ_N is a function indicating, for each state $s \in S_N$, which conditions on requirements must hold (i.e., $\rho_N(s) \subseteq R_N$),*
- *χ_N is a function indicating which capabilities of N are concretely offered in a state $s \in S_N$ (i.e., $\chi_N(s) \subseteq C_N$), and*
- *$\tau_N \subseteq S_N \times 2^{R_N} \times O_N \times S_N$ is a set of quadruples modelling the transition relation (i.e., $\langle s, H, o, s' \rangle \in \tau_N$ means that in state s, and if condition H holds, o is executable and leads to state s').*

Syntactically, to represent $\mathcal{M}_N$ we slightly extend the syntax[2] for describing a TOSCA NodeType. First, we enrich the description of InstanceStates by

---

[2] A more detailed syntax for extended NodeTypes can be found in [5].

introducing the nested elements `ReliesOn` and `Offers`. `ReliesOn` defines ρ_N by enabling the association between states and conditions on requirements, while `Offers` defines χ_N by indicating the capabilities offered in a state. Furthermore, we introduce the element `ManagementProtocol`, to specify the `InitialState` $\bar{s}$ of a protocol, as well as the `Transitions` defining its transition relation τ_N.

The management protocols of the `NodeTypes` in our motivating scenario (Sect. 3) are shown in Fig. 4, where $\mathcal{M}_{WS}$ is the management protocol for Web-Services, $\mathcal{M}_S$ for `Server`, $\mathcal{M}_{OS}$ for `OperatingSystem`, and $\mathcal{M}_{VM}$ for Virtual-Machine. Consider for instance the management protocol $\mathcal{M}_S$ of the `Server` No-

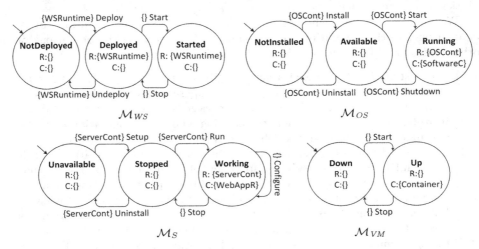

Fig. 4. Management protocols of the `NodeTypes` in our motivating scenario.

deType, typing a *Tomcat* server. Its states S_S are `Unavailable` (initial), `Stopped`, and `Working`, the only requirement in R_S is `ServerContainer`, the only capability in C_S is `WebAppRuntime`, its management operations O_S are `Setup`, `Uninstall`, `Run`, `Stop`, and `Configure`. States `Unavailable` and `Stopped` are not associated with any requirement or capability. State `Working` instead specifies that the capability corresponding to the `ServerContainer` requirement must be provided in order for `Server` to (continue to) work properly. State `Working` also specifies that `Server` provides the `WebAppRuntime` capability when in such state. Finally, all transitions (but those involving operations `Stop` and `Configure`) bind their executability to the availability of the capability that satisfies the `ServerContainer` requirement.

Management protocols (as per Def. 1) allow operations to have non-deterministic effects (e.g., a state may have two outgoing transitions corresponding to the same operation and leading to different states[3]). This form of non-determinism is not acceptable when managing TOSCA applications [8]. We will thus focus

---

[3] Note that the conditions of the two transitions may both hold even if the sets of requirements they refer to are disjoint. Hence the state obtained by performing the operation would be non-deterministic.

on *deterministic* management protocols (i.e., protocols ensuring deterministic effects when performing an operation in a state).

Definition 2. *Let* $N = \langle S_N, R_N, C_N, O_N, \mathcal{M}_N \rangle$ *be a* NodeType. *The management protocol* $\mathcal{M}_N = \langle \overline{s}_N, \rho_N, \chi_N, \tau_N \rangle$ *is* deterministic *if and only if*

$$\forall \langle s_1, H_1, o_1, s_1' \rangle, \langle s_2, H_2, o_2, s_2' \rangle \in \tau_N : (s_1 = s_2 \wedge o_1 = o_2) \Rightarrow s_1' = s_2'$$

4.2 Analysis of Management Protocols

In this section we describe different analyses that can be performed on the management protocol of a TOSCA application, such as checking the validity of a Plan, determining its effects, or discovering Plans that allow to reach certain system configurations.

We first define an *intensional* operational semantics of the management protocol of a single component (viz., a TOSCA NodeType), which models all possible sequences of management operations that could be performed on a component if the conditions on the needed requirements were satisfied by the environment. Formally, the intensional semantics of the management protocol of a NodeType N can be defined by a labelled transition system over configurations that are the states of N.

Definition 3. *Let* $N = \langle S_N, R_N, C_N, O_N, \mathcal{M}_N \rangle$ *be a* NodeType. *The intensional semantics of the management protocol* $\mathcal{M}_N$ *of* N *is modelled by a labelled transition system whose set of configurations is* S_N *and where the transition relation is defined by the following inference rule:*

$$\frac{N = \langle S_N, R_N, C_N, O_N, \mathcal{M}_N \rangle \quad \mathcal{M}_N = \langle \overline{s}_N, \rho_N, \chi_N, \tau_N \rangle \quad \langle s, H, o, s' \rangle \in \tau_N}{s \xrightarrow{\langle H, o \rangle}_N s'}$$

Intuitively, a transition $s \xrightarrow{\langle H, o \rangle}_N s'$ denotes that operation o can be executed on N when N is in state s, and under the hypothesis that condition H holds, making N evolve into state s'.

The intensional semantics of the management protocol of a single NodeType permits to determine the conditions that must hold in the environment for sequences of management operations such as

$$s_0 \xrightarrow{\langle H_1, o_1 \rangle}_N s_1 \xrightarrow{\langle H_2, o_2 \rangle}_N \cdots \xrightarrow{\langle H_h, o_h \rangle}_N s_h$$

to be effectively executable on a NodeTemplate of such NodeType.

We can now define the semantics of the management protocol of a whole application (viz., a TOSCA ServiceTemplate) by suitably composing the intensional semantics of the management protocols of the components (NodeTemplates) that form such application. Formally, the semantics of the management protocol of a ServiceTemplate S can be defined by a labelled transition system over configurations that denote the states of the NodeTemplates of S. Intuitively, a transition

$$G \xrightarrow{\langle o, N_i \rangle}_S G'$$

denotes that operation o can be executed on NodeTemplate N_i when the "global" state of S is G, making S evolve into the new global state G'.

We first formally define the notion of *global state* of a ServiceTemplate and introduce a shorthand notation to denote the capability connected to a requirement in a ServiceTemplate (e.g., to denote Container as the capability connected to the OSContainer requirement in our motivating scenario — Fig. 2).

Definition 4. *A* global state *of* ServiceTemplate S *is denoted by a set*

$$\{(N_1, s_1), \dots, (N_m, s_m)\}$$

where $N_1, \dots, N_m$ is the set of NodeTemplate*s in S, and where s_i is a state of N_i. We denote by $\overline{G}$ the initial global state S in which each* NodeTemplate *is in its initial state (viz., $\overline{G} = \{(N_1, \overline{s}_1), \dots, (N_m, \overline{s}_m)\}$).*

We also denote by $cap_S(r)$ the (partial) function associating a requirement r with the capability connected to r in S by means of a RelationshipTemplate.

We can now formally define the semantics of the management protocols in a ServiceTemplate S. Intuitively, a management operation o can be executed on a NodeTemplate N_i only if all the requirements needed by N_i to perform o are satisfied by the capabilities provided by (other) NodeTemplates in S.

Definition 5. *The semantics of the management protocols in a* ServiceTemplate *S is modelled by a labelled transition system whose configurations are the global states of S, and where the transition relation is defined by the following inference rule:*

$$\frac{\begin{array}{c} G = \{(N_1, s_1), \dots, (N_i, s_i), \dots, (N_m, s_m)\} \\ G' = \{(N_1, s_1), \dots, (N_i, s_i'), \dots, (N_m, s_m)\} \\ s_i \xrightarrow{\langle H, o \rangle}_{N_i} s_i' \quad \forall r \in H : cap_S(r) \text{ is defined} \wedge cap_S(r) \in \bigcup_{j=1}^{m} \chi_{N_j}(s_j) \end{array}}{G \xrightarrow{\langle o, N_i \rangle}_S G'}$$

Definition 5 permits to model the evolution of a ServiceTemplate when a sequence of management operations is executed:

$$G_0 \xrightarrow{\langle o_1, N_{i_1} \rangle}_S G_1 \xrightarrow{\langle o_2, N_{i_2} \rangle}_S \cdots \xrightarrow{\langle o_h, N_{i_h} \rangle}_S G_h.$$

It is worth observing that while Definition 5 checks that the requirements needed by a NodeTemplate N_i to perform an operation o are satisfied by the capabilities provided by the (other) NodeTemplates in S, it does not check whether *after* performing o the requirements assumed by (the states of) all NodeTemplates will continue to be satisfied. We hence introduce the notion of *consistent* global state of a ServiceTemplate.

Definition 6. *A global state $\{(N_1, s_1), \dots, (N_m, s_m)\}$ of a* ServiceTemplate *S is* consistent *if and only if*

$$\forall i \in \{1..m\}, \forall r \in \rho_{N_i}(s_i) : cap_S(r) \text{ is defined} \wedge cap_S(r) \in \bigcup_{j=1}^{m} \chi_{N_j}(s_j).$$

Definitions 5 and 6 allow us to formally characterize the *validity* of a sequence of management operations.

Definition 7. *A sequence $o_1 o_2 \ldots o_n$ of management operations is* valid *from a global state G_0 of a* ServiceTemplate *S if and only if:*

$$G_0 \xrightarrow{\langle o_1, N_{i_1} \rangle}_S G_1 \xrightarrow{\langle o_2, N_{i_2} \rangle}_S \cdots \xrightarrow{\langle o_n, N_{i_n} \rangle}_S G_n$$

and each G_i is a consistent global state.

The validity of a TOSCA Plan descends immediately from Def. 7.

Definition 8. *Let G be a global state of a* ServiceTemplate *S. A* Plan *P for S is* valid *from G if and only if all its sequential traces are valid in G.*

It is easy to see now that the deployment plan (c) of Fig. 3 is valid since, by starting from the initial global state, all its sequential traces are valid (and reach the same global state). Conversely, Plans (a) and (b) in Fig. 3 are not valid as their traces are not valid. More precisely, Plan (a) is not valid since all its sequential traces produce the derivation shown in Fig. 5, and *Apache*:Configure

VMWare	Debian	Apache	Translator	Convertor
Down	NotInstalled	Unavailable	NotDeployed	NotDeployed

⬇ **VMare** : Start

VMWare	Debian	Apache	Translator	Convertor
Up	NotInstalled	Unavailable	NotDeployed	NotDeployed

⬇ **Debian** : Install

VMWare	Debian	Apache	Translator	Convertor
Up	*Available*	Unavailable	NotDeployed	NotDeployed

⬇ **Debian** : Start

VMWare	Debian	Apache	Translator	Convertor
Up	*Running*	Unavailable	NotDeployed	NotDeployed

⬇ **Apache** : Setup

VMWare	Debian	Apache	Translator	Convertor
Up	Running	*Stopped*	NotDeployed	NotDeployed

Fig. 5. Initial evolution according to Plan (a) in Fig. 3.

cannot be executed in the reached global state (because it requires *Apache* to be in state Working, instead of Stopped). On the other hand, Plan (b) is not valid since all its traces start as shown in Fig. 6, and *Apache*:Setup cannot be executed in the reached global state. It indeed requires the capability satisfying *Apache*'s ServerContainer to be provided, but that capability is not provided when *Debian* is not in state Running.

The introduced modelling can be exploited for various other purposes besides checking Plans validity. For instance, valid Plans may not be enough, as their sequential traces may reach different global states. It is thus interesting to characterize deterministic Plans.

VMWare	Debian	Apache	Translator	Convertor
Down	NotInstalled	Unavailable	NotDeployed	NotDeployed

↓ VMare : Start

VMWare	Debian	Apache	Translator	Convertor
_Up_	NotInstalled	Unavailable	NotDeployed	NotDeployed

↓ Debian : Install

VMWare	Debian	Apache	Translator	Convertor
Up	_Available_	Unavailable	NotDeployed	NotDeployed

Fig. 6. Initial evolution according to `Plan` (b) in Fig. 3.

Definition 9. *Let G be a global state of a* `ServiceTemplate` *S. A valid* `Plan` *P for S is deterministic from G if and only if all its sequential traces reach the same global state G'.*

It is also interesting to compute the effects of a valid `Plan` P on the states of the components of a TOSCA `ServiceTemplate`, as well as on the requirements that are satisfied and the capabilities that are available. Such effects can be directly determined from the global state(s) reached by performing the sequential traces of P. Moreover, the problem of finding whether there is a deployment `Plan` which starts from the initial global state $\overline{G}$ and achieves a specific goal (e.g., bringing some components of an application to specific states or making some capabilities available) can be solved with a breadth-first search of the reachable global states. The same approach also works in the case of generic management plans (i.e., plans starting from a generic global state G), and it permits to find the sequential `Plans` (if any) allowing to reach a certain goal from whatever starting G. It also allows to characterize an interesting property that a `ServiceTemplate` may exhibit: if it is possible to reach the intial global state $\overline{G}$ from any G that is reachable from $\overline{G}$ itself, then it is always possible to generate a plan for any (reachable) goal from any (reachable) global state. This ensures reversibility of actions, meaning that whatever G we reach from $\overline{G}$, we can always get back to $\overline{G}$, thus always permitting a (soft) reset of the application.

5   Proof-of-Concept Implementation

We now illustrate the feasibility of our approach by introducing BARREL, a web-based application[4] that permits to edit and analyse management protocols in TOSCA applications. In the following, we shall not deepen into implementation details, but rather focus on how BARREL can be used to edit and analyse existing TOSCA applications.

---

[4] BARREL's interface is written in HTML5, while its back-end is written in JavaScript. The application can be accessed at http://ranma42.github.io/MProt/ with any modern web-browser, like Google Chrome or Mozilla Firefox. The source code is publicly available at https://github.com/ranma42/MProt.

The very first step is to import a CSAR package[5] containing a `ServiceTemplate`, as well as the `NodeTypes` instantiated in its `TopologyTemplate`. Once the CSAR is loaded, the `NodeTypes`' names appear in the left hand pane of BARREL's interface (Available NodeTypes), and by selecting one of them the user can start editing its management protocol (Fig. 7). The management protocol

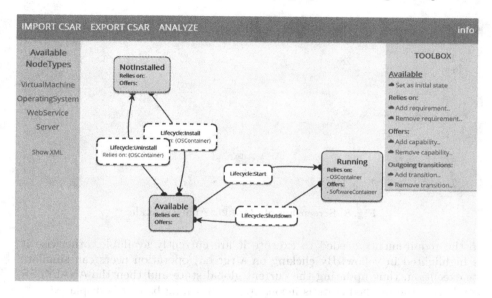

Fig. 7. Screenshot of BARREL: Editing mode.

is visualized in the central pane, by displaying the selected `NodeType`' states and the transitions among these states (if any). By clicking on a state s, a dedicated TOOLBOX opens in the right pane. This TOOLBOX permits editing the current values of $\rho(s)$, $\chi(s)$, and $\tau(s)$, by allowing the user to update the set of requirements on which the selected state s relies, the set of capabilities it offers, and its outgoing transitions. Such updates can also be viewed directly in the XML source of the current `NodeType`, by clicking on the Show XML button in the left pane. Once the `NodeTypes`' management protocols have been edited, the updated CSAR can be downloaded through the EXPORT CSAR functionality.

Users can also analyse the behaviour of the management operations appearing in the imported `ServiceTemplate` by selecting the ANALYZE option in the top menu. As a result, BARREL pops out a window showing the current global state of the application topology (Fig. 8). More precisely, the window lists all the `NodeTemplates` in the `TopologyTemplate`, each associated with its current state, the requirements it relies on, the capabilities it offers and the operation actually available. Each operation is highlighted in green if all the capabilities connected

---

[5] A CSAR (*Cloud Service ARchive*) is a compressed zip file containing the TOSCA definitions describing the cloud application, along with the concrete artefacts implementing its components [15].

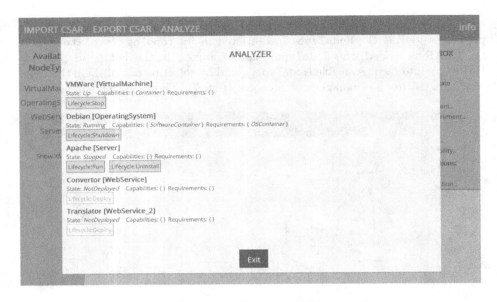

Fig. 8. Screenshot of BARREL: Analysis mode.

to the requirements needed to execute it are currently available, otherwise it is highlighted in yellow. By clicking on a (green) operation users can simulate its execution, thus updating the current global state and then the ANALYZER window. If the reached state is inconsistent, a warning banner is displayed.

With the simple, interactive ANALYZER of BARREL, users can perform the analyses described in Sect. 4.2. For instance, to check whether a Plan is valid, they just need to simulate its sequential traces and check that no inconsistent state is traversed. They can also compute the effects of a valid Plan on states, capabilities and requirements by looking at the initial and final configurations displayed by the ANALYZER window. In this first version of BARREL, developers can only perform these analyses interactively, by manually clicking on the (green) operations and by looking at how they affect the global state[6].

It is worth noting that BARREL is already partially integrated with the Open-TOSCA open source ecosystem [3,14]. BARREL is indeed able to process CSARs developed with the visual editor Winery [14], and it produces CSARs that can be imported in Winery[7].

---

[6] As part of our future work, we intend to extend BARREL in a working prototype capable of automatically performing all the aforementioned analyses.

[7] While Winery imports the CSARs generated by Barrel, it does not properly process the information concerning management protocols. This is obviously because the extension to TOSCA we propose is not yet part of the TOSCA standard, and hence not (yet) supported in the OpenTOSCA open source environment.

6 Related Work

The problem of automating application management is well-known in computer science. In the cloud era, it has become even more prominent because of the complexity of both applications and platforms [9]. This is witnessed by the proliferation of so-called "configuration management systems", like Chef [10] or Puppet [18]. These management systems provide domain-specific languages to model the desired configuration for a software solution, and employ a client-server model to ensure that such configuration is met. However, the lack of a machine-readable representation of how to effectively manage cloud application components inhibits the possibility of performing automated analyses on components' configurations and dependencies.

A first attempt to model the deployment of cloud-based applications was the Aeolus component model [11]. The Aeolus model shares our objective of describing various characteristics of cloud applications' components, including the possibility that component interfaces may vary depending on the internal component state. However, the Aeolus model only permits specifying what is offered and required in a state. Our approach instead allows developers to distinguish the requirements ensuring the consistency of a state from those constraining the applicability of a management operation. This permits to express transitions whose requirements concerns only the applicability of an operation and not the consistency of a state (e.g., the transition $\langle$Unavailable, {ServerContainer}, Setup, Stopped$\rangle$ of the protocol $\mathcal{M}_S$ in Fig. 4). Such kind of transitions cannot be directly modelled in Aelous (without introducing dummy intermediate states). Furthermore, Aelous and other emerging solutions, like Juju [13] or Engage [12], differ from our approach since so far they focus on the *deployment* of a cloud application, rather than on its whole *management*. Aelous, Juju, and Engage also differ from our approach since they are currently not integrated with any cloud interoperability standard.

TOSCA's rich type system has been exploited to devise various techniques that facilitate the the reuse of available services, like [4,7,19]. Those techniques permit to match and adapt (fragments of) existing ServiceTemplates to implement a desired NodeType by checking that the features of the latter are all provided by the former. While those techniques are capable of overcoming various syntactical differences, they do not take into account the behaviour of management operations. Namely, they do not check whether the behaviour of a (fragment of) ServiceTemplate is compatible with the desired behaviour of a NodeType. As our proposal extends TOSCA's type system, it can be naturally exploited to extend the reuse techniques based on TOSCA, like [4,7,19], to account for management behaviour.

Finally, we have investigated the possibility of employing composition-oriented automata (like *interface automata* [1]) to model valid plans directly as the language accepted by the automaton obtained by composing the automata modelling the management protocols of the components of an application. The main drawbacks of such an approach are the size of the obtained automaton (which grows exponentially with the number of application components and hence makes the automaton scarcely readable even for simple applications), and the need of recomputing the automaton whenever a new component is added or its management protocol is modified.

7   Conclusions

In this paper we have proposed an extension of TOSCA to model the behaviour of management operations and their relations with states, requirements, and capabilities. We have then illustrated how such modelling permits to automate different analyses, such as determining whether a management Plan is valid, which are its effects, or which Plans allow to reach certain system configurations. To illustrate the feasibility of the proposed approach, we have developed a proof-of-concept graphical interface that permits to edit NodeTypes' management protocols and to analyze ServiceTemplates' Plans.

It is worth noting that, even if some of the behaviour-aware analyses discussed in Sect. 4.2 have exponential time complexity in the worst case, they still constitute a significant improvement with respect to the state-of-the-art, as currently the development and validation of Plans is performed manually, after delving through the documentation of the application's components.

It is also worth observing that our approach builds on top of, but is not limited to, TOSCA. It can indeed be adapted to other languages for specifying cloud applications (e.g., like CAMP [16] or GENTL [2]), and more in general to any stateful behaviour model of systems that describe states, requirements, capabilities, and operations.

We are currently investigating the possibility of modelling management protocols for cloud-based applications with Petri nets [6], with the objective of expressing some of the analyses described in Sect. 4.2 in terms of well-known Petri net notions (e.g., expressing Plan's validity in terms of firing sequences, or reducing Plan determination to coverability) and hence to possibly exploit some of the many available tools supporting the analyses of Petri nets. We see two other directions for immediate future work. On the one hand, we intend to extend our proof-of-concept BARREL into a working prototype supporting all the analyses described in Sect. 4.2, and to fully integrate it with the Open-TOSCA open source environment [3,14]. On the other hand, as we anticipated in Sect. 6, another interesting direction for future work is to extend the matching and adaptation reuse techniques based on TOSCA [4,7,19] to take into account the management behaviour of cloud-based applications.

References

1. de Alfaro, L., Henzinger, T.A.: Interface automata. In: Proceedings of the 8th European Software Engineering Conference Held Jointly with 9th ACM SIGSOFT International Symposium on Foundations of Software Engineering, ESEC/FSE-9, pp. 109–120. ACM (2001)

2. Andrikopoulos, V., Reuter, A., Sáez, S.G., Leymann, F.: A GENTL approach for cloud application topologies. In: Villari, M., Zimmermann, W., Lau, K.-K. (eds.) ESOCC 2014. LNCS, vol. 8745, pp. 148–159. Springer, Heidelberg (2014)
3. Binz, T., Breitenbücher, U., Haupt, F., Kopp, O., Leymann, F., Nowak, A., Wagner, S.: OpenTOSCA – a runtime for TOSCA-based cloud applications. In: Basu, S., Pautasso, C., Zhang, L., Fu, X. (eds.) ICSOC 2013. LNCS, vol. 8274, pp. 692–695. Springer, Heidelberg (2013)
4. Brogi, A., Soldani, J.: Matching cloud services with TOSCA. In: Canal, C., Villari, M. (eds.) ESOCC 2013. CCIS, vol. 393, pp. 218–232. Springer, Heidelberg (2013)
5. Brogi, A., Canciani, A., Soldani, J.: Modelling the behaviour of management operations in TOSCA. Tech. Rep., University of Pisa, July 2015
6. Brogi, A., Canciani, A., Soldani, J., Wang, P.: Modelling the behaviour of management operations in cloud-based applications. In: Moldt, D. (ed.) Proceedings of the International Workshop on Petri Nets and Software Engineering, PNSE 2015. CEUR Workshop Proceedings, vol. 1372, pp. 191–205. CEUR-WS.org (2015)
7. Brogi, A., Soldani, J.: Reusing cloud-based services with TOSCA. In: INFORMATIK 2014. Lecture Notes in Informatics (LNI), vol. 232, pp. 235–246. Gesellschaft für Informatik (GI) (2014)
8. Brogi, A., Soldani, J., Wang, P.W.: TOSCA in a nutshell: promises and perspectives. In: Villari, M., Zimmermann, W., Lau, K.-K. (eds.) ESOCC 2014. LNCS, vol. 8745, pp. 171–186. Springer, Heidelberg (2014)
9. Buyya, R., Yeo, C.S., Venugopal, S., Broberg, J., Brandic, I.: Cloud computing and emerging IT platforms: Vision, hype, and reality for delivering computing as the 5th utility. Future Generation Computer Systems 25(6), 599–616 (2009)
10. Chef: Opscode. https://www.opscode.com/chef
11. Di Cosmo, R., Mauro, J., Zacchiroli, S., Zavattaro, G.: Aeolus: A component model for the cloud. Information and Computation 239, 100–121 (2014)
12. Fischer, J., Majumdar, R., Esmaeilsabzali, S.: Engage: a deployment management system. In: Proceedings of the 33rd ACM SIGPLAN Conference on Programming Language Design and Implementation, PLDI 2012, pp. 263–274. ACM (2012)
13. Juju: DevOps distilled. https://juju.ubuntu.com
14. Kopp, O., Binz, T., Breitenbücher, U., Leymann, F.: Winery – a modeling tool for TOSCA-based cloud applications. In: Basu, S., Pautasso, C., Zhang, L., Fu, X. (eds.) ICSOC 2013. LNCS, vol. 8274, pp. 700–704. Springer, Heidelberg (2013)
15. OASIS: Topology and Orchestration Specification for Cloud Applications (2013). http://docs.oasis-open.org/tosca/TOSCA/v1.0/TOSCA-v1.0.pdf
16. OASIS: Cloud Application Management for Platforms (CAMP) (2014). http://docs.oasis-open.org/camp/camp-spec/v1.1/camp-spec-v1.1.pdf
17. OASIS: TOSCA Simple Profile in YAML (2014). http://docs.oasis-open.org/tosca/TOSCA-Simple-Profile-YAML/v1.0/TOSCA-Simple-Profile-YAML-v1.0.pdf
18. Puppet: Puppet labs. https://puppetlabs.com
19. Soldani, J., Binz, T., Breitenbücher, U., Leymann, F., Brogi, A.: TOSCA-MART: A method for adapting and reusing cloud applications. Tech. Rep., University of Pisa, March 2015

A Decentralized Approach to Network-Aware Service Composition

Valeria Cardellini[1]([✉]), Mirko D'Angelo[1], Vincenzo Grassi[1], Moreno Marzolla[2], and Raffaela Mirandola[3]

[1] Dip. di Ingegneria Civile e Ingegneria Informatica,
Università di Roma Tor Vergata, Rome, Italy
cardellini@ing.uniroma2.it, vgrassi@info.uniroma2.it, mirko.dng@gmail.com
[2] Dip. di Informatica–Scienza e Ingegneria, Università di Bologna, Bologna, Italy
moreno.marzolla@unibo.it
[3] Dip. di Elettronica, Informazione e Bioingegneria,
Politecnico di Milano, Milan, Italy
raffaela.mirandola@polimi.it

Abstract. Dynamic service composition represents a key feature for service-based applications operating in dynamic and large scale network environments, as it allows leveraging the variety of offered services, and to cope with their volatility. However, the high number of services and the lack of central control pose a significant challenge for the scalability and effectiveness of the composition process. We address this problem by proposing a fully decentralized approach to service composition, based on the use of a gossip protocol to support information dissemination and decision making. The proposed system builds and maintains a composition of services that fulfills both functional and non functional requirements. For the latter, we focus in particular on requirements concerning the composite service completion time, taking into account both the response time and the impact of network latency. Simulation experiments show that our solution converges quickly to a feasible composition and can self-adapt to dynamic changes concerning both service availability and network latency.

Keywords: Peer to peer systems · Service composition

1 Introduction

In this paper we address the problem of discovering and selecting the services needed to dynamically compose a given application developed according to the service-oriented paradigm and deployed in large scale networked systems. We assume that the application is architected as a set of required services logically connected through a workflow that specifies control and data dependencies among them. Such a workflow could be the result of a manual design process, or automatically created by planning approaches. Besides functional requirements concerning the desired service types, we also assume that the resulting

© IFIP International Federation for Information Processing 2015
S. Dustdar et al. (Eds.): ESOCC 2015, LNCS 9306, pp. 34–48, 2015.
DOI: 10.1007/978-3-319-24072-5_3

composition must fulfill non-functional quality of service (QoS) requirements; in particular, we focus on the overall completion time for the service delivered by the composition. Given the large scale environment we are considering, network latency may have a relevant impact on this performance goal.

The composition process must face uncertainty and complexity issues to fulfill both its functional and QoS requirements. Uncertainty is caused by the lack of stable and globally available information about available services, because of reachability problems and service autonomy. Complexity is caused by the potentially high number of required services in an application, spanning from tens up to hundreds or thousands [20], and corresponding candidate functionally equivalent services in the network.

Centralized approaches to service composition can hardly tackle these issues. Rather, they motivate the need of decentralized and self-adaptive approaches to achieve an adequate degree of robustness, resiliency and scalability. Approaches of this kind have already been proposed [9,19], mostly based on the assumption of a decentralized orchestration of the application workflow, using structured or unstructured P2P network architectures.

However, as we argue in Sect. 2, composite services workflows could be orchestrated in a decentralized or centralized way, and network latency affects their overall QoS differently, depending on which orchestration model is used. Hence, a comprehensive QoS-aware approach to service composition should take into account workflows orchestrated according to both models.

In this respect, the main contribution of this paper is a QoS-aware fully decentralized and self-adaptive approach to service composition, whose main features are: (*i*) the ability to deal with composite services workflows orchestrated according to both centralized and decentralized model; (*ii*) the adoption of an unstructured P2P approach to resource discovery and selection, based on the use of a gossip protocol that guarantees resilience to dynamic changes concerning service availability and network latency, and scalability with respect to the system size, thanks to the bounded amount of information maintained and exchanged among nodes. Simulation experiments show that our approach is able to quickly complete the composition process, and to quickly self-adapt to dynamic changes concerning both service availability and network latency.

The paper is organized as follows. We present in Sect. 2 the system model and in Sect. 3 the architecture of the decentralized P2P system and the algorithms for the self-adaptive dynamic service composition. In Sect. 4 we discuss simulation results that assess the system performance. Related works are briefly discussed in Sect. 5. Finally, we conclude and present directions for future work in Sect. 6.

2   System Model

We consider a large scale distributed system consisting of a dynamic set $\mathbf{N}$ of nodes, collectively offering a set $\mathbf{S}$ of *concrete services*. We denote by $node(s)$ the node hosting service $s \in \mathbf{S}$. Both the services in $\mathbf{S}$ and the latency among hosting nodes may dynamically change, because of events such as service providers disabling/enabling services, reachability problems of hosting nodes, or variations in the network topology. We assume that a descriptor is associated with each concrete service, providing information about its functional and non functional characteristics. For the latter, we assume in particular that the descriptor of a service s includes the specification of $resptime(s)$, the estimated completion time of a service request addressed to s. We also assume the availability of function $dist : \mathbf{N} \times \mathbf{N} \rightarrow \Re$ that returns the round-trip latency between a pair of nodes. We discuss in Sect. 3 how it can be implemented in a scalable way, integrated in the overall architecture of the solution we propose.

This system is intended to support the execution of service-based distributed applications dynamically composed according to a workflow that defines control and data dependencies among different services. A workflow W is modeled as a directed acyclic graph (DAG) $W = (\Sigma_W, E_W)$, where:

- Σ_W is a set of nodes. Each node $\sigma \in \Sigma_W$ represents a *required service* for W, labeled with a specification of its functional requirements.
- E_W is a set of edges modeling data and control flow between services. Multiple edges exiting from or entering a node may model XOR, OR, or AND control logic; however, for the purpose of the problem addressed in this paper, we do not need to explicitly specify it.

Given a workflow W, each abstract service $\sigma \in \Sigma_W$ must be bound to a suitable concrete service $s \in \mathbf{S}$ for the workflow to be executed. To this end, we assume that there exists a function $matches : \Sigma_W \times \mathbf{S} \rightarrow [0, 1]$ such that $matches(\sigma, s) = 0$ if the concrete service s does not match the functional requirements of the abstract service σ, and $matches(\sigma, s) > 0$ if some matching exists according to some matching criterion [18,22]. Function $res : \Sigma_W \rightarrow (\mathbf{S} \bigcup \{null\})$ specifies the concrete service bound to an abstract service σ, where $res(\sigma) = s$ if σ is bound to $s \in \mathbf{S}$, $res(s) = null$ otherwise.

When the composition process for a workflow W starts, W has no matching concrete service bound to an abstract one, and can be considered as the template that drives the dynamic composition of the application. Workflow W becomes *fully resolved* when each $\sigma \in \Sigma_W$ is bound to a suitable concrete service, i.e., $res(\sigma) \neq null$ and $matches(\sigma, res(\sigma)) > 0$. Otherwise, W is *partially resolved*.

Centralized and Decentralized Orchestration. Once a workflow has been fully resolved, it may be orchestrated either according to a Centralized Orchestration (CO) or Decentralized Orchestration (DO) model [4]. In the DO model each service receives control and data directly from its immediate predecessors and, once it terminates its task, directly transfers them to its immediate successors. On the other hand, in the CO model interactions among services are mediated by a centralized coordinator, which receives control and data from each service and then transfers them to the suitable successor(s). The CO model simplifies the workflow management, but introduces additional delays caused by the indirect interaction between consecutive services, and may suffer from the typical problems of a centralized solution (bottleneck node, single point of failure). The DO model overcomes these problems, but requires the instantiation of workflow control logic at each node hosting a workflow resource [2,4]. This can be problematic, as such nodes could not be willing to host this logic, or could have limited capabilities that make them not capable of coordinating the workflow operations (as could be the case of nodes involved in Internet-of-Things scenarios). As a consequence, a comprehensive solution for QoS-aware decentralized service composition should consider both CO and DO models, taking into account their different impact on the global QoS. In this respect, an important QoS attribute for a fully resolved workflow is the time required to complete its operations. In the following we precisely define the *worst case completion time* of a fully resolved workflow W, denoted by $wcct(W)$, as a QoS metric based on this attribute, and provide expressions for calculating it in case of workflows orchestrated according to the CO or DO model.

Worst Case Completion Time. We define $wcct(W)$ as the maximum elapsed time from the arrival of a service request to W and the delivery of the final result. Roughly speaking, it corresponds to the length of the longest path in a fully resolved instance of W. For a more precise definition, we introduce the following notation.

Given an abstract service $\sigma \in \Sigma_W$, functions $Pred(\sigma)$ and $Succ(\sigma)$ return the set of predecessors and successors of σ in W respectively, i.e., $Pred(\sigma) = \{\zeta \in \Sigma_W \mid (\zeta, \sigma) \in E_W\}$, and $Succ(\sigma) = \{\tau \in \Sigma_W \mid (\sigma, \tau) \in E_W\}$. A *path* π in W is a sequence of abstract services $\pi = (\sigma_0, \sigma_1, \ldots, \sigma_k)$ such that there exists a dependency between each service and its successor, i.e., $(\sigma_i, \sigma_{i+1}) \in E_W$ for each $i \in \{0, 1, \ldots, k-1\}$. π is a *fully resolved path* if each service in it is bound to a concrete service matching its functional requirements, i.e., $res(\sigma_i) \neq null$ and $matches(\sigma_i, res(\sigma_i)) > 0$ for each $i \in \{0, 1, \ldots, k\}$.

The length $len(\pi)$ of a fully resolved path $\pi = (\sigma_0, \sigma_1, \ldots, \sigma_k)$ in a workflow W is defined as:

$$len(\pi) = \sum_{i=0}^{k} resptime(res(\sigma_i)) + \sum_{i=0}^{k-1} del\left(node(res(\sigma_i)), node(res(\sigma_{i+1}))\right) \quad (1)$$

where $del\left(node(res(\sigma_i)), node(res(\sigma_{i+1}))\right)$ denotes the network delay for transferring control and data from the node hosting $res(\sigma_i)$ to the node hosting $res(\sigma_{i+1})$. This delay depends on the adopted orchestration model and can be expressed as follows for the CO and DO models, respectively:

$$del_{CO}\left(node(R_i), node(R_{i+1})\right) = 2 \cdot dist(node(R_i), node(coord_W)) \quad (2)$$

$$del_{DO}\left(node(R_i), node(R_{i+1})\right) = dist\left(node(R_i), node(R_{i+1})\right) \quad (3)$$

where $R_k := res(\sigma_k)$ and $coord_W$ denotes a resource acting as coordinator of W in the CO case.

From (1) and (2) we see that the path length (and hence the value of $wcct(W)$) in the CO case is the sum of uncorrelated terms: changing the concrete service bound to an abstract service σ has only a local impact, as it does not affect the contribution to the overall path length of concrete services bound to other abstract services in the path. On the other hand, from (1) and (3) we see that the path length in the DO case is the sum of *correlated* terms: changing the concrete service bound to an abstract service σ_i does affect the contribution to the overall path length of concrete services bound to abstract services σ_{i-1} and σ_{i+1}, since the delay for data and control transfer to/from σ_i could change.

Problem Statement. Given the system model described above, the problem addressed in this paper is how to devise a fully decentralized protocol that, given a workflow template W, is able to fully resolve W through a suitable composition of services offered by nodes in **N**, and fulfill a QoS requirement on $wcct(W)$, that can be *threshold-based* (e.g., $wcct(W) < T$ for some suitable threshold T), or *min-based*, requiring the minimization of $wcct(W)$. Given the intrinsic dynamism of the system, the protocol must be able to adapt to modifications of the set of available resources and nodes topology.

3   System Architecture

Figure 1 shows the fundamental components of the architecture that allows achieving the goals stated in the previous section. Each node $n \in$ **N** hosts three macro components: Network Latency Estimator (NLE), Workflow Manager (WM), and Gossip Manager (GM). The cooperation among instances of these three components hosted at each node produces the overall self-adaptive service composition process. In particular, NLE estimates the network delay among pairs of nodes in order to instantiate workflows satisfying the required QoS requirement, as discussed at the end of this section. WM is responsible for starting the composition of a new workflow according to the template received from the application layer, or the repair of an already composed workflow in case of modifications in the available resources. GM implements the decentralized information dissemination and decision-making, leading to the dynamic composition and self-adaptation of workflows according to their functional and QoS requirements. GM instances hosted by different nodes cooperate to this end using a gossip communication model, which leverages epidemic protocols to achieve reliable

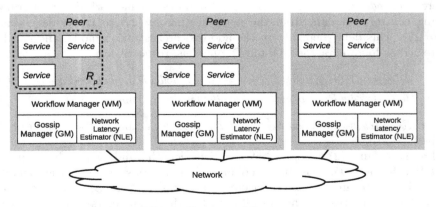

Fig. 1. System architecture.

information exchange among large sets of interconnected peers, also in presence of network instability (e.g., peers join/leave the system suddenly). Although it is in general not possible to analytically estimate the convergence speed of gossip algorithms, it is known that in most cases the number of iterations required to reach a "sufficiently good" solution is proportional to the logarithm of the network size [12]. Indeed, in Sect. 4 we will show that our gossip-based procedure achieves its goal very quickly. The WM and GM components hosted by a node n share a common state made of: (i) the set S_n of concrete services offered by n, (ii) the set $work_n$ of workflows node n is aware of and whose composition is underway, and, (iii) for each $W \in work_n$, the set $C_W = \{C_W(\sigma) \mid \sigma \in \Sigma_W\}$, where $C_W(\sigma)$ is a set of currently known concrete services that could be bound to the required service σ.

The Workflow Manager Component. The WM instance hosted by a node n starts its operations by receiving a fully unresolved or partially resolved workflow W, the former in case of a newly entering workflow, the latter for a workflow under repair. In both cases, WM adds W to the set $work_n$ of workflows under construction. This action triggers a composition phase for W (see Alg. 1). WM also associates W with a globally unique identifier denoted by $id(W)$, which remains associated with all the different instances of W resulting from the decentralized composition process. Hence, given two workflow instances W' and W'', $id(W') = id(W'')$ indicates that they both originate from the same template.

After that, WM enters a stage where it is ready to receive fully resolved instances of W as effect of the operations of the GM components (described below). This stage ends when either a maximum allowed number of candidates has been collected, or a timer expires. Then, WM selects the "best" realization of W from the set of candidates; the selection is based on some criterion that takes into account the requirement on $wcct(W)$ and, possibly, other quality factors (e.g., cost or reliability). Finally, WM sends a commit message to each concrete service bound to an abstract service in the selected W instance, and starts its execution and monitoring.

When the WM monitoring activity detects relevant changes for a workflow W in execution (e.g., the failure of a node hosting one of its services, a change in the actual latency for the interactions with a node), an adaptation action is triggered. It consists in reactivating the workflow composition procedure by inserting a partially resolved instance of W into the set $work_n$. This instance is built differently, depending on the orchestration model adopted for W:

- in the CO case, the instance is built by setting as *unbound* the abstract services originally bound to concrete services whose parameters (response time, latency) changed, while abstract services bound to unaffected concrete services can retain their bindings, because of the uncorrelation among different services.
- in the DO case, the partially resolved instance of W is built by setting as *unbound* the abstract service originally bound to a concrete service whose parameters (response time, latency) changed and, recursively, all services

having at least one of their immediate predecessors set as *unbound* are also set as *unbound*. The rationale is that, as we will see in Alg. 3, binding a concrete service to an abstract service in the DO case depends on the selection performed for its immediate predecessors. Hence, invalidating a service invalidates all its successors.

The Gossip Manager Component. Algorithm 1 describes the core of the gossip algorithm for workflow composition, cooperatively executed by the GM components hosted by peer nodes. The goal of this algorithm is to determine a binding between the unbound abstract services in W, and matching concrete services in $\mathbf{S}$. To achieve this, all nodes iteratively exchange and merge their local state information concerning the workflow(s) whose composition is underway (i.e., the content of set $work_n$ and, for each $W \in work_n$, the corresponding set C_W). The algorithm is parametric with respect to function MERGE() used to this end, since its actual definition depends on the type of orchestration model (centralized or decentralized) that has been adopted to coordinate the workflow operations, as detailed below. Algorithm 1 includes an initialization phase and two concurrent threads: an active thread that starts an interaction by sending a message to a randomly selected node, and a passive thread that responds to messages received from other nodes. In the active thread, node n sends a message to the randomly selected peer p every Δt time units, where the message payload is the content of $work_n$. p is provided by the SELECTRANDOMNODE() function implemented in a underlying layer (e.g., based on the NEWSCAST service [11]). The passive thread listens for messages coming from other nodes. Upon receiving a message containing the set $work_q$ from some node q, the passive threads merges $work_n$ and $work_q$ (line 10). After that, it checks whether some workflow becomes fully resolved by effect of the merging procedure. If so, the fully resolved workflow is sent to the node that initiated its composition. In the next two subsections we complete the definition of the gossip-based service composition procedure by specifying the MERGE() function passed as input to Alg. 1, for the CO and DO scenario, respectively.

State Merging Under the CO Model. Algorithm 2 implements the MERGE() function for the CO scenario where $wcct(W)$ is computed based on (2). MERGE() treats the resolution of each $\sigma \in \Sigma_W$ separately, aiming at the minimization of its completion time independently of the other services in Σ_W. Thanks to the uncorrelation among different services, as remarked in Sect. 2, this local minimization eventually leads also to the minimization of the overall value of $wcct(W)$. As a consequence, the gossip-based procedure will make the system eventually able to deliver one or more fully resolved instances of W that fulfill the min-based requirement on $wcct(W)$. For the same reason, the threshold-based requirement can be eventually fulfilled, provided that resources suitable to this purpose exist in the system (i.e. if the achievable minimum value for $wcct(W)$ is less than the required threshold).

Algorithm 1. GM algorithm executed by node n

1:   $work_n \leftarrow \emptyset$
2:   **procedure** ACTIVETHREAD
3:      **loop**
4:        Wait Δt
5:        $p \leftarrow$ SELECTRANDOMNODE()
6:        Send $\langle work_n \rangle$ to p
7:   **procedure** PASSIVETHREAD
8:      **loop**
9:        Receive $\langle work_q \rangle$ from q
10:      $work_n \leftarrow$ MERGE($work_n, work_q$)
11:      **for all** $W \in work_n$ s.t. W is fully resolved **do**
12:        Send $\langle W \rangle$ to the initiator

Algorithm 2. Merge state information of n and q under a CO scenario

1:   **procedure** MERGE($work_p, work_q$)
2:      $work_n \leftarrow work_n \cup work_q$
3:      **for all** $W \in work_n$ **do**
4:        $W' \leftarrow \{w \in work_n - id(w) = id(W)\}$
5:        **for all** $\sigma \in \Sigma_W$ **do**
6:          $C_W(\sigma) \leftarrow C_W(\sigma) \cup C_{W'}(\sigma) \cup \{s \in S_n$ s.t. $matches(\sigma, s) > 0\}$
7:          **if** $C_W(s) \neq \emptyset$ **then**
8:            $s_{\text{best}} \leftarrow \arg\min_{s \in C_W(\sigma)} \{resptime(s) + dist(node(s), node(coord_W))\}$
9:            $C_W(\sigma) \leftarrow \{s_{\text{best}}\}$
10:         bind s_{best} to σ
11:      $work_n \leftarrow work_n \setminus \{W'\}$

State Merging Under the DO Model. Algorithm 3 implements the MERGE() function for the DO scenario where $wcct(W)$ is computed according to (3). Differently from the centralized case, minimizing $wcct(W)$ cannot be decomposed into the local problems of minimizing the completion time of each abstract service $\sigma \in \Sigma_W$. This makes finding the optimal solution computationally infeasible [14]. Therefore, Alg. 3 adopts a heuristic procedure that tries to determine a "good enough" composition, without a strict guarantee that an optimal solution will be found. The procedure is based on a greedy approach similar to the ones proposed in [9,19], which resolves services in Σ_W on a step-by-step basis, starting from the initial node of W: indeed, a required service σ is bound to a matching concrete service only if all preceding services in $Pred(\sigma)$ have already been resolved (line 7). The rationale for this mechanism is that only when $Pred(\sigma)$ is fully resolved, it is possible to know the worst case increment to the path length caused by resources in the set of known candidates for σ, and to select the one causing the minimal increment (lines 7–9). Once σ has been resolved, the algorithm no longer tries to modify its binding (line 5), even if some better resource could be discovered in next rounds of the algorithm. This avoids

Algorithm 3. Merge state information of n and q under a DO scenario

---

1: **procedure** MERGE($work_n, work_q$)
2:     $work_n \leftarrow work_n \cup work_q$
3:     **for all** $W \in work_n$ **do**
4:         $W' \leftarrow \{w \in work_n - id(w) = id(W)\}$
5:         **for all** $\sigma \in \Sigma_W$ s.t. σ is not resolved **do**
6:             $C_W(\sigma) \leftarrow C_W(\sigma) \cup C_{W'}(\sigma) \cup \{s \in S_n \text{ s.t. } matches(\sigma, s) > 0\}$
7:             **if** $resolved(Pred(\sigma))$ **then**
8:                 $s_{best} \qquad\qquad \leftarrow \qquad\qquad \arg\min_{s \in C_W(\sigma)}\{resptime(s) \quad +$
        $\max_{\sigma' \in Pred(\sigma)}\{dist(node(s), node(res(\sigma')))\}\}$
9:                 bind s_{best} to σ
10:             **else**
11:                 keep in $C_W(\sigma)$ at most $K_{\max}$ concrete services s with smallest
        $resptime(s)$
12:     **for all** $W \in work_n$ **do**
13:         $W' \leftarrow w \in work_n$ such that $id(w) = id(W)$
14:         $W_{worst} \leftarrow \arg\max_{w \in \{W, W'\}}\{max_{\pi \in \Pi_w}(len_{DO}(\pi))\}$
        // Π_W is the set of all resolved paths in W
15:         $work_p \leftarrow work_p \setminus \{W_{worst}\}$

---

cascading effects on successors of σ, which could lead to combinatorial explosion of the number of possible alternatives. However, it could prevent the discovery of a better solution. Hence, this greedy approach ensures that the system progresses towards the fulfillment of its functional requirement (i.e., the full resolution of W), but without a strict guarantee of eventually achieving the minimum value for $wcct(W)$, differently from the CO case.

As a final note, we point out that both merging algorithms guarantee that at each round of the gossip algorithm the total amount of exchanged information for the composition of a workflow W is upper bounded by $N \cdot |W|$, where N is the number of peer nodes and $|W|$ is the size of the W representation. This makes the composition procedure scalable, as its complexity at each round grows at most linearly with the number of nodes and workflow size.

Network Delay Estimation. Estimating the network delay between pairs of peer nodes plays a crucial role for the selected QoS metric ($wcct$) driving the QoS-aware composition process. Indeed, in this context, the communication delay for the interactions with services located at different nodes could have a non-negligible impact, as some services could be offered by distant cloud servers. However, estimating the latency among services located at different nodes would in principle require probing all pairwise link distances, which would not scale with high numbers of concrete services and hosting nodes. For this reason the NLE components (see Fig. 1) collectively implement a *network coordinates* (NC) system that provides an accurate estimate of the round-trip latency between any two network locations, without the need of an exhaustive probing. The NLE components maintain the NC system through a decentralized algorithm [6] with linear complexity with respect to the number of network locations, thus ensuring scalability. Moreover, as this NC algorithm adopts a gossip-based information dissemination scheme, the NLE components operations are easily integrated with the overall approach to service composition described above.

4 System Assessment

In this section we present a set of simulation experiments to assess the performance of the algorithms implementing the decentralized service composition. We evaluate the proposed approaches for the CO and DO scenarios over a large P2P network by exploiting the event-driven engine of PeerSim [16], a widely used discrete event simulator for P2P systems. We implemented the overlay network and the system architecture described in Sect. 3 on top of PeerSim. We initialized the P2P network topology with a specific number of nodes (by default 1000), modeled according to the scale-free Barabasi-Albert graph with power-law degree $\gamma = 3$. We set the replication degree of each resource to 5. For each concrete service s, value $resptime(s)$ is linearly distributed in the range $[100, 140]$ ms. We randomly select the nodes that host concrete services, without placing any concrete service on the workflow initiator; moreover, each node hosts a single concrete service. Such a service placement allows us to evaluate the performance of the algorithms in a worst case scenario.

For the workflow, we considered a layered structure, where each layer has one or more activities. We experimented with various alternatives, ranging from a "long" workflow with n layers and characterized by a sequence of n activities and 1 activity per layer, to a "short" workflow, characterized by having a single service in the first and last layers and $n - 2$ parallel services in the middle layer, to a line workflow, where all services are in parallel on a single layer. For space reason, we report the results only for the long workflow, which represents a worst case scenario for the decentralized orchestration. If not otherwise specified, the sequential workflow has 10 distinct activities.

We modeled the network latency as a uniform random variable in the range $[10, 130]$ ms, which is consistent with Internet latency values. The NC system described in Sect. 3 is maintained by means of the Vivaldi algorithm [6]. With the described setting, each gossip round requires about 1 s.

For each experimental scenario, we run a set of 1000 experiments, each corresponding to a different network topology and a different random allocation of the services to the network nodes. Most of the experiments assume a single workflow to be resolved within $30s$, which, in our setting, represents a reasonable timeout for the resolution time (in the experiments that terminate with a fully resolved workflow, the resolution time is almost always less than $10s$).

In the discussed experiments, we mainly focus on the average *resolution time* as performance index, which is the time required for the initiator to receive a fully resolved workflow averaged out the 1000 experiments. Specifically, we consider both the *threshold resolution time* and the *first resolution time*. The first is the time to receive a fully resolved instance of the workflow W that satisfies its

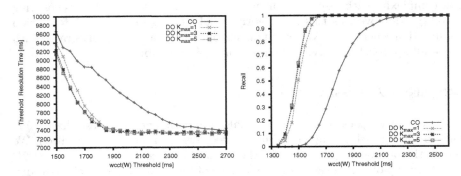

Fig. 2. Base scenario. (a) Resolution time vs. $wcct(W)$ threshold. (b) Recall vs. $wcct(W)$ threshold.

$wcct(W)$ threshold requirement, while the latter is the time to receive the first fully resolved workflow. As additional performance index we consider the *recall*, which measures the system's ability to timely provide a fully resolved workflow. It is computed as the ratio of the number of experiments where the workflow is fully resolved within the timeout to the total number of experiments.

In the first set of experiments, we consider the base scenario, with 1000 network nodes and a long workflow with 10 activities. Figs. 2a and 2b show the threshold resolution time and the recall for the CO and DO models, when the $wcct(W)$ threshold varies. For the DO case, the peer can retain at most $K_{\max}$ candidate resources with the smallest execution time (see Alg. 3). We observe that the system gets more quickly and with a higher success probability a fully resolved workflow matching the threshold-based requirement in the DO case than in the CO case, because it is advantaged by the intrinsic greater efficiency of DO workflows, which makes more likely to match that requirement. For example, when the $wcct(W)$ threshold is set to 1.7 s, DO with $K_{\max} = 1$ finds the solution in less than 8 gossip rounds (8 s) and with a 99.5% probability, while CO requires almost 9 rounds (8.85 s) but with a low success probability equal to 29%. The DO curves show that the $K_{\max}$ parameter does not impact significantly on the performance; therefore, in the remaining experiments, we set $K_{\max} = 1$, thus saving storage space on the peer and network bandwidth.

We now analyze with Fig. 3 the scalability of the CO and DO models with respect to the number of nodes in the network, the length of the sequential workflow, and the resource replication degree. In these experiments, we consider the first resolution time as performance metric. We observe that under such a metric the performance achieved by the two orchestration models is quite similar: keeping in $C_W(s)$ the matching resources as soon as they are discovered alleviates the performance penalty the DO model could suffer by the step-by-step composition. As expected, when the number of network nodes increases (see Fig. 3a), the resolution time augments as well, since the resources are more spread in the network and a large number of peers needs to be contacted. However, increasing by one order of magnitude the size of the network just requires two additional gossip rounds to fully resolve the workflow. In the remaining experiments, we set again the number of network nodes equal to the default value (1000). When the workflow length increases (see Fig. 3b), the resolution time grows as well, because a larger number of services needs to be resolved, but such increase is quite limited: changing the number of activities from 10 to 60 increases the resolution time only by 11.2% and 11.5% for CO and DO, respectively. Figure 3c shows that keeping the workflow length set to 10 sequential activities and increasing the replication degree of resources available for each service in the same response time range [100, 140] ms, the first resolution time quickly decreases, because finding a good resource requires less message exchange.

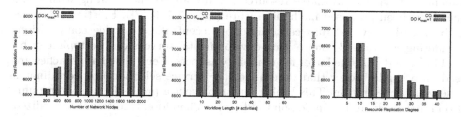

Fig. 3. Scalability analysis: first resolution time vs. (a) number of network nodes; (b) workflow length; (c) replication degree of resources.

Finally, we examine in Fig. 4 the ability of the proposed approach to quickly self-adapt to dynamic changes concerning both service availability and network latency. Differently from the previous sets of experiments, we now consider 30 concurrent long workflows to resolve, and inject the failure of either 10% of network nodes (Fig. 4a) or 10% of network links (Fig. 4b) at 10 and 20 s simulation times. Each long workflow is randomly composed by choosing 10 distinct activities between 20 available ones; all the other parameters take the default value. As performance metric, we consider the percentage of fully resolved workflows as the time flows and set the *wcct* threshold requirement to 1.9 s. As explained in Sect. 3, the WM component that detects the failure reactivates the workflow composition procedure. We see from Fig. 4 that the repair of workflows

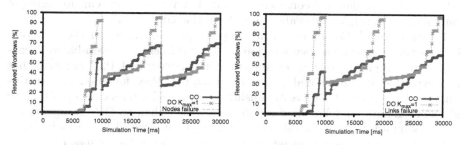

Fig. 4. Self-adaptation. (a) Failure of network nodes. (b) Failure of network links.

orchestrated according to the DO model is faster and more extensive than that achieved by the CO model, whose repair is slower and limited to less than 70% of the workflows. The reason is that even if CO needs to repair only the failed nodes or links, it is penalized by the higher communication latency between consecutive services which makes harder to stay below the required threshold.

5   Related Work

The dynamic service composition problem in pervasive computing systems has different challenging aspects, mainly related to possible changes in the environment and types of available resources. Many approaches dealing with these issues have been proposed in the literature (e.g., [5,7–9,17]). Existing solutions can be broadly divided into centralized or decentralized service composition. Considering *centralized* composition environments, surveys on the topic can be found in [3] and [10], the latter for reliability aspects. Centralized approaches are based on a single broker that determines the service selection and coordinates the service orchestration. This broker may represent a processing and communication bottleneck, and a single point of failure. Therefore, traditional centralized techniques are not sufficient to address the application needs in dynamic and heterogeneous decentralized environments, and various recent works have focused on *decentralized* approaches to service composition on top of P2P overlay networks. Broadly speaking, there are two main families of P2P overlay networks: *structured* and *unstructured* overlays.

Structured Overlay Networks are tightly controlled and are generally based on a Distributed Hash Table (DHT) for resource and data management. Groba and Clarke [9] propose a service composition protocol that invokes service providers in ad hoc networks with the goal of minimizing the impact of topology changes and reducing failures. The proposed approach supports parallel service flows, but presents some limits with respect to composite complexity, network density, and service demand. Repantis et al. [19] focus on stream processing applications and propose a service composition approach where the component discovery phase exploits a structured P2P network and precedes the probe-based composition phase. We also mention the work in [15], that proposes DANS, a decentralized multimedia workflow processing system. DANS exploits a DHT and deals with scalability considering redundancy in the system, in terms of availability of multiple nodes able to perform the same task.

Unstructured Overlays do not impose any constraint on the structure of the network, and allow peers to join and leave freely. A gossip-based decentralized technique for service composition in unstructured P2P networks has been exploited by Furno and Zimeo [7]. However, they focus on cooperative semantic discovery and composition using each peer's local service repository by means of semantic matchmaking capabilities, rather than on QoS-aware composition; therefore, their proposal can complement our own. The works in [8,21] propose QoS-driven gossip-based approaches to resolve hierarchies of component dependencies. However, they do not consider issues concerning workflow orchestration and impact of network delays on the overall system QoS. Other decentralized service composition methods include nature-inspired approaches. Mostafa et al. [17] propose a decentralized composition mechanism based on the notion of stigmergy, taking inspiration from the interactions exhibited by social insects to coordinate their activities. However, they focus on trust measures as a criterion for service selection, without considering the latency issue, and leave open the question of how the decentralized mechanism could be architected. A physics-inspired approach based on the friction concept is presented in [1], with the goal of minimizing the waiting time of service requests. However, only sequential workflows are supported and latencies between services are not taken into account. Multi-agent techniques have also been investigated to deal with service composition in mobile ad hoc and pervasive environments, e.g., [5].

6 Conclusions

In this paper we have presented a decentralized approach to network-aware service composition, based on the use of an epidemic protocol for information dissemination. Differently from most previous works that only focus on service composites with decentralized orchestration, we explicitly consider the case of centrally orchestrated service composites, and the different impact these two orchestration models have on a decentralized network-aware procedure for service composition. Simulation experiments show that our approach can quickly build a service composite fulfilling given functional and QoS requirements, and can self-adapt to changes concerning resource availability and network latency. Moreover, the proposed gossip-based procedure requires a bounded amount of information to be exchanged and maintained at each peer for each composite service, independently of the overall number of peers in the system, thus guaranteeing scalability.

We plan to extend our approach along several directions: (i) consider multiple QoS attributes; (ii) explicitly take into account resources offered at different levels (e.g., IaaS, PaaS, SaaS) and investigate whether this would require a refinement of our approach; (iii) assess whether hierarchical gossiping protocols [13] can improve the scalability of our approach; (iv) extend the present work to workflow graphs with cycles (observe that, in case an upper bound can be given to the number of times a cycle is executed, the extension is straightforward).

Acknowledgments. V. Cardellini acknowledges the support of ICT COST Action IC1304 ACROSS.

References

1. Ahmed, T., Srivastava, A.: Minimizing waiting time for service composition: a frictional approach. In: Proc. of IEEE ICWS 2013, pp. 268–275 (2013)
2. Atluri, V., Chun, S.A., Mukkamala, R., Mazzoleni, P.: A decentralized execution model for inter-organizational workflows. Distrib. Parallel Databases **22**(1) (2007)

3. Cardellini, V., Casalicchio, E., Grassi, V., Iannucci, S., Presti, F.L., Mirandola, R.: MOSES: A framework for QoS driven runtime adaptation of service-oriented systems. IEEE Trans. Software Eng. **38**(5), 1138–1159 (2012)

4. Chafle, G.B., Chandra, S., Mann, V., Nanda, M.G.: Decentralized orchestration of composite web services. In: Proc. of WWW Alt. 2004, pp. 134–143. ACM (2004)

5. Cruz Torres, M.H., Holvoet, T.: Self-adaptive resilient service composition. In: Proc. of 2nd Int'l Conf. on Cloud and Autonomic Computing (2014)

6. Dabek, F., Cox, R., Kaashoek, F., Morris, R.: Vivaldi: a decentralized network coordinate system. In: Proc. of ACM SIGCOMM 2004, pp. 15–26 (2004)

7. Furno, A., Zimeo, E.: Self-scaling cooperative discovery of service compositions in unstructured P2P networks. J. Parallel Distrib. Comput. **74**(10), 2994–3025 (2014)

8. Grassi, V., Marzolla, M., Mirandola, R.: Qos-aware fully decentralized service assembly. In: Proc. of SEAMS 2013, pp. 53–62. IEEE (2013)

9. Groba, C., Clarke, S.: Opportunistic service composition in dynamic ad hoc environments. IEEE Trans. Serv. Comput. **7**, 642–653 (2014)

10. Immonen, A., Pakkala, D.: A survey of methods and approaches for reliable dynamic service compositions. Serv. Oriented Comput. Appl. **8**(2), 129–158 (2014)

11. Jelasity, M., Kowalczyk, W., van Steen, M.: Newscast computing. Tech. Rep. IR-CS-006.03, Dept. of Computer Science, Vrije Universiteit (2003)

12. Kempe, D., Dobra, A., Gehrke, J.: Gossip-based computation of aggregate information. In: Proc. of SFCS 2003, pp. 482–491 (2003)

13. Kermarrec, A.M., Massoulié, L., Ganesh, A.J.: Probabilistic reliable dissemination in large-scale systems. IEEE Trans. Parallel Distrib. Syst. **14**(3), 248–258 (2003)

14. Klein, A., Ishikawa, F., Honiden, S.: SanGA: A self-adaptive network-aware approach to service composition. IEEE Trans. Serv. Comput. **7**(3), 452–464 (2014)

15. Kwon, G., Candan, K.S.: DANS: decentralized, autonomous, and network-wide service delivery and multimedia workflow processing. In: Proc. of ACM MULTIMEDIA 2006, pp. 549–558 (2006)

16. Montresor, A., Jelasity, M.: PeerSim: a scalable P2P simulator. In: Proc. of 9th Int'l Conf. on Peer-to-Peer Computing, pp. 99–100 (2009)

17. Mostafa, A., Zhang, M., Bai, Q.: Trustworthy stigmergic service composition and adaptation in decentralized environments. IEEE Trans. Serv. Comput. (2015)

18. Paolucci, M., Kawamura, T., Payne, T.R., Sycara, K.: Semantic matching of web services capabilities. In: Horrocks, I., Hendler, J. (eds.) ISWC 2002. LNCS, vol. 2342, pp. 333–347. Springer, Heidelberg (2002)

19. Repantis, T., Gu, X., Kalogeraki, V.: Qos-aware shared component composition for distributed stream processing systems. IEEE Trans. Parallel Distrib. Syst. **20**(7), 968–982 (2009)

20. Schuhmann, S., Herrmann, K., Rothermel, K., Boshmaf, Y.: Adaptive composition of distributed pervasive applications in heterogeneous environments. ACM Trans. Auton. Adapt. Syst. **8**(2), 10:1–10:21 (2013)

21. Sykes, D., Magee, J., Kramer, J.: FlashMob: distributed adaptive self-assembly. In: Proc. of SEAMS 2011, pp. 100–109. ACM (2011)

22. Val, E.D., Rebollo, M., Vasirani, M., Fernández, A.: Utility-based mechanism for structural self-organization in service-oriented MAS. ACM Trans. Auton. Adapt. Syst. **9**(3), 12:1–12:24 (2014)

On the Integration of Automatic Deployment into the ABS Modeling Language

Stijn de Gouw[1,2], Michael Lienhardt[4], Jacopo Mauro[4(✉)],
Behrooz Nobakht[1,3], and Gianluigi Zavattaro[4]

[1] SDL, Amsterdam, Netherlands
[2] CWI, Amsterdam, Netherlands
[3] Leiden University, Leiden, Netherlands
[4] University of Bologna/INRIA, Bologna, Italy
jmauro@cs.unibo.it

Abstract. In modern software systems, deployment is an integral and critical part of application development (see, e.g., the DevOps approach to software development). Nevertheless, deployment is usually overlooked at the modeling level, thus losing the possibility to perform deployment conscious decisions during the early stages of development. In this paper, we address the problem of promoting deployment as an integral part of modeling, by focusing on the Abstract Behavioral Specification (ABS) language used for the specification of models of systems composed of concurrent objects consuming resources provided by deployment components. We extend ABS with class annotations expressing the resource requirements of the objects of that class. Then we define a tool that, starting from a high-level declaration of the desired system, computes a model instance of such system that optimally distributes objects over available deployment components.

1 Introduction

Nowadays it is more and more frequent to observe an integration among the application development and deployment phases. The most popular approach in this specific context, is the one promoted by the DevOps community that aims at the automation of deployment starting from application-dependent deployment information. Modeling languages for deployment have been already proposed [9,13,19]. In this paper we take a complementary approach: we intend to investigate the integration of deployment within an existing modeling language, thus allowing for the reasoning about deployment at the application modeling level in a declarative way. Driven by a use-case considered in the ENVISAGE FP7 European Project, we integrate automatic deployment in the ABS (Abstract Behavioural Specification) language [1]. ABS has a formal semantics [15] and

Supported by the EU projects FP7-610582 *Envisage: Engineering Virtualized Services* (http://www.envisage-project.eu) and FP7-644298 *HyVar: Scalable Hybrid Variability for Distributed, Evolving Software Systems* (http://www.hyvar-project.eu).

© IFIP International Federation for Information Processing 2015
S. Dustdar et al. (Eds.): ESOCC 2015, LNCS 9306, pp. 49–64, 2015.
DOI: 10.1007/978-3-319-24072-5_4

is used to model systems based on asynchronously communicating concurrent objects distributed over deployment components that can be seen as containers offering to objects the resources they need to run.

The considered use case is given by the Fredhopper Cloud Services, which offer search and targeting facilities on a large product database to e-Commerce companies. Depending on the specific profile of an e-Commerce company Fredhopper has to decide the most appropriate customized deployment of the service. Currently, such decisions are taken manually by an operation team which decides customized, hopefully optimal, service configurations taking into account the tension among several aspects like the level of replications of critical parts of the service to ensure high availability, the costs of the virtual computing resources to acquire, and the necessity of some clients to keep their data private. These relevant aspects are considered only at deployment time and not during the application modeling and development.

We envisage several advantages from the anticipation at the modeling level of aspects related with deployment. On the one hand, this allows for an early analysis of different alternative deployments, thus providing the operation team with a valuable decisions support. On the other hand, it is possible to detect the need for additional iterations in the system design in case the results of the deployment analysis are not satisfactory. In this way, it is not necessary to test real installations of the system in order to detect design decisions having a negative impact on the system deployment.

Within the ENVISAGE project, the Fredhopper Cloud Services have been already modeled with the ABS language. This language is therefore the suitable candidate to lift for taking into account also deployment aspects. The approach that we present for integrating deployment into ABS is based on three main pillars: (i) software artifacts are enriched with the indication of their functional dependencies and the quantification of the resources they require in order to be properly executed, (ii) a high-level language for the declarative specification of the desired deployment allowing to express the minimal requirements for the desired system (e.g., the basic components that must be present or the number of replica of a given service to guarantee high availability), (iii) an automatic engine that, taking as input the local requirements of the single software artifacts and the global expectations on the desired system, computes a fully specified deployment that satisfies both kinds of constraints and minimize the total deployment costs. Summarizing, the first main contributions of the paper is the extension of ABS with the possibility to annotate class definitions with deployment information. Several deployment scenarios can be considered and, for each of them, it is possible to indicate specific functional and resource-dependent requirements. The second contribution is the definition of DDLang, a domain specific language allowing for the high-level declarative specification of the desired deployment. Moreover, we also provide an implementation of *Model-Driven Deployment Engine* (MODDE), a tool that given the set of available ABS classes (annotated with their deployment information) and the declarative specification in DDLang of the desired system, computes an ABS main program that creates the needed deployment components and deploys on them the required objects. The deployment components are taken from a description of the available computing resources (each one with an associated cost) given to MODDE as an additional input.

It is worth to mention that in the implementation of MODDE we have taken advantage of two already available tools: the configuration engine Zephyrus [4] to support the computation of the optimal allocation of objects over deployment components, and the Metis planner [17] for the generation of the sequence of actions to be executed by the generated ABS main program. We have decided to leverage on already available tools that are not tailored to a specific modeling language, to realize an easily portable and adaptable framework for model-driven deployment. In fact, if an alternative modeling language is considered instead of ABS, it will be possible to adapt our approach simply by extending that modeling language with the deployment annotations, and by modifying only those (limited) parts of MODDE that depend on ABS. Our declarative deployment language DDLang can be indeed applied to any other object-oriented modeling language as it has no particular dependencies on the specific aspects of ABS.

The paper structured as follows. In Section 2 we present the extension to the ABS modeling language for the definition of models extended with deployment information. The declarative deployment language DDLang is presented in Section 3 while Section 4 discusses the implementation of MODDE. Section 5 discuss the test of our approach on the Fredhopper Cloud Services use case. Before some concluding presented in Section 7, Section 6 discuss the related literature.

2   Annotated ABS

In this section we will briefly describe the ABS language focusing only on those aspects that are concerned with deployment: namely classes, objects instantiation, interfaces, and deployment components. Moreover, we present our extension of ABS with class annotations expressing the deployment requirements of the objects obtained as instances of such classes.

2.1   ABS

The ABS language is designed to develop executable models. It targets distributed and concurrent systems by means of concurrent object groups and asynchronous method calls. Here, we will recap just the specific linguistic features of ABS to support the modeling of the deployment; for more details we refer the interested reader to the ABS project website [1].

The basic element to capture the deployment in ABS is the *deployment component*, which is a container for objects/services.

```
DeploymentComponent small = new DeploymentComponent("m1",
    map[Pair(Memory,500), Pair(CPU,1)]);
DeploymentComponent large = new DeploymentComponent("m2",
    map[Pair(Memory,1500), Pair(CPU,4)]);
```

```
[DC: large]  Service  s1  =  new  Service();
[DC: large]  Service  s2  =  new  Service();
[DC: small]  Balancer  b  =  new  Balancer(list[s1,s2]);
```

In the ABS code above, the two deployment components small and large are
initially created. Every deployment component has an associated identification
string and a set of provided resources. Next, three objects are created: the first
two are services that are located on the large deployment component, while
the last one is a balancer located on the small deployment component. Notice
that the balancer receives as initialization parameters a list with the references
to the two service objects. In ABS it is possible to declare interface hierarchies
and define classes implementing them.

```
interface EndPoint { }
interface ReverseProxy extends EndPoint { }
class Balancer(List<Service> services) implements
    ReverseProxy { ... }
```

In the excerpt of ABS above, the ReverseProxy service is declared as an interface
that extends EndPoint, and the class Balancer is defined as an implementation
of this interface. Notice that the initialization parameters required at object
instantiation are indicated as parameters in the corresponding class definition.

2.2   ABS Annotations

Ideally, we would like to have a measure of the resource consumption associated
to every object that can be created. In this way we can have a precise estimation of the resources needed by the overall system and take deployment decisions
accordingly. We do not focus on pre-defined resources. In our context a resource
is simply a measurable quantity that can be consumed by the ABS program.
Common resources that a service can consume are memory or CPU clock cycles.
We require an annotation for every relevant class that can be involved in the
automatic generation of the main program that deploys the system. Intuitively,
an annotation for the class C describes: (i) the maximal resource consumption of
an object obj of the class C, (ii) the requirements on the initialization parameters
for class C (for instance, at least two services should be present in the initialization list of a load balancer), and (iii) how many other objects in the deployed
system can use the functionalities provided by obj.

An example of an annotated ABS (i.e., the specification of the Query API
service of the Fredhopper Cloud Services) is shown in Listing 1.1.

In general, as can be seen from the grammar of the ABS annotations reported
in Table 1, given a class C, an annotation ann is simply a list of comma separated
expressions expr where the expressions are of the following types.

– Name(X): associates a name X to the annotation. The name, also called *scenario name* or simply scenario, identifies unequivocally the annotation in
  case of different annotations for the same class C, each one representing a
  different way for deploying objects of that class. This expression can be left

Table 1. Grammar of ABS annotations.

```
1 ann
2   : '[Deploy: scenario[' expr (',' expr)* ']]';
3 expr
4   : 'Name(' STRING ')'
5   | 'MaxUse(' INT ')'
6   | 'Cost(' STRING ',' INT ')'
7   | 'Param(' STRING ',' paramKind ')';
8 paramKind
9   : User
10  | 'Default(' STRING ')'
11  | Req
12  | 'List(' INT ')';
```

```
1 interface IQueryService extends Service {
2   List<Item> doQuery(String q); }
3 [Deploy: scenario[
4   MaxUse(1),
5   Cost("CPU", 1), Cost("Memory", 400),
6   Param("c", Default("CustomerX")),
7   Param("ds", Req)]]
8 class QueryServiceImpl(DeploymentService ds, Customer c)
9   implements IQueryService { ... }
```

Listing 1.1. Fredhopper Query API

unspecified in at most one of the annotations of a class: in this case the name is set to the default value Def.

- MaxUse(X): indicates that an object obj of class C can be used in the creation of at most X other objects. This parameter expresses the constraint that in the specified deployment scenario, obj can provide its functionalities only to a limited number of other client objects. By default, if this field is absent, an unlimited number of client objects is considered.
- Cost(r, X): indicates that an object obj of class C consumes at most X units of the resource r.
- Param(param, kind): indicates how the initialization parameters param for class C must be instantiated when an object obj of class C is deployed. There are four different cases:

  1. User: the user has to enter the parameter name. This happens when only the user knows how to specify the parameter value. In this case, the automatic deployer leaves the parameter unspecified and the user will have to manually instantiate it.
  2. Default(X): the parameter must be set to the default value X.

3. Req: the parameter is required to be defined by MODDE: here, MODDE is responsible to first create an appropriate object and then pass it as parameter when obj is instantiated.
4. List(X): the parameter requires a list of at least X objects (where X is a natural number) that should be defined by MODDE. Similar to what happens with the Req parameter, X objects should be created and their list passed as parameter when obj is instantiated.

Let us now consider the annotated ABS code of Listing 1.1. Abstracting away the implementation details, the Query API has been modeled as a QueryServiceImpl class implementing the interface IQueryService. The interface and the class QueryServiceImpl are defined in ABS at Lines 2 and 8. The annotation for the class QueryServiceImpl is introduced before the class definition, at Line 3. The annotation at Line 4 specifies that an object of QueryServiceImpl may be used as parameter only once during the creation of other objects. Line 5 associates some resource costs to an object of QueryServiceImpl. In particular, in this case an object of class QueryServiceImpl can consume up to 4GB of memory and 1 CPU. Lines 6 and 7 annotate the single initialization parameters of the class. QueryServiceImpl has two parameters: ds, an object implementing the DeploymentService interface, and the customer c. The ds parameter is set as a required parameter. This means that before deploying an object obj of QueryServiceImpl, it is necessary to deploy an object implementing DeploymentService and pass this object as initialization parameter to obj. The customer parameter is instead set to a default value, in this case CustomerX.

Multiple annotations are possible for the same class to identify different ways to deploy the same type of object. For instance, consider the possibility that the object of class QueryServiceImpl for a different customer requires 2GB of memory instead of 4GB and 2 CPUs. To capture this we can add before the class definition the following annotation.

```
[Deploy: scenario[ Name( "NewCustomer")
    MaxUse(1),
    Cost("CPU", 2), Cost("Memory", 200),
    Param("c", Default("NewCustomer")),
    Param("ds", Req) ]]
```

This annotation represents a deployment scenario identified by NewCustomer (Line 1) that consumes a different amount of resources and considers a different default value for the c parameter.[1]

3 DDLang

When a system deployment is automatically computed, a user expects to reach specific goals and could have some desiderata. For instance, in the considered

---

[1] Please note the annotation in Listing 1.1 represents the default scenario (Def) since the Name annotation is not defined.

Table 2. DDLang grammar.

```
1 spec
2   : expr comparisonOP expr | spec boolOP spec | 'true' |
3   | 'not' spec | '(' spec ')' ;
4 expr
5   : 'DC[' resourceFilter '|' simpleExpr ']'
6   | 'DC[' simpleExpr ']'
7   | expr arithmeticOP expr | simpleExpr ;
8 resourceFilter
9   : STRING comparisonOP INT
10  | resourceFilter ';' resourceFilter ;
11 simpleExpr
12  : exprNoDC comparisonOP exprNoDC
13  | simpleExpr boolOP simpleExpr |
14  | 'true' | 'not' spec | '(' spec ')' ;
15 exprNoDC :
16  INT | 'INTERFACE[' STRING ']'
17  | 'CLASS[' STRING ']' | 'CLASS[' STRING ':' STRING ']'
18  | exprNoDC arithmeticOP exprNoDC ;
19 comparisonOP : '<=' | '<' | '=' | '>=' | '>' ;
20 arithmeticOP : '+' | '-' | '*' ;
21 boolOP : 'and' | 'or' | 'impl' | 'iff' ;
```

Fredhopper Cloud Services use case, the goal is to deploy a given number of
Query Services and a Platform Service, possibly located on different machines
(e.g., to improve fault tolerance).

All these goals and desiderata can be expressed in the *Declarative Deployment Language* (DDLang): a language for stating the constraints that the final
configuration should satisfy. As shown in Table 2 that reports the DDLang grammar defined using the ANTLR tool,[2] a constraint is a specification **spec** of basic
constraints **expr comparisonOP expr** (Line 2) combined using the usual logical
connectives. These basic constraints specify how many elements (e.g., classes,
interfaces, or deployment components) the user desires to create. An expression
expr could identify different kinds of basic quantities: (i) an integer value, (ii)
the number of objects implementing an interface **I** (denoted **INTERFACE[I]** -
Line 16), (iii) the number of objects of a class **C** (denoted **CLASS[C]** - Line 17).
In this last case, it is also possible to indicate the number of objects of a class **C**
deployed following a given scenario **S** (**CLASS[C : S]** - Line 17).

With this expressiveness it is possible to add constraints that abstract away
from the deployment components. For instance, one might require the deployment of at least 2 objects implementing the interface **IQueryService** and exactly
1 object of class **PlatformServiceImpl** by using the following expression.

---

[2] ANTLR (ANother Tool for Language Recognition) - http://www.antlr.org/

```
INTERFACE[IQueryService] >= 2 and CLASS[PlatformServiceImpl]
   = 1
```

More complex quantities are concerned with deployment components. These are expressed (Line 5) with the notation DC[filter | simpleExpr] where filter is a sequence of constraints on the resources provided by the deployment component and simpleExpr is an expression. DC[filter | simpleExpr] denotes the number of deployment components that satisfy the resource constraints of filter and that contain objects satisfying the expression simpleExpr. For instance, we can specify that no deployment component having less than 2 CPUs should contain more than one object of class QueryServiceImpl as follows.

```
DC[ CPU <= 2 | CLASS[QueryServiceImpl] >= 2 ] = 0
```

It is interesting to notice that using such constraints it is also possible to express co-location or distribution requests. For instance, for efficiency reasons it could be convenient to co-locate highly interacting objects or, for security or fault tolerance reasons, two objects should be required to be deployed separately. For instance, in the considered case study, we require that an object of class QueryServiceImpl must be always co-installed together with an object of class DeploymentServiceImpl. This can be achieved as follows.

```
DC[CLASS[QueryServiceImpl] > 0 and CLASS[
   DeploymentServiceImpl] = 0 ] = 0
```

4 Deployment Engine

MODDE is the tool that we have implemented to generate an ABS main program realizing a deployment of objects, obtained as instantiations from a set of annotated classes, which satisfies constraints expressed in DDLang. The tool relies on scripts that integrate Zephyrus and Metis. Zephyrus [4] is a tool that generates, starting from a description of the target application, a fully detailed architecture indicating which components are needed and how to distributed them. Metis [17] is a planner that generates a deployment plan to bring the current state of a deployed application to the new, desired one. These tools are used following the workflow depicted in Figure 1. More precisely, MODDE takes three distinct inputs: the ABS program annotated as discussed in Section 2, the user desiderata formalized as constraints in the language DDLang defined in Section 3, and the list of available deployment components expressed as described below.

The list of components is given as a JSON object having two properties: DC_description, which describes the different types of deployment components, and DC_availability, that specifies the number of available instances for each of these types. A deployment component type is identified by a name, the list of the resources it provides and a cost that the user has to pay in order to use it. For instance the following JSON object defines the possibility of using 5 c3.large and 3 c3.xlarge Amazon AWS instances as deployment components.

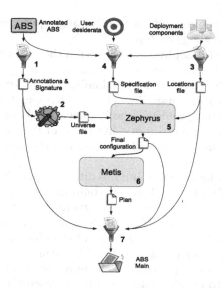

Fig. 1. MODDE execution flow

```
{ "DC_description": [
  { "name" : "c3.large", "cost" : 105,
    "provide_resources" : {"CPU" : 2, "Memory" : 375} },
  { "name" : "c3.xlarge", "cost" : 210
    "provide_resources" : {"CPU" : 4, "Memory" : 750} } ],
  "DC_availability": {
    "c3.large" : 5, "c3.xlarge" : 3 } }
```

The `c3.large` AWS machine is identified as a deployment component type that provides 2 CPUs and 3.75 GB of RAM. When used, this type of deployment component cost 105 credits per hour.

When MODDE is executed, the first step builds an abstract syntax tree of the annotated ABS program, retrieving all the annotations and the class signatures. This step (step 1 in Figure 1) is performed by a Java program that outputs a JSON file. In the second step, the output of the annotation extraction is processed to generate the universe file of components required by Zephyrus [4]. Zephyrus requires as input a representation of the components to deploy following the Aeolus model specification [5].[3] Moreover, to compute the optimal allocation of these components, Zephyrus requires two additional inputs: a description of all locations where components can be installed and the requirements imposed on the final configuration. These two additional inputs are computed in steps 3 and 4 (see Figure 1) from the description of the deployment components and the user desiderata. In particular, in step 3, every deployment component available is translated as a Zephyrus location, associated with the resource capacities it

---

[3] For space reasons, the details of the encoding of ABS objects into the Aeolus model are presented in the companion technical report [6].

provides. In step 4, the constraints in the DDLang input are translated into the specification request language of Zephyrus.

When all the inputs for Zephyrus are collected the solver is launched (step 5). The execution of Zephyrus is the most computation intensive task. Indeed, Zephyrus needs to solve the problem of finding the optimal allocation of the components that satisfy the user desiderata which can be seen as a generalization of the bin packing problem, a well known NP-hard problem [11]. Even though this theoretical complexity is quite high, in practice in our tested scenarios Zephyrus was able to successfully compute the optimal solution in few seconds.

Since Zephyrus can be used to minimize different quantities we use it to minimize the total cost of all the deployment components. The output of Zephyrus lists the objects that need to be deployed, where they are deployed, and their dependencies. For the generation of the ABS main program, the only remaining missing information is the deployment order of the objects creation. To get this information, in step 6, we launch Metis [17]. This planner takes in input the final configuration produced by Zephyrus and the universe file obtained at step 2 and computes the actions to be performed in order to reach the final configuration.

After the generation of the Metis plan we have all the information to generate the ABS main program. The deployment components to be used are created as computed by Zephyrus. Then, following the order of the state changes computed by Metis, the new objects are created and located in the corresponding deployment components. In case an object requires other objects as initialization parameters, the required objects are passed based on the bindings among the components as defined by Zephyrus.

MODDE is written in Python (∼1k lines of code) with the exception of the annotation extractor which is written for convenience in Java (∼500 lines of code). MODDE is publicly available from https://github.com/jacopoMauro/abs_deployer.

5   Use Case

To demonstrate the feasibility of our approach, we use as a case study the deployment of the Fredhopper Cloud Services that drives over 350 global retailers with more than 16 billion in online sales every year. A typical customer of Fredhopper is a web shop, and an end-user is a visitor of the web shop.

The services offered by Fredhopper are exposed at endpoints. In practice, these services are implemented to be RESTful and accept connections over HTTP. Typically, software services are deployed as *service instances*. Each instance offers the same service and is exposed via the Load Balancing Service, which in turn offers a service endpoint. Requests through the endpoint are then distributed over the instances. Depending on the expected number of requests from end-users or the expected service throughput, more or less instances may be deployed and be exposed through the same endpoint. This calls for specific customized deployments of the Fredhopper Cloud Services.

Table 3. Code metrics of the Fredhopper Cloud Services ABS model

Metric	Value
Lines of Code	1282
Classes	13
Interfaces	16
Data Types	8
Functions	31

All the services are modeled in ABS. Table 3 summarizes the main code metrics of the Fredhopper Cloud Services ABS implementation.

To test our approach we first collected the resource consumption of instances of the most relevant classes in the ABS model. The numbers are based on real-world log files of customers of the in-production Java version of the Fredhopper Cloud Services system. CPU usage was inferred from business logs, and garbage collection logs were used to determine the memory consumption. We then associated cost annotations to the involved classes with the calculated figures. In our context, a deployment component can be considered to be an Amazon AWS instance. We defined the capacity of each resource for several AWS instance types in the locations file.[4] The price used in the cost attribute of each AWS instance type concerns on-demand instances in the US East region running Linux.[5]

We created several deployment scenarios based on the varying requirements of different customers. For instance, web shops with a large number of visitors require more Query Service instances than smaller web shops. In general, this requires a scalable, and fault tolerant system with a proportionate number of Query Service instances to handle computational tasks and network traffic and return the query results sufficiently quickly.

The deployment configuration also has to satisfy certain requirements. For instance, for security reasons, services that operate on sensitive customer data should not be deployed on machines shared by multiple customers. On the other hand, some services should be co-located with other services, for example, deploying an instance of the Query Service to a machine requires the presence of the Deployment Service on that same machine. A user can install the framework on AWS instances, exploiting the elasticity of the cloud to dynamically adapt the number of the Query Services. In the modeling of the framework, the API to control the cloud resources is defined as a class that implements the `Infrastructureservice` interface. Since this interface in reality is provided by Amazon itself, there is no need to deploy also an object implementing it on the customer AWS instances. To model this, we define a deployment component called `amazon_internals` that has no cost (the Amazon API is available to all its customers for free).

---

[4] A full list of AWS instance types, with associated capacity for each resource, can be found at http://aws.amazon.com/ec2/instance-types/

[5] http://aws.amazon.com/ec2/pricing/

We have automatically generated ABS deployments for several scenarios. We report only the result obtained by MODDE when 2 instances of the Query service are required for a customer,[6] which is a simple but illustrative and common case.

```
DeploymentComponent m1.large_1 =
  new DeploymentComponent("m1.large_1", map[Pair(Memory,750),
      Pair(CPU,2)]);
DeploymentComponent m1.large_2 =
  new DeploymentComponent("m1.large_2", map[Pair(Memory,750),
      Pair(CPU,2)]);
DeploymentComponent m1.xlarge_1 =
  new DeploymentComponent("m1.xlarge_1", map[Pair(Memory,1500
      ), Pair(CPU,4)]);
DeploymentComponent m1.xlarge_2 =
  new DeploymentComponent("m1.xlarge_2", map[Pair(Memory,1500
      ), Pair(CPU,4)]);
DeploymentComponent amazon_internals =
  new DeploymentComponent("amazon_internals", map[]);

[DC: amazon_internals] InfrastructureService
  o1 = new InfrastructureServiceImpl();
[DC: m1.xlarge_1] LoadBalancerService o2 = new
    LoadBalancerServiceImpl();
[DC: m1.large_1] DeploymentService o3 = new
    DeploymentServiceImpl(o1);
[DC: m1.large_2] DeploymentService o4 = new
    DeploymentServiceImpl(o1);
[DC: m1.xlarge_2] MonitorPlatformService
  o5 = new PlatformServiceImpl(list[o3,o4], o2);
[DC: m1.large_2] IQueryService o6 = new QueryServiceImpl(o4,
    CustomerX);
[DC: m1.large_1] IQueryService o7 = new QueryServiceImpl(o3,
    CustomerX);
[DC: m1.xlarge_2] ServiceProvider o8 = new
    ServiceProviderImpl(o5, o2);
```

A graphical representation of the deployment generated by this ABS main can be seen in Figure 2. Deployment components are depicted as boxes containing the objects and arrows between an object a towards and object b represents the use of b as a parameter for the creation of a.

At a first sight, the deployment configuration suggested by MODDE differs from the one used in-production which uses only instances of type c3.xlarge (one for the Platform Service and the Service Provider, one for the Load Balancer, two for the two Query and Deployment Service pairs).

---

[6] The input files for MODDE implementing this use case can be found at https:// github.com/jacopoMauro/abs_deployer/tree/master/test. Please note that MODDE generates long names for objects and components. Here, for the sake of brevity, we renamed these identifiers with shorter strings.

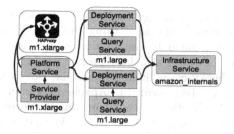

Fig. 2. Example of automatic objects allocation to deployment components.

This discrepancy is due to the fact that we allowed MODDE to use all the possible AWS instances. However, Amazon is continuously updating its instances with new, better, and possibly cheaper ones. Currently, the machines of type m1 have been deprecated and new m1 machines could not be acquired any more. The optimal solution computed by MODDE can therefore be only used by customers that have already m1 running machines. New customers have to rely instead on machines of type m3 and c3.

If MODDE is executed taking into account just the new m3 and c3 AWS instances, the computed configuration obtained is exactly the one currently adopted by the operations team, thus proving its optimality.

As can be seen from this example, tool support is extremely helpful to understand what the optimal deployment scenario is in the presence of external changes, such as the appearance of new machines. With a proper estimation of the cost, using MODDE, the computation of the optimal deployment scenario is trivial and does not require a deep knowledge of the external environment conditions. This is of crucial importance because it facilitates computing the price of the final product that may vary due to external conditions such as the possibility of using (or not using) a virtual machine.

6   Related Work

The deployment of applications and services has been extensively studied in the literature. Many popular system management tools exist to that end: CFEngine [3], Puppet [16], MCollective [21], and Chef [20] are just a few among the most popular ones. Despite their differences, such tools allow to declare the components that should be installed on each machine, together with their configuration files. The burden of specifying *where* components should be deployed, and how to interconnect them is left to the system administrator or cloud engineers, let alone in solving the difficult problem of optimal resource allocation.

As of today, most of the industrial products, offered by big companies, such as Amazon, HP and IBM, rely on the holistic approach where a complete model for the entire application is defined and the deployment plan is then derived in a top-down manner. In this context, one prominent work is represented by the TOSCA (Topology and Orchestration Specification for Cloud Applications) standard [19], promoted by the OASIS consortium for open standards. TOSCA proposes an XML-like rich language (or YAML) to describe an application. Deployment plans are usually specified using the BPMN or BPEL notations, i.e., workflow languages defined in the context of business process modeling. TOSCA specifications, however, still lack proper tooling and technology support for large-scale industry cases. Following similar philosophies, but focusing more on cloud aspects, are Terraform [14], Apache Brooklyn [2], and other tools supporting the Cloud Application Management for Platforms protocol [18].

To the best of our knowledge there are no works that deal with deployment at the modeling level, providing a tool that automatically computes optimal target configurations from a declarative specification. Two recent efforts, Feinerer's work on UML [8] and Engage [10], are more similar to our approach as they both rely on a solver to plan deployments. Feinerer's work is based on the UML component model, which includes conflicts and dependencies, but lacks the aspects concerning virtual machines and deployment. Engage, on the other hand, offers no support for conflicts in the specification language. Neither Feinerer's work nor Engage allows to find a deployment that uses resources in an optimal way, minimizing the number and cost of needed (virtual) machines.

Other domain specific languages for the deployment of applications in the clouds have been proposed, e.g., the component based application model of [7], CloudML [13], and CloudMF [9]. All these approaches mainly aim at modeling the entities involved in the cloud and effective and efficient deployment engines are still to be developed for them.

7   Conclusions

In this paper we have proposed a new way to tackle and unify the modeling of a distributed system together with its deployment. We followed a model-driven approach that allows the user to specify the deployment aspects in a declarative way, without requiring in-depth knowledge of the system to be deployed. We focused and used our approach on the ABS modeling language, but we are not restricted to it: other languages such as SmartFrog [12] that have primitives to handle the deployment aspects can be used as well, provided that annotations related to the execution costs of the system are used.

We tested our approach on an industrial case study from the e-Commerce company Fredhopper. The results are encouraging since the deployment solutions resemble those (manually) devised by the operations team proving their optimality. Clearly, any automated tool that can give quicker and better evaluations of the deployment configuration based on a rigorous formal approach is a big step forward compared to the current practice since devising the best deployment setting is a complex, time consuming process that requires in-depth domain specific knowledge.

Based on the feedback from the operations team at Fredhopper, as future work, we will improve MODDE further addressing some of its limitations. For instance, we would like to find the best deployment configuration given a user-specified maximal cost and a maximal resource consumption. We also intend to add support for annotations with parametric costs that depend on the class parameters. Moreover, we would also like to tackle the computational aspects involved in the process of finding the optimal configuration allowing users to exploit heuristics such as local search techniques to quickly get good but possibly sub-optimal solutions.

References

1. Abstract behavioral specification language. http://www.abs-models.com/
2. Apache Software Foundation. Apache Brooklyn. https://brooklyn.incubator. apache.org/
3. Burgess, M.: A Site Configuration Engine. Computing Systems 8(2) (1995)
4. Cosmo, R.D., Lienhardt, M., Treinen, R., Zacchiroli, S., Zwolakowski, J., Eiche, A., Agahi, A.: Automated synthesis and deployment of cloud applications. In: ASE (2014)
5. Cosmo, R.D., Mauro, J., Zacchiroli, S., Zavattaro, G.: Aeolus: A component model for the cloud. Inf. Comput. 239 (2014)
6. De Gouw, S., Lienhardt, M., Mauro, J., Nobakht, B., Zavattaro, G.: On the Integration of Automatic Deployment into the ABS Modeling Language. Technical report, Inria Sophia Antipolis (2015)
7. Etchevers, X., Coupaye, T., Boyer, F., Palma, N.D.: Self-configuration of distributed applications in the cloud. In: CLOUD (2011)
8. Feinerer, I.: Efficient large-scale configuration via integer linear programming. AI EDAM 27(1), 37–49 (2013)
9. Ferry, N., Chauvel, F., Rossini, A., Morin, B., Solberg, A.: Managing multi-cloud systems with CloudMF. In: NordiCloud, vol. 826, pp. 38–45. ACM (2013)
10. Fischer, J., Majumdar, R., Esmaeilsabzali, S.: Engage: a deployment management system. In: PLDI (2012)
11. Garey, M.R., Johnson, D.S.: Computers and Intractability: A Guide to the Theory of NP-Completeness. W. H. Freeman & Co. (1990)
12. Goldsack, P., Guijarro, J., Loughran, S., Coles, A.N., Farrell, A., Lain, A., Murray, P., Toft, P.: The SmartFrog configuration management framework. Operating Systems Review 43(1), 16–25 (2009)
13. Gonçalves, G.E., Endo, P.T., Santos, M.A., Sadok, D., Kelner, J., Melander, B., Mångs, J.: CloudML: An integrated language for resource. service and request description for D-Clouds. In: CloudCom (2011)
14. HashiCorp. Terraform. https://terraform.io/
15. Johnsen, E.B., Hähnle, R., Schäfer, J., Schlatte, R., Steffen, M.: ABS: A core language for abstract behavioral specification. In: Aichernig, B.K., de Boer, F.S., Bonsangue, M.M. (eds.) FMCO 2010. LNCS, vol. 6957, pp. 142–164. Springer, Heidelberg (2011)
16. Kanies, L.: Puppet: Next-generation configuration management. ;login: The USENIX Magazine 31(1) (2006)
17. Lascu, T.A., Mauro, J., Zavattaro, G.: A planning tool supporting the deployment of cloud applications. In: ICTAI (2013)

18. OASIS. Cloud Application Management for Platforms. http://docs.oasis-open.org/camp/camp-spec/v1.1/camp-spec-v1.1.html
19. OASIS. Topology and Orchestration Specification for Cloud Applications (TOSCA) Version 1.0. http://docs.oasis-open.org/tosca/TOSCA/v1.0/cs01/TOSCA-v1.0-cs01.html
20. Opscode. Chef. http://www.opscode.com/chef/
21. Puppet Labs. Marionette collective. http://docs.puppetlabs.com/mcollective/

A Heterogeneous Approach for Developing Applications with FIWARE GEs

Simone Di Cola[1], Cuong Tran[1], Kung-Kiu Lau[1], Antonio Celesti[2], and Maria Fazio[2]([✉])

[1] School of Computer Science, The University of Manchester,
Manchester M13 9PL, UK
{dicolas,ctran,kung-kiu}@cs.man.ac.uk
[2] Facoltá di Ingegneria Contrada di Dio, S. Agata,
Universitá Degli Studi di Messina, 98166 Messina, Italy
{acelesti,mfazio}@unime.it

Abstract. The European Commission funded FIWARE project aims to support the development of a European cloud, and a rich catalogue of generic components called Generic Enablers (GEs). However, the lack of an efficient approach and tool for developing applications using GEs hinders their adoption. This paper tries to fill this gap by proposing an approach based on a component model, along with its related tool, that allows heterogeneous composition of GEs and non-GE components. The approach is validated with a case study where a content delivery application is developed.

Keywords: Cloud · FIWARE · Generic enabler · Component model · Heterogeneous composition

1 Introduction

FIWARE [3] is an initiative funded by the European Commission whose aim is to ease the development of smart applications by means of an open cloud-based infrastructure that offers a catalogue of ready-made components called Generic Enablers (GEs). Each GE offers a number of general-purpose functions through public and royalty-free APIs.

Developing an application using FIWARE GEs means constructing a software system by composing GEs with non-GEs software components [2]. In current state of the art, GEs can be used in a workflow, or composed in a GE bundle[1].

In a workflow, GE instances are orchestrated. Workflow activities invoke specific services on GE instances which are already deployed on some servers.

C. Tran—Research leading to these results has received funding from the EU ARTEMIS Joint Undertaking under grant agreement no. 621429 (project EMC2) and from the Technology Transfer Board (TSB) on behalf of the Department for Business, Innovation & Skills, UK.

[1] http://catalogue.fiware.org/bundles

© IFIP International Federation for Information Processing 2015
S. Dustdar et al. (Eds.): ESOCC 2015, LNCS 9306, pp. 65–79, 2015.
DOI: 10.1007/978-3-319-24072-5_5

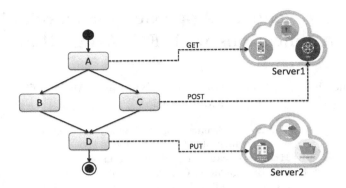

Fig. 1. A workflow using Generic Enablers.

For instance, Fig. 1 depicts a workflow where three activities A, C, and D invoke respectively *GET*, *POST* and *PUT* methods to GE instances on Server1 and Server2.

A bundle, in contrast, is a template that dictates a possible composition of specific GEs directly interacting with one another. Such composition is described informally as configuration instructions to be manually performed when participating GEs are deployed. As such, composition is not concrete until deployment time. Moreover, complex control flows or data transformations usually need to be developed afresh as services sitting between GEs.

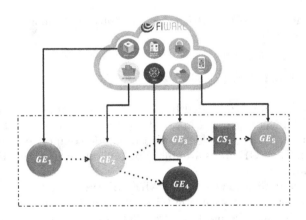

Fig. 2. A GE bundle.eps

Fig. 2 depicts an example of bundle which consists of five GEs. Those GEs can be configured so that GE_1 can call GE_2 which can call GE_3 and GE_4. GE_3 calls services in CS_1 which then calls GE_5.

We argue that both mechanisms are inefficient in developing GE-based applications. A workflow requires that all participant components expose WSDL or

RESTful services. This represents a heavy-weight solution [6], which is sometimes not even applicable (e.g. for a GUI component). A bundle composes a set of GEs, but it needs to be customized in order to result in an application. Furthermore, the composition is informally described, and has to be performed manually.

In this paper, we present a component model [8], and its related tool [1] that has been extended for constructing GE-based applications. Our solution supports heterogeneous systems because it allows composition of GE and non-GE software components. Such components are hierarchically composed by means of predefined (exogenous) composition connectors.

To show the effectiveness of our approach, we construct a simple case study for the provisioning of multimedia contents. It includes three GEs and two non-GE components, which are composed in a meaningful application.

The paper is organized as follows: Section 2 presents related work in the literature. Section 3 introduces our component model. Details on how to use our component model for heterogeneous composition of GEs and non-GE components are then presented in Section 4. A content delivery application is presented in Section 5 as a case study to evaluate our solution. Details of the implementation of the related workflow in X-MAN are discussed in Section 6. Section 7 summarizes the advantages and limitations of the presented solution, and identifies future work that we intend to pursue.

2 Related Work

There have been a number of efforts to exploit FIWARE GEs technology. In the ENVIROFI project [5], domain specific GEs were identified and developed for six domains. The work reported in [17] presents an interesting utilisation of FIWARE to handle IoTs, smart environment devices, data and services by using a semantic approach within the FIWARE core platform. The work described in [19] illustrates an application for sensor driven FI applications used as a motion sensor cloud service. A solution for healthcare developed exploiting FIWARE technologies is presented in [2]. In [20], an application for text mining based on the BigData GE is developed and presented.

In supporting developing GEs and GE-based applications, a tool set called FI-CoDE[2] was developed. Essentially, it consists of several Eclipse plug-ins for GE-based software projects. Apart from generic functionalities such as collaborative development, task management, version control and testing, it provides a Java code generator to yield GEs clients. There is no support for building GE bundles or composing GEs with non-GEs components.

In the area of service composition, workflow is the de facto standard approach. A workflow can be defined using a suitable language such as BPEL [21], BPMN [18], or JOpera Visual Composition Language (JVCL) [16]. A workflow can be turned into a service by giving it a WSDL, or RESTful interface. One representative work is BPEL for REST [14], which offers a heterogeneous mechanism

---

[2] http://catalogue.fiware.org/tools/fi-code-tools

to compose RESTful and WSDL services. For homogeneous RESTful services composition, JOpera [15] provides a visual modelling language for workflows. A JOpera workflow can be compiled into a RESTful service.

Following the same idea, the FIWARE catalogue contains a special GE called Ericsson Composition Engine (ECE) [13]. It consists of a composition editor for creating composed service skeletons, and a composition execution engine. Offering its own graphical language, the editor allows users to model event-driven service executions and data flows. A configure service skeleton can then be instantiated into a workflow and executed within the composition execution engine.

RESTful services can be aggregated in a web application with web widgets and data sources by means of mashup [11,22]. The mechanism to perform a mashup is still a workflow. However, mashup cannot be used on non-web software components and applications.

In component-based development, SCA [12] is a component model that allows us to create heterogeneous composition of various components which may be implemented as Java classes, RESTful, and WSDL services. SCA does not explicitly define control and data flows in a composition.

3   Our Component Model

Our approach is based on an extended version of the X-MAN component model [7], with three kinds of first-class entities: *components, connectors,* and *services.*

Components. There are two types of components: *atomic*, and *composite*. They are both fully encapsulated, i.e. they have no external functional dependencies.

An *atomic component* (Fig. 3a) is a unit of computation. Its `computation unit` (CU) contains the implementation of the `services` $(S_1, \ldots, S_m)$ it exposes via the `invocation connector` (IC).

Its behaviour can be specified in the language of state charts (Fig. 3b): when a service S_i is invoked, a transition occurs from the initial state to the state in which S_i is executed; when S_i's computation ends, the component reaches

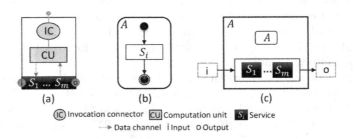

Fig. 3. An atomic component and its functional model.

its end state. Data to and from the CU is provided and retrieved via `service` parameters. The activity chart in Fig. 3c shows parameters as external activities, and services as internal ones. The latter are controlled by the control activity A defined by the state chart in Fig. 3b.

Atomic components are composed into *composite components* by means of *composition connectors*.

Connectors. *Composition connectors* are (exogenous) control structures that coordinate the execution of the components they compose. They are `Sequencer` (*SEQ*) and `Selector` (*SEL*), which provide sequencing and branching respectively.

The component Q in Fig. 4a is built by sequencing n atomic components $A_1 \ldots A_n$. Similarly, the same atomic components composed by a selector results in the composite component B in Fig. 5a. The state chart for Q (Fig. 4b) is

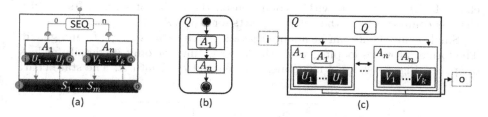

Fig. 4. A composite component with sequencer and its functional model.

composed from the state charts for $A_1 \ldots A_n$ by sequencing them in the order specified in *SEQ*. Similarly, the state chart for B (Fig. 5b) is composed from the state charts for $A_1 \ldots A_n$ by branching according to the condition in *SEL*.

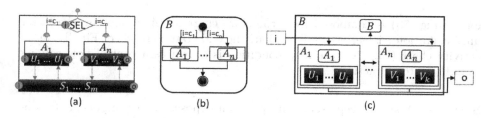

Fig. 5. A composite component with selector and its functional model.

The activity charts for Q (Fig. 4c) and B (Fig. 5c) are composed from those of $A_1 \ldots A_n$. Data flow among activities mirrors the data flow among the corresponding services. The control activity B receives a control flow input needed to perform branching decisions.

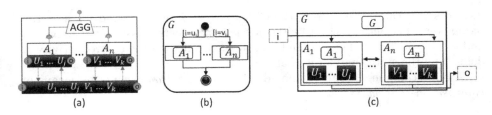

Fig. 6. A composite component with aggregator and its functional model.

Apart from composition connectors, X-MAN also defines an `aggregator` connector (AGG), which aggregates in a new composite component the services exposed by its sub-components. An aggregated component effectively provides a *façade* to the aggregated services. In Figure 6a, the component G is built by aggregating the services exposed by components $A_1 \ldots A_n$. Like the composite component B, the state chart for G is composed by branching among the state charts for $A_1 \ldots A_n$, but with a condition on the choice of service. Its activity chart is composed from the activity charts for $A_1 \ldots A_n$.

Single components can be adapted by `adapters` such as `loop` (L) and `guard`. The former provides looping, while the latter gating (we omit its details for lack of space). Fig. 7a shows a component A adapted by L into R. The state chart

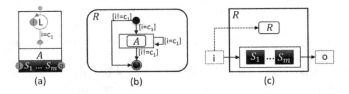

Fig. 7. A component with loop and its functional model.

for R (Fig. 7b) is composed from the state chart for A by looping the latter until condition i is verified; failing that, the end state is reached. Finally, in its activity chart (Fig. 7c), the loop condition is shown as a control flow coming from the external activity i.

Services. A *service* represents an operation exposed by a component. It contains two main entities: parameters, and service references. *Parameters* are inputs and outputs, while *service references* specify services in sub-components that contribute to the provided operation.

As already stated, an atomic component exposes services implemented by its CU. For example, the atomic component A in Fig. 3a offers m services named as $S_1 \ldots S_m$.

On the other hand, a composite component, or an adapted one, exposes services resulting from the coordination of the ones exposed by its sub-components.

For instance, the composite component Q in Fig. 4 exposes m services $(S_1 \ldots S_m)$ resulting from sequencing services $U_1 \ldots U_j$ and $V_1 \ldots V_k$ from sub-components $A_1 \ldots A_n$ respectively. Moreover, the adapted component R in Fig. 7a has its services realised by conditionally repeating invocation to $S_1 \ldots S_m$ services of the original component A.

Clearly, any architecture in X-MAN is a service-oriented one. Moreover, we can hierarchically and compositionally build larger service-oriented architectures from existing ones. This leads to the next section where we detail our composition of GEs.

4   Heterogenous Composition

Our approach allows heterogeneous composition of GEs and X-MAN components to construct applications, i.e. composite components. To that end, a suitable mechanism needs to be devised.

A Generic Enabler (GE) is encapsulated, by definition. Its provided services are fully implemented and available via a RESTful interface. The interface can be formally specified in WADL [4], or informally as text.

Taking into account the aforementioned characteristics, it is sound to map a GE into a X-MAN atomic component, albeit a special one. In Fig.8, a GE atomic component is depicted as a white cube. The computation unit of a GE atomic component is always remote. Therefore, a GE atomic component needs to maintain an URL pointer to a GE instance. This pointer can be specified at design time or later when an instance of a GE atomic component is instantiated. Such a pointer is named as Based_URI in Fig. 9a.

In addition, the services of a GE need to be mapped to the ones of a GE atomic component. Usually, GEs expose RESTful services and are thus resource-oriented. There are four possible CRUD operations namely *POST*, *GET*, *PUT* and *DELETE*. As in Fig. 9(a) for each operation, the mapping yields a service-oriented counterpart in a GE atomic component. For instance, mapping for four RESTful services GET /res1, PUT /res1, POST /res1, and DELETE /res1 produces four services called sGetRes1, sPutRes1, sPostRes1, sDeleteRes1 respectively.

Furthermore in our mapping, a RESTful service usually has a dynamic URI which is constructed from a base URI. The dynamic part is influenced by the parameters for that service. Parameters can be either in the *path* or in the *query* part of a URI. For any situation, the mapping specifies those parameters in the resulting service as its inputs. For each input, the name, data type, order and an attribute indicating whether the parameter is path or query based is specified. Outputs for a RESTful service include status code and data. The status code indicates a provisional response of the service call, while the data is the result of service execution. Our mapping creates two outputs respectively for both of them.

In Fig. 9b, we give details of an example of our mapping. A RESTful service offers a GET method to access a resource called res1. From its API documentation, it accepts three mandatory parameters param1, param2 and param3, and

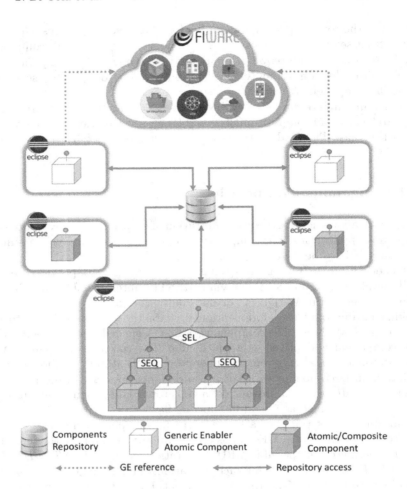

Fig. 8. Approach overview.

an optional `param4`. The former two parameters are path-based, separated by '/', while the latter two are query-based, following '?' and delimited by '&'. Our mapping yields a new service which is described in three parts. The core part specifies the service name, resource location relatively to the base URI and the method as `sGetRes1`, `/res1` and `GET` respectively. The input part has four inputs `param1`, `param2`, `param3` and `param4` matching the ones of the service. The data types of these inputs are identified from the API. From the same source, the order, optionality default values of inputs are identified. The output section consists of two outputs which are `status_code` and `data`. `status_code` is always an integer while `data` can be of a type matching one stated in the API.

Once GE atomic components are defined, they can be composed with other components by means of X-MAN composition connectors to yield a composite X-MAN component. Such a composite component is in fact a GE-based application.

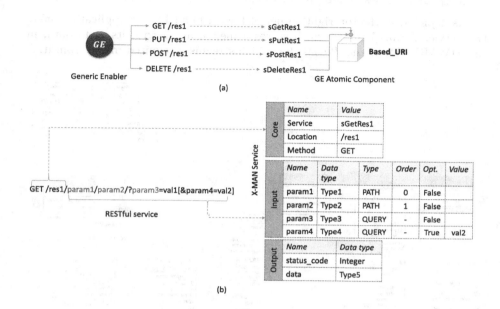

Fig. 9. Mapping of GE to GE atomic component.

It can be delivered, or stored in our repository (Fig. 8) in order to be further composed.

5   Case Study: A Content Delivery Application

Figs. 10 and 11 depict a simplified content delivery application. The application stores multimedia data in an object storage system. Whenever an authorised client asks for a content, the application stores his information, verifies its availability and delivers it if found. Moreover, for performance analysis, the response time is also returned.

To develop this application we compose three GE atomic components (Cosmos, ObjectStorage and Kurento), with two X-MAN components (Logger, Adapter):

- Cosmos offers cluster-based data persistence and functionality for processing vast amounts of data; we use it to store and search content meta-data.
- ObjectStorage provides robust, and scalable object storage functionality; we use it to store actual media content.
- Kurento implements an abstraction layer for multimedia capabilities; we use it to stream media contents to clients.

- **Logger** logs clients' credentials, and calculates the response time.
- **Adapter** analyses **Cosmos** result to extract relevant content meta-data.

As depicted in the top right corner of Figs. 10 and 11, the application offers two services: *StoreMedia*[3], which stores a media, along with its meta-data, in the FIWARE cloud, and *PlayMedia*, which streams a required media from it.

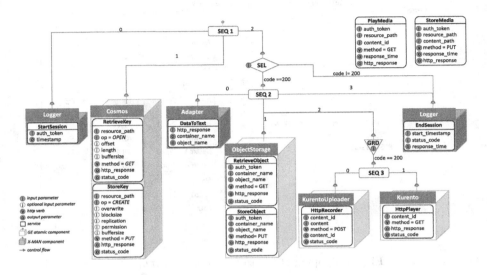

Fig. 10. A content delivery application (control flow)

To access a content, a client needs an authentication token, the path of the required media, and the media id. Following the order of the root connector (SEQ 1) in Fig. 10, the application first invokes the service *StartSession*, which logs information about the callee (extracted from the provided authorisation token), and returns the actual timestamp. The latter will be used by another instance of *Logger* to calculate the response time (Fig. 11).

Once the request is logged, the service *RetrieveKey* of the GE atomic component **Cosmos** is invoked. The mapped API (Fig. 12) requires the resource path (optional parameters have been omitted for simplicity), and returns its content. If the resource is found, then the *DataToText* service parses its content, and returns two parameters, i.e. *container_name*, and the *object_name*. The former are used by the service *RetrieveObject*, which maps to the counterpart API in Fig. 12, to return the object content in the response body. If the return code is 200, the *http_response* is redirected to the service *HttpRecorder*. The latter, using the corresponding API in Fig. 12, uploads the object content to the Kurento Media Server. Finally, the *content_ID* is passed to the Kurento *HTTPPlayer* service (Fig. 11), which returns a JSON object containing the content URL.

---

[3] We omit its details to simplify our discussion. Indeed, other X-MAN components are needed to upload content to **Cosmos**, and **ObjectStorage**.

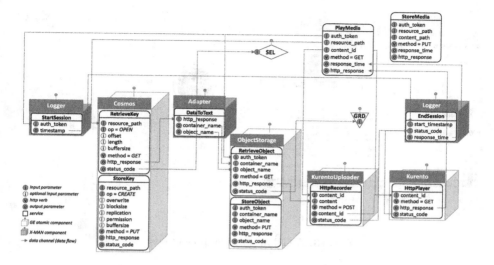

Fig. 11. A content delivery application (data flow)

Component	Service	HTTP Method	RESTful API mapped
Cosmos	RetrieveKey	GET	http://\<host\>:\<port\>/webhdfs/v1/\<path\>?op=OPEN [&offset=\<LONG\>][&length=\<LONG\>][&buffersize=\<INT\>]
ObjectStorage	RetrieveObject	GET	http://\<host\>:\<port\>/v1/\<account\>/\<container\>/\<object\>
Kurento	HttpRecorder	POST	http://\<host\>:\<port\>/\<app_logic_path\>/\<ContentID\>
Kurento	HttpPlayer	GET	http://\<host\>:\<port\>/\<app_logic_path\>/\<ContentID\>

Fig. 12. RESTful APIs mapped

6   Implementation

Based on the new X-MAN tool [1], two extensions are developed. The first extension is to implement GE atomic components while the second one is to support heterogeneous composition. To that end, the meta-model is extended to capture the mapping results, i.e. core, inputs and outputs.

Our code generator is then extended to support the new extensions. The generated code for GE atomic components is essentially to perform invocations to GEs' RESTful services. For those invocations implementation, we use the Jersey library.[4]

In Fig. 13 we illustrate the design of the `ObjectStorage` GE atomic component in our tool. It offers two services *RetrieveObject* and *StoreObject*, each of which has three input and two output parameters. The base URI is captured by the data element (circle with letter d), specified at deployment time.

---

[4] https://jersey.java.net/

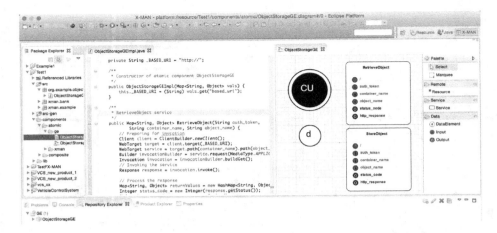

Fig. 13. A GE atomic component.eps

The generated source code shows how the RESTful service is invoked with the specified inputs.

Once designed, components are deposited in a repository (bottom Fig. 13), and later retrieved to be composed into the application as in Figs. 10 and 11.

The source code of the application is then generated by our tool. As part of code generation, we specify the application to be packaged as a 'war' file, which is then deployed on a Tomcat[5] server. In order to test our application, we developed a simple web page (hosted by the same server) which provides an interface to take end-users' requests and pass them to the application. The media if found and returned from the application is then played via an embedded video player. The client is depicted in Fig. 14.

7   Discussion and Conclusion

We have defined and implemented an approach to developing GE-based applications based on an extended version of the X-MAN component model. Our approach presents novel heterogeneous composition mechanisms that exploit the power of the FIWARE ecosystem. Unlike heterogeneous composition in BPEL for REST, we compose software components with RESTful services. In comparison with JOpera, our applications are not limited to the middle tier of an MVC architecture. For instance, we can compose the application in our case study with an X-MAN component implementing a GUI that replaces the Web client. On another note, SCA does provide a component model for heterogeneous composition. However, unlike our approach, it does not provide explicit control flow. In addition, it requires a "glue" component to be developed afresh to act as coordinator.

---

[5] http://tomcat.apache.org/

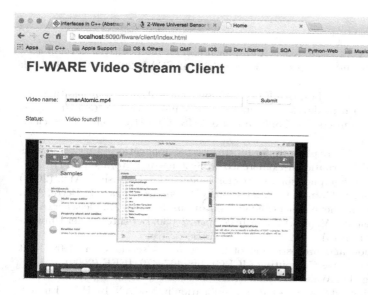

Fig. 14. A client of the content delivery application.eps

Currently, applications can make use of existing FIWARE bundles which already composes certain GEs. The composition in these bundles is carried out by an 'active' GE such as `Orion` which implements the *Observer* pattern [10]. Orion is called by a 'publisher' GE and it then actively notifies 'subscriber' GEs. X-MAN composition connectors are Turing complete. It implies that we can use them to construct any complex control logics including the *Observer* pattern.

Our approach however has some limitations. The mapping we presented, although defined to be applied automatically, requires human effort to be performed. It is because currently GEs' interfaces are described informally by textual documentation. Whilst this may be adequate for human consumption, the lack of a machine processable format such as WADL hinders our mapping. When this limitation is removed in the future, our approach can be improved accordingly.

GE catalogue currently supports programmatically access through a RESTful API. However, the results seem to be out of sync with the actual GEs. This poses a challenge for development tools like ours to integrate the GE catalogue with our component repository. Such integration when possible will allow seamless application development.

As future work, we plan to investigate an integration with FIA Project Management Plugin[6] to provide a complete environment for FIWARE users and developers. Finally, we intend to extend the X-MAN component model to support concurrency [9].

---

[6] http://catalogue.fiware.org/enablers/fia-project-management-plugin

References

1. Di Cola, S., Tran, C.M., Lau, K.K.: A graphical tool for model-driven development using components and services. In: Proceedings of SEAA 2015 - MOCS Track (2015)
2. Fazio, M., Celesti, A., Marquez, F.G., Glikson, A., Villari, M.: Exploiting the fiware cloud platform to develop a remote patient monitoring system. In: IEEE Symposium on Computers and Communications (ISCC). IEEE Computer Society, Larnaca, June 2015
3. Glikson, A.: Fi-ware: Core platform for future internet applications. In: Proceedings of the 4th Annual International Conference on Systems and Storage (2011)
4. Hadley, J.: Wadl (web application description language). GlassFish, WADL (2009)
5. Havlik, D., Soriano, J., Granell, C., Middleton, S.E., van der Schaaf, H., Berre, A.J., Pielorz, J.: Future internet enablers for vgi applications. In: Page, B., Fleischer, A.G., Göbel, J., Wohlgemuth, V. (eds.) EnviroInfo, pp. 622–630. Berichte aus der Umweltinformatik, Shaker (2013)
6. He, K.: Integration and orchestration of heterogeneous services. In: 2009 Joint Conferences on Pervasive Computing (JCPC), pp. 467–470. IEEE (2009)
7. He, N., Kroening, D., Wahl, T., Lau, K.K., Taweel, F., Tran, C., Rümmer, P., Sharma, S.: Component-based design and verification in X-MAN. In: Proc. Embedded Real Time Software and Systems (2012)
8. Lau, K.-K.: Software component models: Past, present and future. In: Proceedings of the 17th International ACM SIGSOFT Symposium on Component-Based Software Engineering, pp. 185–186. ACM (2014)
9. Lau, K.K., Ntalamagkas, I.: Component-based construction of concurrent systems with active components. In: Proc. 35th EUROMICRO Conference on Software Engineering and Advanced Applications (SEAA 2009), pp. 497–502. IEEE (2009)
10. Lau, K.-K., Ntalamagkas, I., Tran, C.M., Rana, T.: (Behavioural) design patterns as composition operators. In: Grunske, L., Reussner, R., Plasil, F. (eds.) CBSE 2010. LNCS, vol. 6092, pp. 232–251. Springer, Heidelberg (2010)
11. Liu, X., Hui, Y., Sun, W., Liang, H.: Towards service composition based on mashup. In: 2007 IEEE Congress on Services, pp. 332–339. IEEE (2007)
12. Marino, J., Rowley, M.: Understanding sca (2009)
13. Niemöller, J., Fikouras, I., de Rooij, F., Klostermann, L., Stringer, U., Olsson, U.: Ericsson composition engine-next-generation in. Ericsson Review **2**, 22–27 (2009)
14. Pautasso, C.: BPEL for REST. In: Dumas, M., Reichert, M., Shan, M.-C. (eds.) BPM 2008. LNCS, vol. 5240, pp. 278–293. Springer, Heidelberg (2008)
15. Pautasso, C.: Composing RESTful services with JOpera. In: Bergel, A., Fabry, J. (eds.) SC 2009. LNCS, vol. 5634, pp. 142–159. Springer, Heidelberg (2009)
16. Pautasso, C., Alonso, G.: The jopera visual composition language. J. Vis. Lang. Comput. **16**(1–2), 119–152 (2005). doi:10.1016/j.jvlc.2004.08.004
17. Ramparany, F., Galan Marquez, F., Soriano, J., Elsaleh, T.: Handling smart environment devices, data and services at the semantic level with the fi-ware core platform. In: 2014 IEEE International Conference on Big Data (Big Data), pp. 14–20, October 2014
18. Silver, B.: BPMN method and style, vol. 2. Cody-Cassidy Press Aptos (2009)

19. Stravoskoufos, K., Sotiriadis, S., Preventis, A., Petrakis, E.: Motion sensor driven gesture recognition for future internet application development. In: The 5th International Conference on Information, Intelligence, Systems and Applications, IISA 2014, pp. 372–377, July 2014

20. Villaseñor, E., Estrada, H.: Informetric mapping of "big data" in fi-ware. In: Proceedings of the 15th Annual International Conference on Digital Government Research, dg.o 2014, pp. 348–349. ACM, New York (2014). http://doi.acm.org/10. 1145/2612733.2619954

21. Weerawarana, S., Curbera, F., Leymann, F., Storey, T., Ferguson, D.F.: Web services platform architecture: SOAP, WSDL, WS-policy, WS-addressing, WS-BPEL. WS-reliable messaging and more. Prentice Hall PTR (2005)

22. Yu, J., Benatallah, B., Casati, F., Daniel, F.: Understanding mashup development. IEEE Internet Computing 12(5), 44–52 (2008)

Elastic Application-Level Monitoring for Large Software Landscapes in the Cloud

Florian Fittkau$^{(\boxtimes)}$ and Wilhelm Hasselbring

Software Engineering Group, Kiel University, 24098 Kiel, Germany
{ffi,wha}@informatik.uni-kiel.de

Abstract. Application-level monitoring provides valuable, detailed insights into running applications. However, many approaches often only employ a single analysis application. This analysis application may become a performance bottleneck when monitoring several programs resulting in reduced monitoring quality or violated service level agreements of the monitored applications.

We present an approach for elastic, distributed application-level monitoring for large software landscapes consisting of several hundreds of applications by utilizing cloud computing. Our approach dynamically inserts and removes worker levels to circumvent overloading the analysis master application without interrupting or pausing the actual live analysis of the monitored data. To evaluate our approach, we conduct an experiment in which we generate load – following a real workload pattern – on web applications in a 24 hour experiment.

In our experiment, 160 monitored JPetStore instances generate roughly 20 million analyzed method calls per second in the peak. Furthermore, two worker levels are dynamically started and removed in line with the imposed workload on the monitored applications. The experiment shows that our monitoring approach is capable of live analyzing several millions of monitored method calls per second without overloading the analysis master application.

Keywords: Application-level monitoring · Elasticity · Cloud computing

1 Introduction

Enterprises often run and administer large and complex software landscapes featuring hundreds of running applications [12]. Since most of them evolve over decades, the comprehension of those landscapes often gets lost due to missing documentation, changing business requirements, or employees, for example. Application-level monitoring can support in the comprehension process such large software landscapes [6]. However, most approaches only feature one analysis node for the monitored data which provides poor scalability – especially in cloud environments where the monitored applications adapt to the imposed workload.

© IFIP International Federation for Information Processing 2015
S. Dustdar et al. (Eds.): ESOCC 2015, LNCS 9306, pp. 80–94, 2015.
DOI: 10.1007/978-3-319-24072-5_6

In this paper, we present an elastic, distributed application-level monitoring approach to circumvent this overuse of a single analysis node. Our approach dynamically inserts and removes preprocessing worker levels depending on the actual utilization of the analysis master. The change of the system takes place without interrupting the actual analysis of the monitored data.

Furthermore, we present a thorough evaluation of the described approach in which our monitoring solution monitors 160 elastically scaled web applications and analyzes several millions of method calls per second. To facilitate the verifiability and reproducibility of our results, we provide a data package [4] containing all our experimental results and source code.

In summary, our main contributions are:

- an elastic, distributed application-level monitoring approach which dynamically inserts and removes worker levels, and
- a thorough evaluation of the approach incorporating 160 scaled web applications and several millions of analyzed method calls per second.

The remainder of this paper is organized as follows. Section 2 states the addressed problem. Afterwards, our approach for elastic, distributed application-level monitoring is described. A 24 hour experiment for applying the concept is presented in Section 4 as evaluation. Related work is discussed in Section 5. Finally, we draw the conclusions and illustrate future work in Section 6.

2   Problem Statement

Employing only a single analysis node for live processing the monitoring data can easily become a bottleneck. For example, in our evaluation described in Section 4, the analysis would operate at full capacity after receiving load from only four monitored applications. In general, this number is determined by the amount of monitoring and the hardware for the analysis node. However, eventually every node will be fully utilized if the workload rises to some point. Cloud computing aims to provide – perceived – infinite scalability for the monitored applications and therefore, this should also apply to the monitoring solution.

Application-level monitoring tools, e.g., Kieker [9], typically offer three configurable strategies, what should be done when the analysis cannot process the current monitoring data. The first strategy simply terminates the monitoring. Since this requires a manual restart of the application to start monitoring again, this behavior is undesirable for a high monitoring quality. However, this typically does not affect the service-level agreements (SLAs) of the monitored applications.

The second strategy discards new monitoring records until a space in the monitoring queue is available. Therefore, this behavior is similar to sampling which only monitors method calls on a defined interval, e.g., every 10th request. This strategy typically imposes no SLA violations at the expense of a reduced monitoring quality. However, it can automatically recover when the workload drops and thus is typically preferable over the first strategy and therefore, often employed in practice.

The third strategy uses blocking until a free space in the monitoring queue becomes available. While this behavior seems appealing on first sight, it can violate the SLAs when the analysis node takes a long time to recover from its high workload. The SLA violations are caused by the waiting of the application for finishing the writing of the monitored data. Therefore, it is not processing user requests often leading to loss in revenue due to annoyed customers.

This situation can become even more expensive, if the capacity manager utilizes the waiting user requests for its upscaling condition for the applications. Since only one analysis node is employed, the newly started application would also wait for the analysis node to finish. Therefore, the capacity manager might keep starting new instances until some node limit is reached and the service provider has to pay for application nodes that are waiting for the analysis of the monitoring data.

Based on the chosen strategy, either the quality of the SLAs or the monitoring quality is reduced in the circumstance of a fully utilized analysis node. One way to postpone this problem is an analysis node with a high number of CPU cores and a high amount of RAM. However, the analysis must be designed to utilize an infinite number of CPU cores and if the workload rises, the number of CPU cores must be increased according to the peeks in the workload. Hence, they become superfluous during low workload.

3   Elastic, Distributed Application-Level Monitoring

In this section, we describe how we employ an elastic, scalable monitoring approach to circumvent the overutilization of a single analysis node by dynamically adding or removing preproccesing levels.

We start by outlining our basic idea. Then, our general scalable architecture is described. Afterwards, the analysis component, which enables the connection of multiple analysis workers in series, is explained. Then, we illustrate the scaling process for multiple worker levels. Lastly, assumptions and limitations of our approach are discussed.

3.1   Idea

Fig. 1 illustrates the basic idea of our elastic, distributed application-level monitoring. When the analysis master impends to become overutilized, a new worker level is dynamically added in front of it. Similar to the MapReduce pattern [3], each worker on the new level analyzes one part of the monitoring data. To circumvent an overutilization of the workers, the associated worker applications are scaled within their worker level. With this preprocessing step, the Master is only required to combine the analysis results. Eventually with rising workload, the merging of the results impends to overload the Master again. Then, a second level is dynamically inserted between the first level and the Master. In theory, this behavior can continue infinitely.

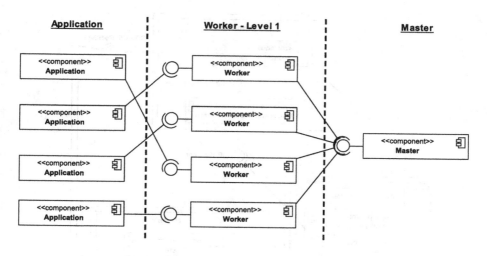

Fig. 1. Basic idea of dynamic worker levels

3.2   Scalable Architecture

Next, we show our general scalable architecture. Fig. 2 displays this architecture including our capacity manager CapMan and one master node. Therefore, it represents the initial state when only a small amount of monitoring data has to be analyzed. In our architecture, the capacity manager includes the workload generation and its load balancing for our experiment due to convenience reasons. Therefore, the applications are accessed by CapMan to simulate user requests. A System Monitor records the CPU utilization of the application nodes and sends this utilization to CapMan. CapMan uses these values, in addition to the outstanding request count from the workload generation, for scaling the applications. This cycle forms the employed load generation on the applications and their automatic elastic scaling.

Every application contains a Monitoring component. At its start, it requests an IP address from the Monitoring LoadBalancer. This request contains a loadbalancing group property to determine the kind of application which the Monitoring component wants to access. For example, the applications use analysis to reflect their wish to write monitoring data on an analysis node. In Fig. 2, the shown state only exists of one analysis node, i.e., the master node. Therefore, the Monitoring component receives the IP address of the master node and sends its monitoring data to the master analysis application. After a defined interval, the Monitoring component again fetches an IP address from the Monitoring LoadBalancer and if necessary connects to the newly received IP address. Therefore, the monitoring data is distributed to different nodes when multiple nodes (e.g., on a worker level) are available. This results in an approximate equal utilization of the target nodes. Similar to the application nodes, the CPU utilization of the analysis nodes is sent by a System Monitor to CapMan

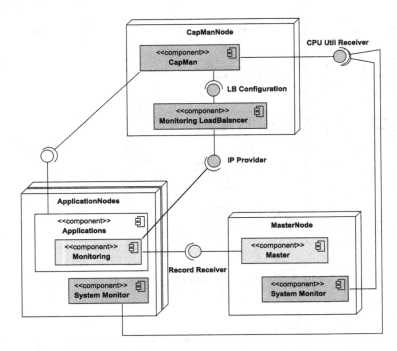

Fig. 2. Our scalable monitoring architecture

which uses these values for scaling the analysis nodes. If a new analysis node is started by CapMan, the IP address of the newly started node is registered in the Monitoring LoadBalancer under a defined loadbalancing group property.

3.3 Analysis Component

To enable a series connection of the different worker levels, the analysis component follows the activities shown in Fig. 3. The monitoring data is received via a TCP connection and a record reconstruction step creates record objects. A record object can contain, for example, a monitored method call (and its data like the method duration), an ID-to-String-mapping, or general meta data. ID-to-String-mappings are an important concept for reducing the transferred data by replacing Strings with an integer representation before sending. The record objects are passed to the trace reconstruction step which links the loose method call records to an execution trace representing the full execution path of one user request. Afterwards, the traces are passed to a trace reduction activity. The chance of same traces typically increases when multiple user requests are conducted. For example, most of the users will access the main page of a website which will often generate the same execution trace in an application. To save network bandwidth and CPU cycles on the next analysis node in the chain, similar traces are reduced to one trace class. For monitoring how many times the

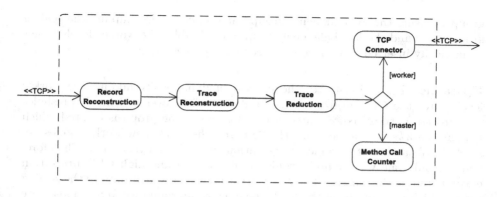

Fig. 3. Activities in the analysis component (worker and master)

trace class was called, it contains an attribute *called times* and runtime statistics (e.g., minimum and maximum duration) for the monitored method calls. To be able to determine which host might behave differently, the runtime statistics are formed on a per host basis.

If an analysis node is started as a worker node, the trace classes are sent to the next analysis node in line via a TCP connector which sends these trace classes as serialized single record objects again. If the analysis node is running as the master node, it simply counts the processed monitored method calls in our example. However, these trace classes can also be used for, e.g., creating a model of the monitored applications as we do it for our ExplorViz [6] visualization.

3.4   Scaling Process

In Fig. 4, the state from Fig. 2 is visualized in a simplified form. The boxes with dashed lines represent one scaling group, i.e., a group of applications which is scaled independently by a capacity manager. The name of each scaling group is displayed at the top. There are two scaling groups: Application and Master. Arrows illustrate accesses to the target scaling group. The label of an arrow is the `loadbalancing group` name used to request an IP address from the `Monitoring LoadBalancer`. In the initial state, the applications access the `Master` scaling

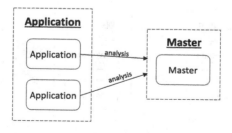

Fig. 4. Initial state before scaling

group by using the loadbalancing group name *analysis*. Decoupling the scaling group name and the loadbalancing group name enables the worker levels to get dynamically inserted or removed between each processing level.

Upscaling. Fig. 5 illustrates the process of dynamically adding one worker level. After the CPU utilization of the `Master` rises over a defined threshold, this process is triggered. At first, a new loadbalancing group is created which is named *worker-1* and contains the `Master`. Then, *two* new worker nodes are started. We assume the same configuration on each analysis node. Therefore, starting only one worker node would result in the same high CPU utilization encountered on the `Master`. The new worker nodes send their data to the scaling group which is resolved by the loadbalancing group name *worker-1*. This state is visualized in Fig. 5a. After the worker application on the nodes are started, the two workers are added to the loadbalancing group *analysis* and the `Master` is removed from it. The final state is illustrated in Fig. 5b. Notably, the order of adding and removing loadbalancing groups is important because the analysis should not be paused during the scaling process.

Downscaling. The downscaling process follows the upscaling process in reverse order. However, we employ a different scaling condition. Our first approach was

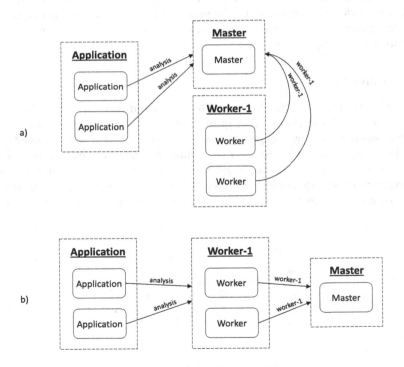

Fig. 5. Activities forming the upscaling process

using the analogous CPU utilization of the `Master` when it falls below a defined threshold. However, this condition is independent from the amount of nodes in the previous worker level. Therefore, it would also trigger when the previous worker level contains, e.g., 10 nodes and shutting down all of them would typically result in an overutilization of the `Master`. This could be lifted by only downscaling when there are exactly two nodes of the previous worker level left. However, this still contains no statement about the utilization of the previous worker level. For example, both workers might be heavily utilized. Hence, we use the CPU utilization of the previous worker level as downscaling condition. When only two nodes are left in the previous worker level and the average CPU utilization falls below a defined threshold in this scaling group, it is shut down and removed by following the upscaling process in analogous reverse order. Therefore, downscaling is not delaying or pausing the analysis either.

3.5   Assumptions and Limitations

For being able to reduce the traces on one worker, similar execution traces have to be generated by the applications in one processing interval (e.g., 5 seconds). From our observations, web applications often impose similar traces if the behavior is not user-specific. However, if every trace is different from another, our worker concept will not work.

A further limitation is imposed by the round-robin connection of the worker nodes. Each worker connects to a new node on a regular basis. Therefore, a common state between the worker and its target node has to be reestablished each time. For instance, the ID-to-String-mapping is shared between both nodes. Therefore, for each new connection this mapping must be communicated to the target node. If this exchange takes too much processing time, our approach may not work. This limitation could probably be lifted by proper caching techniques which stays as future work.

4   Experimental Evaluation

In this section, we present an experiment for evaluating our elastic, distributed application-level monitoring approach. We start by describing the used workload curve and the experimental setup. Then, the results of the experiment are discussed and a summary is presented. At last, we identify threats to validity.

4.1   Workload

Our employed workload curve can be seen in Fig. 6. The access pattern of our object system was modeled after a real web application access pattern which is detailed in [11].

The workload curve represents a day-night-cycle workload pattern which can be considered typical for regional websites. It starts with a rising workload until six o'clock when about 1,000 requests per second are conducted. Then, the load

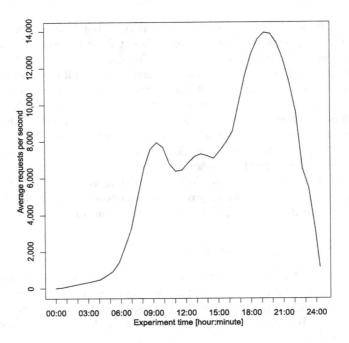

Fig. 6. Employed workload curve

peaks at nine o'clock with about 8,000 requests per second. Afterwards, it slightly decreases to about 7,000 requests per second. In the evening at around eight o'clock p.m., the request count peaks with about 14,000 requests per seconds. Then, it falls to about 1,000 requests per second at midnight and shortly behind this point in time, it drops to no requests for our experiment.

4.2   Experimental Setup

We utilize our private cloud running OpenStack[1] containing seven servers. Each server has two Intel Xeon E5-2650 (2.8 GHz, 8 cores) CPUs, 128 GB of RAM, and a 400 GB SSD. Therefore, the total amount of resources are 112 CPU cores, 896 GB of RAM, and 2.8 TB of disc space. Since every core also features Hyper-threading, we configured our cloud to have a maximum of 224 virtual cores.

As object system, we utilize the web application JPetStore[2] written in Java. As the name suggests, it is a software for setting up a small web shop for pets. We monitor all method calls in the *com.ibatis* package which contains source code written by the authors of JPetStore and all method calls in the *org.apache.struts* package which significantly contributes to the generation time of one web page.

Two flavors – resource configurations in OpenStack terms – are used in our experiment. The first one is a small flavor which is used by every dynamically

---

[1] https://www.openstack.org

[2] http://ibatisjpetstore.sf.net

started instance (Master, Worker, and JPetStore nodes). It consists of one virtual CPU (VCPU), 3 GB of RAM, and 10 GB disc space. With this configuration, we are able to start a total count of 224 possible instances. The second flavor is only used by the capacity manager node. Since this node also contains the `Monitoring LoadBalancer` and generates the workload, it should be guaranteed to have sufficient resources for its tasks. Therefore, the capacity manager node runs with 8 VCPUs, 16 GB of RAM, and 80 GB disc space which reduces the maximum count of dynamically started instances of the small flavor to 216.

A large setup cost for this experiment was imposed by tuning the operating system of the physical server (Debian Sid) to process the large amount of requests per second. In the default configuration, this request amount is detected as potential denial of service attack and thus the requests are dropped. For example, we had to tune the number of usable TCP ports, TCP state timeouts, the maximum open files, and the NAT connection tracking tables. For potential replications, our experimental package contains the relevant configuration files. Furthermore, we provide the virtual machine image used for all our instances to reduce the setup costs.

The configuration of our capacity manager `CapMan` contains three scaling groups, i.e., for the Master, the workers (as prototype for dynamically started levels), and the JPetStores. The Master scaling group uses a threshold of 40 % average CPU utilization to trigger the insertion of a new worker level. `CapMan` always calculates the average CPU utilization over a time window of 120 seconds to reduce the impact of short utilization spikes. The prototype of a worker scaling group is configured with a downscaling condition of a value below 15 % average CPU utilization. A new instance is started if the average CPU utilization is above 45 %. In the JPetStore scaling group, an instance is shut down when the average CPU utilization falls below 27 %. For upscaling, the outstanding requests are counted and when these are above 200, a new instance is started. In contrast to the other scaling groups, the start time of a new instance is not negligible. Therefore, 16 seconds are waited during booting since Jetty must be started and JPetStore must be deployed.

4.3 Results and Discussion

Fig. 7 shows the resulting JPetStore instance count and the average CPU utilization of the Master node in our experiment. In general, the count of the JPetStore instances follows the workload curve and peaks at 160 instances. The only exception is the instance count not reducing after the first peak in the workload at hour nine. This is caused by the 27 % average CPU utilization downscaling condition which could be further reduced to also scale down in this situation.

Notably, since the workload curve is reflected in the JPetStore instances, the general scaling in accordance to the imposed workload is functioning. We now take a closer look at the CPU utilization of the Master, the started worker levels, and the monitored method calls per second.

With the constantly rising workload, the CPU utilization of the Master also constantly increases until approximately hour three. At this time, a new worker

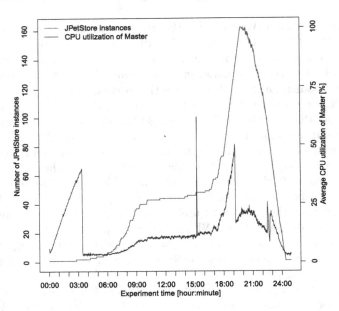

Fig. 7. JPetStore instance count and average CPU utilization of Master node

level is started since the average CPU utilization of the Master rises above 40 %. The started analysis nodes are visualized in Fig. 8 where this circumstance can also be seen. After the successful insertion of the worker level, the CPU utilization of the Master drops to about 3 %. Notably, at this point in time only two JPetStore instances are started. This is reasonable since about 400,000 method calls per seconds need to be analyzed.

After hour three, the CPU utilization of the Master node only rises slightly to 11 % while the JPetStore instance count drastically increases to about 40 instances in hour ten. The work induced by the analysis of the monitoring data is distributed to the workers in the first worker level where the instance count increases to 20 instances till hour ten.

In hour 15, a short peak of about 62 % in the Master CPU utilization can be seen. Since it only occurred for about one minute and has a difference of about 50 % to the previous and afterwards values, this peak is an anomaly. During other runs on our private cloud, we often observed this behavior when another instance is started on the same physical host. Therefore, we implemented an anomaly detection algorithm in our capacity manager for this circumstance and thus no new worker level is started in hour 15.

The JPetStore instance count is rising again from hour 15 till hour 20 peaking in 160 instances. Therefore, the instance count of the workers in the first worker level is also increasing which peaks at about 50 instances in hour 20. Since the Master has to receive and merge the traces from those instances, its CPU utilization also rises until hour 19. Then, the CPU utilization is once again above the 40 % threshold which results in a newly inserted worker level.

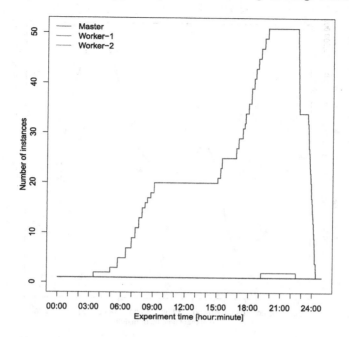

Fig. 8. Analysis nodes and number of instances in each level

Afterwards, the Master CPU utilization drops to about 17 %. This drop is not as large as the previous one but still it circumvents the overutilization of the Master node.

In hour 20, the workload approximately decreases until hour 24. This leads to a reduction of the JPetStore instances and therefore, also the analysis nodes are reduced. At first, the second worker level is completely removed in hour 22 resulting in an increase of the CPU utilization on the Master node. The worker instances in the first worker level are also reduced until hour 24 is reached. Then, also the first worker level is removed resulting in the initial configuration where only the Master node is analyzing the monitored data.

Fig. 9 visualizes the monitored and analyzed method calls per second. In general, it follows the requests per second of the workload and peaks in about 20 million analyzed calls per second. The only exception is a short spike in hour 22. This resulted from a too fast shutdown of one analysis node in the second worker level which can be circumvented by increasing the shutdown delay of analysis nodes in higher worker levels.

4.4 Summary

Summarizing the results, our elastic, distributed application-level monitoring approach shows feasible to circumvent the overutilization of the Master node in spite of a rising workload. Furthermore, the Master node employs only a

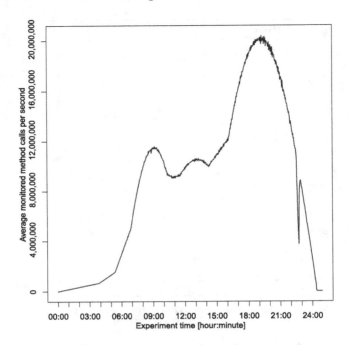

Fig. 9. Average monitored and analyzed method calls per second

single VCPU. Therefore, during low workload on the monitored applications, the minimum costs for monitoring incur.

4.5   Threats to Validity

We conducted our experiment on our private cloud with scaling of JPetStore instances. For external validity, it should also be evaluated in other environments and with other applications. The same applies to the employed workload curve and the amount of conducted monitoring.

Our experiment involved two worker levels due to having only 216 VCPUs available. The results for a third worker level might be different. Further experiments are required to show if the third worker level still circumvents the overutilization of the Master node.

Furthermore, similar traces are generated by accessing JPetStore. We assume that our monitoring approach will behave differently if this assumption is not satisfied. This should be also investigated in further experiments.

5   Related Work

Brunst and Nagel [2] present a parallel analysis infrastructure. They focus on massive parallel systems with thousands of processor cores. In contrast, we focus on the monitoring and analysis of applications running on typical business servers or in cloud environments.

Meng et al. [10] propose a Monitoring-as-a-Service solution for monitoring cloud infrastructures. To monitor the complex infrastructure of Cloud data centers, they developed a scalable and flexible monitoring topology consisting of different services. Compared to our approach, they focus on monitoring the virtualized data center environment.

Hilbrich and Muller-Pfefferkorn [7] describe a concept of a scalable job centric monitoring infrastructure. Their approach features multiple layers of short and long time storage of the monitored data. Contrary, we directly analyze the monitored data after gathering it without a persistent storage.

The ECoWare Infrastructure [1] consists of three types of components, i.e., the execution environment, processors, and a dashboard. In contrast to our approach, they use a message bus for their analysis and do not provide multiple analysis levels.

In [5], we presented a first idea of utilizing multiple worker levels. However, at this time, the count of worker levels was statically determined at the start of the system, i.e., not adapting to the actual workload. Furthermore, we only presented the idea without evaluating the concept of worker levels.

In general, our approach exhibits similarities to the MapReduce pattern [3]. However, in contrast to our approach, it does not dynamically insert or remove preprocessing levels according to the actual workload.

Capacity management approaches utilizing the monitored data for their scaling decisions, e.g., SLAstic [8], are also related to our approach, since they must analyze the monitored data just after it was observed. To the best of our knowledge, none of these approaches utilizes dynamically inserted or removed worker levels as presented here.

6   Conclusions

In this paper, we presented our elastic, distributed application-level monitoring approach to circumvent the overuse of a single analysis master application. We dynamically insert and remove preprocessing worker levels depending on the actual utilization of the analysis master without interrupting the analysis of the monitored data. In our presented 24 hour experiment, 160 monitored JPetStore instances generated roughly 20 million analyzed method calls per second in the peak. It showed that our approach is feasible and is capable of live analyzing several millions of monitored method calls.

For replications of our experiment and extensions of our approach, we provide an experimental package [4] containing the used programs as executables, written source code under the Apache 2.0 License, server settings, virtual machine image, and raw experimental results.

Future work includes implementing and evaluating caching techniques for enhancing the state exchange between the analysis node. Furthermore, since our experiment only involved two worker levels, we aim to conduct an even larger experiment with more worker levels to investigate the applicability to thousands of monitored applications. In addition, our approach should be evaluated with different cloud environments and different monitored applications, e.g., RUBiS, to investigate the effect of these variables.

References

1. Baresi, L., Guinea, S.: Event-based multi-level service monitoring. In: Proc. of 20th Int. Conf. on Web Services (ICWS 2013). IEEE, June 2013
2. Brunst, H., Nagel, W.E.: Scalable performance analysis of parallel systems: Concepts and experiences. In: Proc. of the 10th Conf. on Parallel Computing: Software Technology, Algorithms, Architectures, and Applications. Elsevier (2003)
3. Dean, J., Ghemawat, S.: MapReduce: a flexible data processing tool. Communications of the ACM 53(1), 72–77 (2010)
4. Fittkau, F., Hasselbring, W.: Data for: Elastic application-level monitoring for large software landscapes in the cloud (2015). doi:10.5281/zenodo.19296
5. Fittkau, F., Waller, J., Brauer, P.C., Hasselbring, W.: Scalable and live trace processing with Kieker utilizing cloud computing. In: Proc. of the Symposium on Software Performance: Joint Kieker/Palladio Days 2013. CEUR Workshop Proceedings, vol. 1083, November 2013
6. Fittkau, F., Waller, J., Wulf, C., Hasselbring, W.: Live trace visualization for comprehending large software landscapes: The ExplorViz approach. In: Proc. of the 1st Int. Working Conf. on Software Visualization (VISSOFT 2013), September 2013
7. Hilbrich, M., Muller-Pfefferkorn, R.: Identifying limits of scalability in distributed, heterogeneous, layer based monitoring concepts like SLAte. Comp. Sc. 13(3) (2012)
8. van Hoorn, A., Rohr, M., Gul, I.A., Hasselbring, W.: An adaptation framework enabling resource-efficient operation of software systems. In: Proc. of the Warm Up Workshop (WUP 2009) for ICSE 2010. ACM, April 2009
9. van Hoorn, A., Waller, J., Hasselbring, W.: Kieker: A framework for application performance monitoring and dynamic software analysis. In: Proc. of the 3rd Int. Conf. on Performance Engineering (ICPE 2012). ACM, April 2012
10. Meng, S., Liu, L., Soundararajan, V.: Tide: Achieving self-scaling in virtualized datacenter management middleware. In: Proc. of the 11th Int. Middleware Conf. (Middleware 2010). ACM (2010)
11. Rohr, M., van Hoorn, A., Hasselbring, W., Lübcke, M., Alekseev, S.: Workload-intensity-sensitive timing behavior analysis for distributed multi-user software systems. In: Proc. of the First Joint WOSP/SIPEW Int. Conf. on Performance Engineering (WOSP/SIPEW 2010), pp. 87–92. ACM (2010)
12. Vierhauser, M., Rabiser, R., Grünbacher, P.: A case study on testing, commissioning, and operation of very-large-scale software systems. In: Proc. of the 36th Int. Conf. on Software Engineering (ICSE Companion 2014). ACM (2014)

Evaluation of the Employment of Machine Learning Approaches and Strategies for Service Recommendation

Jens Kirchner[1,2]([✉]), Andreas Heberle[1], and Welf Löwe[2]

[1] Karlsruhe University of Applied Sciences, Karlsruhe, Germany
{Jens.Kirchner,Andreas.Heberle}@hs-karlsruhe.de
[2] Linnaeus University, Växjö, Sweden
{Jens.Kirchner,Welf.Lowe}@lnu.se

Abstract. Service functionality can be provided by more than one service consumer. In order to choose the service with the highest benefit, a selection based on previously measured experiences by other consumers is beneficial. In this paper, we present the results of our evaluation of two machine learning approaches in combination with several learning strategies to predict the best service within this selection problem. The first approach focuses on the prediction of the best-performing service, while the second approach focuses on the prediction of service performances which can then be used for the determination of the best-performing service. We assessed both approaches w. r. t. the overall optimization achievement relative to the worst- and the best-performing service. Our evaluation is based on data measured on real Web services as well as on simulated data. The latter is needed for a more profound analysis of the strengths and weaknesses of each approach and learning strategy when it gets harder to distinguish the performance profile of the service candidates. The simulated data focuses on different aspects of a service performance profile. For the real-world measurement data, 97 % overall optimization achievement and over 82 % best service selection could be achieved within the evaluation.

1 Introduction

Service-Oriented Computing (SOC), Software as a Service (SaaS), Cloud Computing, and Mobile Computing indicate the development of the Internet into a market of services. With little to no knowledge about the service implementation or the system environment, service consumers can dynamically and ubiquitously consume service functionality. Besides the actual functionality, service consumers are interested in the service performance, which is expressed in its non-functional properties (NFPs) such as response time, availability, or monetary costs. In such a service market, the same service functionality may be provided by several competing service providers. Among these similar services, service consumers are interested in the service which fits best to their (NFP) preferences. In particular, consumers are interested in the actual experienced performance.

© IFIP International Federation for Information Processing 2015
S. Dustdar et al. (Eds.): ESOCC 2015, LNCS 9306, pp. 95–109, 2015.
DOI: 10.1007/978-3-319-24072-5_7

One of the major characteristics of a service market such as the Internet is perpetual change. Entering and leaving service providers as well as the complexity of service dependencies and environments make service selection and recommendation a challenge. Our service recommendation framework uses a collaborative knowledge base of consumption experiences of similar consumers in the past to predict the performance of a service in a certain consumer-based call context. This is used to recommend the best-fit service candidate to a consumer, considering his/her preferences [1,2]. Since the experienced performance at consumer side is influenced by a consumer's call context, e. g., calling time and location, the performance has to be predicted based on this context. Furthermore, performance is different for different consumers who value the NFPs of a service differently. For instance, some consumers are more interested in a fast response time and rather neglect higher monetary charges than others who want to have a service for free and rather experience higher response times. Therefore, service value is individual and it has to be determined individually whether a service is actually best-fit in a specific context. Considering these aspects, we analyzed two machine learning approaches which are based on classification and regression in combination with learning strategies for an optimal employment within service recommendation. Our practical assessment is based on real-world measurement data as well as profile-guided simulation data which addresses certain aspects of changes in the performance behavior of services for a more fine-grained analysis.

2   Recommendation Background and Framework

As written above, perpetual change is one of the major characteristics of the Internet as a service market. Among similar functional services, the selection of a service instance is based on one or more NFPs. NFPs have different scales of measurement with different optimization functions. For example, response time is a ratio scale with an optimization towards the minimum. The availability of a service at a specific time is nominal: a service is either available or not. In such a case, the optimization focus is to select a service instance which has the highest (maximum) probability of being available. When the selection of a service instance is based on more than one NFP, NFP data has to be normalized in order to be comparable and calculable. In such a case, not all NFPs are equally important, so their importance has to be weighted and taken into account [2]. In [1], we introduced our framework which optimizes service selection based on consumer experience, call context, and preferences (utility). Within this paper, the focus is set on the machine learning approaches which can be employed for service recommendation in general, and which can be implemented within our framework. Figure 1 depicts how the broker component in our framework works and where machine learning methods are employed. Constantly collecting the measurement data of service calls, the data is then pre-processed for the learning of each NFP of a service instance considering the contexts of the service calls from where the data derives. The NFPs/performance of each service instance are learned and constitute a background model. For each utility function and each

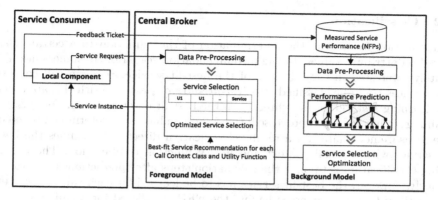

Fig. 1. Foreground and Background Model within our Framework [2]

context, this model contains the utility value of each service instance. Within each utility function and call context, the instance with the highest utility value is considered to be the best-fit service instance among functionally similar services. This best-fit service is saved in a foreground model to provide good performance within the time-critical recommendation process. It is updated with relearned background model information within intervals and on detected change. Once again, since preferences vary among all service consumers, the best-fit service instance is individual for each utility function.

3   Employment of Machine Learning Approaches

Initially introduced in [2,3], for the employment within our framework, we follow two machine learning approaches for service recommendation.

3.1   Regression

In machine learning, regression aims at the prediction of numerical values based on attribute values. Within our focus, regression can be used to predict each NFP value (e. g., the expected response time) based on call context values (e. g., calling time and weekday). The drawback is that learning has to be conducted for each NFP individually and the actual utility value for the best-fit determination has to be calculated. These higher efforts, however, have several benefits at the same time. For each NFP and call context combination, the NFP value has only to be predicted once, while the best-fit service can be calculated for each preference (utility function) individually. Furthermore, since each service's utility value is calculated (based on the expected NFP values) and considered, the ranking of second, third, etc. best-fit services can be used to achieve a higher overall performance gain. Note that utility optimization does not require a high accuracy of selecting the best-fit if the second best-fit achieves an almost as high utility gain. Also, underdog and quick starter strategies can also be implemented, since the performance data of services of calls of the past still remain.

3.2 Classification

Classification focuses on the determination of the affiliation to a certain class based on attribute values. In the recommendation scenario, consumers are ultimately interested in the selection of the best-fit service. So for a call context, the services could be classified into *best-fit* and *non-best-fit*. With this approach, the learning method focuses directly on the best-fit determination. For this, the training set has to be pre-processed: the champion has to be determined based on the measurement data. As a result, classification directly determines the best-fit service within a call context and utility function combination. The benefit using classification is to omit the calculation steps after prediction. Disadvantageously, however, the best-fit service has to be learned for each call context and each utility function; whereas having the NFPs predicted for a call context as an intermediate step, the best-fit service can be calculated for other utility functions without new learning. Furthermore, old service instances are automatically not further considered and, hence, sorted out. Disadvantageously, underdogs can never prove themselves since the approach is only focused on best-fit service recommendation and non-best-fit are neglected or not invoked at all. Also, there is no differentiation among non-best-fit services, which is important in a non-accurate prediction in order to still create a high utility gain.

4 Research Question

In [2,3], we showed that in general a classification- and regression-based approach can be employed for service recommendation. Additionally to these initial analyses, the present paper focuses on the research question regarding optimal learning strategies for the employment of machine learning approaches in service recommendation within a real-world scenario and focusing on certain performance behavior profiles. Within this, the following sub-questions address different aspects which need to be analyzed: What is the optimal size for the training dataset of a learning model in this context? How long is a trained model reliable for good service recommendation? Which learning strategy is better: incremental learning or sliding windows? Based on that, is drift detection implemented by a learning method better to cope with change? Is there a difference in the accuracy of service recommendation for different learning approaches when the services' performance profile becomes more and more similar?

5 Analysis of the Learning Approaches

For the conduction of the analysis, we developed a Java-based software that uses Weka[1] and MOA[2] as machine learning frameworks. Both were chosen because of their extensive collection of classical and state of the art methods and their

---

[1] http://www.cs.waikato.ac.nz/ml/weka/

[2] http://moa.cms.waikato.ac.nz/

Table 1. Evaluation Indicators

Overall Achievement	It indicates the optimization degree in per cent between the response time of the worst service towards the response time of the best service for each prediction case: $\left(1 - \frac{RT_{Prediction} - RT_{Best}}{RT_{Worst} - RT_{Best}}\right) \cdot 100$
Best Choice	It expresses the amount in per cent of the prediction of the actual best(-fit) service candidates.

high automation degree. Based on good initial results in regression [2], we chose the Fast Incremental Model Tree with Drift Detection (FIMT-DD) algorithm for regression. FIMT-DD focuses on time-changing data streams with explicit drift detection [4]. For classification, we chose DecisionStump[3], which showed the highest accuracy in initial experiments.

There are several aspects relevant for the evaluation of machine learning methods such as speed, accuracy, scalability, robustness, and interpretability [2,5,6]. Since service consumers are interested in the improvement of the performance they experience, we chose accuracy and performance as key indicators. As our focus is not set on the complexity of multi-target NFP optimizations, we reduce utility to the (arguably) most important NFP which is *response time*. The performance gain is therefore not based on a utility value, which is the weighted sum of different NPFs, but an *overall performance achievement* between the response time of the worst-performing service and the best-performing service. Second indicator is *best choice* to reflect the top-selection accuracy. The definitions of both indicators are listed in Table 1. Recall, service recommendation is an optimization problem. Hence, performance gain is more important than a high accuracy of selecting the best-performing service, since a slightly worse second best might still create a high performance gain which would not be reflected in best choice.

Regression is able to exploit continuous (date)time values. For classification, additional enhanced time attributes were added. Furthermore, in addition to the basic attributes *date*, *time*, and *response time*, we added further attributes to each measurement entry in order to provide statistically enhanced data with focus on natural periods. The additional attributes were added to all datasets. Note that these additional attributes (Table 2) only consider attribute values of previous records, since the current response time value of each record is part of the actual learning.

Due to different prerequisites of the two machine learning approaches, additional approach-specific pre-processing had to be conducted. Using regression, each NFP of each service instance has to be learned individually. Hence, the datasets had to be filtered into sub-datasets for each service. Classification is only interested in the best service at each moment in time. Therefore, the dataset had to be filtered so that only the records of the fastest services remained.

---

[3] http://weka.sourceforge.net/doc.dev/weka/classifiers/trees/DecisionStump.html

Table 2. Statistical Enhancement of Attributes

DayOfMonth	Extracted day of month from date
Hour	Extracted hour from time
Weekday	Determined nominal day of week from date *(class. only)*
Workingday	True is weelday is Monday to Friday *(class. only)*
RT_Xmin_AVG $X = \{61, 121, 181, 361, 721, 1441, 2881, 7201, 10081\}$	Response time mean of all records (chronologically) within the last 1, 2, 3, 6, 12 hours, and 1, 2, 5, 7 days
RT_X_AVG $X = \{40, 80, 160, 240\}$	Response time mean of the previous x records (chronologically; without consideration of any other attribute)
RT_X_AVG_Hour $X = \{4, 12, 20, 28\}$	Response time mean of the previous x records within the same hour value (1, 3, 5, 7 days of the same nominal hour)
RT_X_AVG_Weekday $X = \{4, 8, 16\}$	Resp. time mean of the prev. x records within the same weekday value (1, 2, 4 weeks of the same nom. day of w.)

Furthermore, the response time attribute is not directly used in classification, only indirectly for determining the best-fit service in the training set. Therefore, we removed the response time attribute for learning. After pre-processing, each dataset had to be divided into a training and a validation sub-set. Because of chronological aspects, the dataset could only be split into training and validation sets. N-fold cross validation could not be applied for that reason. In contrast to initial analyses, we conducted a sliding split point evaluation. For each analysis of an aspect, the split point between training set and validation set was iterated day by day. Depending on the period (and window sizes), it could result in a statistical mean of up to $\frac{n}{24m} - 1$ iterations (for the measurement input 170 iterations per scenario), for n data entries and m data records per hour (one record for each service).

5.1   Learning Strategies

In order to address the research questions related to the optimal learning strategies, we conducted the following scenarios. For both scenarios, we applied a prediction window of various sizes in order to determine the optimal training/prediction interval ratio for the updates of the foreground model (Figure 1).

Incremental Learning. This scenario continuously updates the learning model. Any strategies on changes and their impact on the model have to be dealt by the learning method such as drift detection.

Sliding Window Learning. This learning scenario applies a fixed window of previous measurements for the training of the learning model.

5.2   Measurement Data

The measurement data was gained from four real-world stock quote Web services [1]. The services are functionally similar, so they can be substituted.

The measurement period for this dataset was 185 days and contained 16,441 measurement entries. Each entry contained the date, time, the consumed service, and the measured response time. Within this period, each Web service was called on an hourly basis and its response time during this call was measured; hence, four data entries per hour. If a service was not available or timed out (30,000 ms), its entry was not added to the set.

5.3 Simulation Scenarios

The simulation of measurement data enabled to challenge machine learning approaches and to analyze their performance in certain scenarios. Within the measured real-world Web services, the statistical characteristics showed easily distinguishable performance profiles of the services. In order to compare the strengths and weaknesses of the machine learning approaches in more challenging scenarios, where the service profiles are harder to distinguish, we step by step approximated these profiles. For each profile, learning approach, and learning strategy combination, we conducted approximation iterations in 10 % steps until their profiles were fully identical (up to random noise).

Normal Distribution Profiled Data. As a baseline of every service profile, we assumed normally distributed response times of Web services around a mean value (with a certain standard deviation and variance). We created[4] normally distributed response time data for four services with a similar initial mean (vertical shift), standard deviation, and variance as the four measured Web services. This mean response time gets approximated step by step. Fully approximated, their statistical mean is identical.

Cyclic Spikes Up/Down. We generated two profiles with response times normally distributed around the same mean but with cyclic/periodic spikes which go in one profile up and in the other profile down. Spikes going up simulate services that have suddenly longer response times, while spikes going down simulate sudden response time improvements. For their creation, we used a saw tooth generator[5] in combination with an iceberg filter which are added to the basic normal distribution line. Again, all created services are similar. They are distinguished only in their horizontal shift. Fully approximated, their horizontal shift is identical.

Acyclic Spikes Up/Down. This profile has several acyclic spikes and different levels shifts in combination with an iceberg filter. Using several cyclic spikes in spikes generations with very long periods in combination with pulse train shifts[6] and the iceberg filter, a complete acyclic/aperiodic behavior could be simulated. Again, all services have the same mean response time and in a fully approximated case, their spikes are overlapping.

---

[4] Java implementation based on http://info.michael-simons.eu/2013/02/21/java-implementation-of-excels-statistical-functions-norminv/.

[5] Cf. Saw tooth generation using Fourier series http://mathworld.wolfram.com/FourierSeriesTriangleWave.html

[6] Fourier series expansion was used; cf. http://en.wikipedia.org/wiki/Pulse_wave

6 Results

The results presented in this section are mean values. For each input dataset, each evaluation scenario was conducted on a sliding iteration with sliding start, split, and end points in order to get statistically profound results.

6.1 Measurement Data

Based on the initially analyzed Web Services [3], we used an extended measurement dataset of over six months of four functionally substitutable real-world Web services. In contrast to the initial analysis, we conducted sliding iterations with sliding start, split, and end points. The purpose of these sliding iterations is to statistically equalize any start, split, or end point, so that the results are not influenced by any selected point. Within the evaluation of the two learning approaches, we used two general learning scenarios. The first scenario trains the learning model on an incremental basis, while the second uses a sliding window for training. For the window scenarios, we evaluated different window sizes.

Addressing the question whether increment or window learning is better, Table 3 shows the results of the incremental learning scenarios with prediction windows of 1 and 28 days. Within the overall optimization achievement of response time as well as the best choice indicator, there is not much deterioration of the predictions of the upcoming day to four weeks. However, the standard deviation of the results decreases for the wider prediction window; especially, in the case of the FIMT-DD, which we presume already due to its drift detection.

Analyzing optimal sliding training window sizes and the reliability within increasing prediction window sizes, we conducted sliding iterations with different window sizes for training and prediction. Table 4 reveals the statistical mean values for the analyzed training window sizes, while Table 5 for the analyzed prediction window sizes. Again, the analysis data revealed not much difference between the different window sizes in the overall achievement indicator, while there is a difference in the best choice indicator (Table 5). For the classification approach using DecisionStump, small prediction windows achieve better best choice indicator values than wider ones. Regression-based FIMT-DD remains more or less steady regardless of the window size. In direct comparison, the classification-based determination of the best-fit service is in general slightly better (in the case of a prediction window size of one day). In Figure 2(b), it seems that for the DecisionStump approach, a smaller prediction window results in a better best choice indicator, while for FIMT-DD a wider prediction window leads to a steadier best choice prediction (similar best choice mean, but a smaller standard deviation). Recall, the indicators introduced in Table 1 focus on different aspects. While the best choice indicator focuses on the accuracy in the overall prediction of the actual best-fit service (employing machine learning methods as well a calculation steps), the overall achievement indicator expresses the degree of optimization. Although it is desirable to always predict the best service candidate, for an optimization it is not necessary if the second-best creates a similarly high optimization benefit.

Table 3. Different Prediction Windows within Incremental Learning

Win. Size	*DecisionStump*				*FIMT-DD*			
	Achievement		**Best Choice**		**Achievement**		**Best Choice**	
Prediction	*mean*	σ	*mean*	σ	*mean*	σ	*mean*	σ
1	97.10 %	6.10 %	82.26 %	22.89 %	97.04 %	3.89 %	73.35 %	21.47 %
28	96.34 %	2.23 %	72.77 %	22.94 %	97.02 %	1.60 %	72.78 %	13.59 %

Table 4. Sliding Window Scenario with Different Training Windows

Win. Size	*DecisionStump*				*FIMT-DD*			
	Achievement		**Best Choice**		**Achievement**		**Best Choice**	
Training	*mean*	σ	*mean*	σ	*mean*	σ	*mean*	σ
1	96.50 %	3.93 %	74.76 %	22.74 %	97.13 %	2.35 %	73.52 %	16.67 %
10	97.29 %	3.21 %	80.85 %	20.83 %	97.23 %	2.36 %	73.94 %	16.89 %
20	97.37 %	3.18 %	79.90 %	22.51 %	97.38 %	2.29 %	74.74 %	16.87 %
40	97.70 %	2.97 %	81.31 %	25.42 %	97.93 %	1.66 %	78.86 %	14.50 %
60	98.32 %	2.53 %	89.72 %	12.70 %	98.16 %	1.63 %	81.89 %	13.20 %
120	97.45 %	4.36 %	89.79 %	4.25 %	97.48 %	2.00 %	72.97 %	13.87 %

Table 5. Sliding Window Scenario with Different Prediction Windows

Win. Size	*DecisionStump*				*FIMT-DD*			
	Achievement		**Best Choice**		**Achievement**		**Best Choice**	
Prediction	*mean*	σ	*mean*	σ	*mean*	σ	*mean*	σ
1	97.86 %	4.81 %	85.61 %	17.27 %	97.48 %	3.55 %	75.76 %	21.43 %
7	97.42 %	3.52 %	83.48 %	17.33 %	97.54 %	1.95 %	75.87 %	16.27 %
14	97.31 %	2.91 %	82.06 %	18.18 %	97.56 %	1.53 %	75.87 %	12.92 %
28	97.16 %	2.22 %	79.73 %	19.52 %	97.63 %	1.16 %	76.44 %	10.71 %

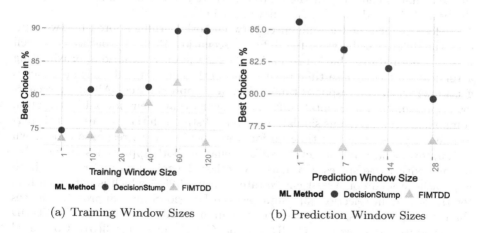

(a) Training Window Sizes   (b) Prediction Window Sizes

Fig. 2. Best Choice Means of Different Window Sizes with Measurement Data

6.2 Simulated Scenarios

Based on the very good results of the measurement data and the results regarding the optimal window sizes for training and prediction, we now challenged both learning approaches with generated data. In contrast to the measured Web services with their quite distinctive characteristics, we generated the behavior of services with the simulation scenarios (profiles) introduced in Section 5.3. The services within a scenario have similar profiles but distinguish themselves in isolated focused aspects. Like the measurement data, the training on the generated datasets is also conducted on a sliding iteration basis. Additionally, we approximated each profile in 10 % steps until they were identical (disregarding some random noise) in order to address the last research sub-question. Presumably, the results of the machine learning approaches are supposed to get worse during the approximation. Still, the results of each approximation step reveal how good the learning approaches can cope with the challenge which the respective scenario focused on. The mean values in the illustrations were gained from the sliding window approach with a training window size of seven days and a prediction window of one day. This was the overall optimal combination for the measured real-world scenario. The generated input provided data for a period of six weeks in total. Since the simulated data followed a profile-guided generation, a longer period would not lead to different results in this case. Figure 3 depicts the best choice results for each machine learning approach. Figure 4 shows the correspondent overall achievement figures. Since the achievement is defined relatively between the best and worst service performances and since these performances are approximated step by step, there is not much difference between both figures with their different accuracy criteria "best choice" and "overall achievement", resp.; especially, when the approximation approaches 100 %. For the cyclic and acyclic profiles, the non-best services perform equally since there is no vertical shift. Hence, the overall achievement depends only on whether finding the best choice or not. Therefore, for these profiles, there is not much difference between the best choice and the overall achievement indicators.

Before we focus on the differences between both learning approaches, we compare the differences between the different scenarios. Both approaches cope well with the normal distribution scenario. This is the only scenario approximating a vertical shift (response time mean), and both methods and their approaches get worse when the response time means are approximated. All other scenarios approximate a horizontal shift. That means that their normal distribution component is and remains similar. They only distinguish themselves in their performance spikes (response time up for worse performance; response time down for improvements). In the acyclic spike scenarios, both approaches are not able to cope with these spikes. No matter whether the spikes go up or down, both approaches remain on a best choice rate of around 25 % which is not much better than random selection [3]. However, the DecisionStump approach achieves slightly better results. Comparing the remaining cyclic scenarios, the FIMT-DD can show its strengths (see CyclDown and CyclUp in Figure 3(b)). Compared to the classification-based approach illustrated in Figure 3(a), the FIMT-DD

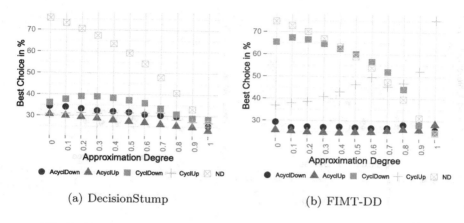

(a) DecisionStump   (b) FIMT-DD

Fig. 3. Best Choice Mean using Sliding Windows within the Scenarios

achieves much higher best choice (and overall achievement) figures. The profiles of each service are taken into account, while this information is lost using the classification approach, which is illustrated in the charts in Figures 3 and 4. Our question, whether it makes any difference if the spikes go up (a service gets suddenly worse) or the spikes go down (a service gets suddenly better), could be answered. According to the results, illustrated in the figures, it does make a difference whether the spikes go up or down. FIMT-DD is in both cases significantly better. However, if a service gets suddenly worse among similar services (spikes down), it can be learned better than the other way around. It seems to be easier to learn an outstanding service whereas it seems to be more difficult to recognize a service getting worse within the optimization focus of similar well performing services. The presumed reason for that could be that spikes down (improvement of a single service) are changes within the optimization focus.

Having a closer look at the cyclic up illustration in Figure 3(b) and Figure 4(b), the indicator values get better with a higher approximation degree. This seems to be odd. One explanation could be that the regression-based approach focuses on the prediction of the performance behavior of each service as a pre-step for the actual best service determination, while the classification-based approach only focuses on the direct learning of the best fit service. However, the spikes up scenario simulates the opposite. Furthermore, considering the generation of the cyclic down and up scenario, their profiles are inverted on a higher level. The differences between the results in the figures also appear to be inverted. Still, the results for this scenario require further analysis, since a total approximation of this profile and its normal distribution part should develop similarly to the fully approximated normal distribution scenario.

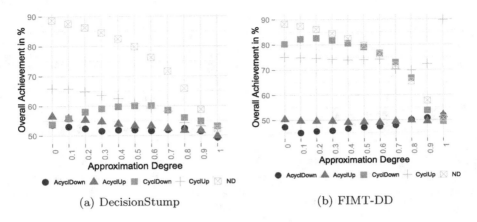

(a) DecisionStump   (b) FIMT-DD

Fig. 4. Overall Achievement Mean using Sliding Windows within the Scenarios

6.3   Overall Results Conclusion

Both learning approaches achieved high overall optimization achievement results within the validation using real-world measurement data. Considering the best choice indicator, the classification-based approach could achieve higher values, however, with a higher standard deviation. Since real world-measured Web services have different profiles, which are easy to distinguish, challenging simulation scenarios showed the strengths and weaknesses of each approach. The regression-based approach for the prediction of the actual performance of each service candidate could prove its strengths in a cyclic behavior scenario. The consideration of a ranked determination of best services is especially beneficial since second-best service candidates can also still create an almost high optimization benefit. The normal distribution scenario showed that if the competitive service candidates mainly distinguish themselves vertically within the optimization focus, both machine learning approaches achieve equally good results.

6.4   Threats to Validity

The analysis is based on measured and generated data. Addressing an emerging future market, it is difficult to find freely consumable and functionally similar services. Therefore, the measurement data bases only on four Web services. The NFP behavior of Web services are diverse, therefore, the characteristics of other services may show different results. Nonetheless, with generated data of various scenarios as well as their approximation, we could analyze the strengths and weaknesses in detail. This would not be possible if the analysis is only based on measurement data.

7   Related Work

In [2], we introduced our service recommendation framework with an initial implementation using machine learning. We also determined appropriate machine learning frameworks which can be employed for service recommendation in general. First evaluations of the classification- and regression-based approaches were described in [3]. In these evaluations, we only had measurement input for 34 days. Furthermore, we did not conduct a sliding window approach. However, using different start, split, and end points can lead to different evaluation results. A sliding-conduction-based evaluation, which we used for the evaluation of the results of this paper, leads to more statistically profound results. In contrast to relative indicators (comparison to random selection), we used absolute indicators in this paper. Furthermore, in this paper, the generated simulation data focused specifically on general, presumable aspects of the performance behavior of services, which is beneficial for general evaluation of both approaches focusing on performance-behavior-based changes within a service market. Approaches using collaborative filtering (CF) for service recommendation also focus on the exploitation of shared knowledge about services in order to recommend services to similar consumers before the actual consumption on an automated basis (cf. [7–10]). Machine learning, in general, can also be used in CF. In contrast to the filtering of external decision results in CF, our approach determines the individual best-fit service based on previously measured performance data, individual preferences, and calculated utility values. With the call context and utility function approach, in our framework, new consumers can already benefit from existing knowledge. CF approaches also do not take into account that consumers can have different optimization goals or preferences and only some approaches [8,9] consider differences between consumers regarding their context. In [11], the authors tackle the lack of consideration of a consumer's preferences and interests; however, they do not take consumer context into account. The authors of [12,13] describe approaches to tackle the mentioned cold-start problem within CF. In [14], the authors used data mining methods for the service discovery. For the recommendation of services, trust and reputation are also important aspects. They can be understood in the security meaning, but also in a reliability context. For the latter, there are approaches which focus on a trust/reputation-based service recommendation [15–19]. Timelines within contexts are an important aspect. We leave this information to be handled by machine learning methods (apart from initial preparations). For detailed learning aspects on this context detail, we refer to the field of time series analysis.

8   Conclusion

With the sliding iterations of the input set, we conducted a statistically profound analysis of a classification- and regression-based machine learning approach for service recommendation. Both learning approaches achieved very high overall optimization achievement results within the validation using real-world measurement data. In contrast to the best choice indicator, for which both approaches also achieved high values, the overall achievement figure also takes into account the optimization achievement when recommending non-best-fit service candidates. The overall optimization achievement is more significant than the best choice indicator since it considers the actual utility/performance gain.

Considering the various training windows, the overall achievement figures remain similar when processing the measurement data. However, with an increasing training window size of up to 60 days, the best choice indicator improves for both approaches. For both approaches, the sliding window training strategy achieved better results than incremental learning. Although the classification approach achieved better best choice figures than the regression-based approach, both have similar overall achievements. So, the strength of the regression-based approach is the indirect ranking within the non-best services. Although the FIMT-DD regression method focuses on drift detection, a sliding training window achieved better results than the incremental learning approach.

In order to challenge both approaches and analyze their strengths and weaknesses in detail, we created profile-guided simulation data and re-conducted the analysis. Additionally, we approximated each generation scenario and re-run each analysis on each approximation step. For a normal distribution scenario, both approaches achieved similar good results. As expected, an increasing approximation degree resulted in less optimization achievement. In the acyclic case, both approaches did not achieve good results. However, the classification-based approach was slightly better. The regression-based approach achieved very good results within the cyclic profile scenario. Focusing on the best choice indicator, the approaches cope better with the scenarios with sudden performance improvements (spikes down) than with sudden performance decreases (spikes up). The unexpected improvements in the cyclic up scenario within the approximation steps require further analysis.

This work raised further future work questions: So far we have focused on a classification- and regression-based approach. Other approaches such as cyclic regression methods should be also evaluated. Also, other presumable behavior scenarios such as sudden death or continuously de-/increasing performance of services can be used for the analysis of the machine learning approaches. Furthermore, service recommendation also has an impact on the actual NFPs (e. g., NFP values of best-fit services might become worse due to over-consumption because of service recommendation), which also needs to be analyzed. In case of considerable negative effects, new strategies have to be found. Last but not least, strategies which aim at giving underdogs a chance to improve and quick starter strategies have to be found.

References

1. Andersson, J., Heberle, A., Kirchner, J., Löwe, W.: Service level achievements - distributed knowledge for optimal service selection. In: IEEE European Conference on Web Services (ECOWS) (2011)

2. Kirchner, J., Karg, P., Heberle, A., Löwe, W.: Appropriate machine learning methods for service recommendation based on measured consumer experiences within a service market. In: Int. Conf. on Advanced Service Computing (2015)
3. Kirchner, J., Heberle, A., Löwe, W.: Classification vs. Regression - Machine learning approaches for service recommendation based on measured consumer experiences. In: IEEE 11th World Congress on Services (SERVICES) (2015)
4. Ikonomovska, E., Gama, J., Džeroski, S.: Learning model trees from evolving data streams. Data Mining and Knowledge Discovery 23(1) (2011)
5. Han, J., Kamber, M.: Data Mining: Concepts and Techniques, 2nd edn. Elsevier, Morgan Kaufmann (2006)
6. Kotsiantis, S.B.: Supervised machine learning: A review of classification techniques. Informatica (31) (2007)
7. Zheng, Z., Ma, H., Lyu, M., King, I.: QoS-aware Web service recommendation by collaborative filtering. IEEE Trans. on Services Computing 4(2) (2011)
8. Tang, M., Jiang, Y., Liu, J., Liu, X.: Location-aware collaborative filtering for QoS-based service recommendation. In: IEEE Int. Conf. on Web Services (ICWS) (2012)
9. Kuang, L., Xia, Y., Mao, Y.: Personalized services recommendation based on context-aware QoS prediction. In: IEEE Int. Conf. Web Services (ICWS) (2012)
10. Yang, R., Chen, Q., Qi, L., Dou, W.: A QoS evaluation method for personalized service requests. In: Gong, Z., Luo, X., Chen, J., Lei, J., Wang, F.L. (eds.) WISM 2011, Part II. LNCS, vol. 6988, pp. 393–402. Springer, Heidelberg (2011)
11. Kang, G., Liu, J., Tang, M., Liu, X., Cao, B., Xu, Y.: AWSR: active Web service recommendation based on usage history. In: IEEE Int. Conf. on Web Services (ICWS) (2012)
12. Yu, Q.: Decision tree learning from incomplete QoS to bootstrap service recommendation. In: IEEE Int. Conf. on Web Services (ICWS) (2012)
13. Ahmed, T., Srivastava, A.: A data-centric and machine based approach towards fixing the cold start problem in web service recommendation. In: IEEE Students' Conference on Electrical, Electronics and Computer Science (SCEECS) (2014)
14. Nayak, R., Tong, C.: Applications of data mining in web services. In: Zhou, X., Su, S., Papazoglou, M.P., Orlowska, M.E., Jeffery, K. (eds.) WISE 2004. LNCS, vol. 3306, pp. 199–205. Springer, Heidelberg (2004)
15. Yao, J., Tan, W., Nepal, S., Chen, S., Zhang, J., De Roure, D., Goble, C.: Reputationnet: a reputation engine to enhance servicemap by recommending trusted services. In: IEEE Int. Conf. on Services Computing (SCC) (2012)
16. Zhang, J., Votava, P., Lee, T., Adhikarla, S., Kulkumjon, I., Schlau, M., Natesan, D., Nemani, R.: A technique of analyzing trust relationships to facilitate scientific service discovery and recommendation. In: IEEE International Conference on Services Computing (SCC) (2013)
17. Huang, K., Yao, J., Fan, Y., Tan, W., Nepal, S., Ni, Y., Chen, S.: Mirror, mirror, on the web, which is the most reputable service of them all? In: Basu, S., Pautasso, C., Zhang, L., Fu, X. (eds.) ICSOC 2013. LNCS, vol. 8274, pp. 343–357. Springer, Heidelberg (2013)
18. Li, L., Wang, Y., Lim, E.-P.: Trust-oriented composite service selection and discovery. In: Baresi, L., Chi, C.-H., Suzuki, J. (eds.) ICSOC-ServiceWave 2009. LNCS, vol. 5900, pp. 50–67. Springer, Heidelberg (2009)
19. He, Q., Yan, J., Jin, H., Yang, Y.: ServiceTrust: supporting reputation-oriented service selection. In: Baresi, L., Chi, C.-H., Suzuki, J. (eds.) ICSOC-ServiceWave 2009. LNCS, vol. 5900, pp. 269–284. Springer, Heidelberg (2009)

Business Process Adaptability Metrics for QoS-Based Service Compositions

Raffaela Mirandola[1], Diego Perez-Palacin[1], Patrizia Scandurra[2(✉)],
Michele Brignoli[2], and Andrea Zonca[2]

[1] Politecnico di Milano, Milano, Italy
{raffaela.mirandola,diego.perez}@polimi.it
[2] DIGIP, Università degli Studi di Bergamo, Dalmine (BG), Italy
patrizia.scandurra@unibg.it, {m.brignoli,a.zonca}@studenti.unibg.it

Abstract. Modern service-oriented software applications, like those envisioned in cloud computing scenarios, operate in highly dynamic and often unpredictable environments that can degrade their quality of service. Therefore, it is increasingly important to efficiently and effectively manage the adaptation of such service compositions while guaranteeing quality attributes, such as availability, performance or cost. Within this context, software metrics to quantify the adaptability of a business process in orchestrating distributed services are highly demanded in conjunction with techniques for evaluating other system quality attributes. This paper proposes a set of software metrics to quantify the adaptability of a service-oriented application when services are composed dynamically trough a business process. The paper also proposes an approach for analyzing tradeoffs between the application adaptability and a quality of service such as availability. The feasibility of the approach is illustrated through a case study carried out with a tool we have developed.

1 Introduction

The SOA promise of agility and flexibility is recognized in the ability to change the business processes as market changes. To this end, it introduces a separate layer in the architecture, the *Business Process Layer*, for business processes and flows. This layer covers process representation and composition, and provides building blocks for orchestrating or choreographing the set of required atomic or composite services from the underlying *Service Component Layer*. Loosely-coupled services are aggregated to constitute a business process aligned with business goals and able to rapidly change as the market condition changes [5].

Modern service-oriented software applications, like those envisioned in cloud computing scenarios, are increasingly reliant on business processes built from multiple distributed software services that must be suitably composed to

This work is supported in part by the Italian Ministry of Research within the PRIN project GenData 2020 and by the EU-FP7-ICT-610531 SeaClouds project.

S. Dustdar et al. (Eds.): ESOCC 2015, LNCS 9306, pp. 110–124, 2015.
DOI: 10.1007/978-3-319-24072-5_8

meet some specified functional and non functional requirements. These service-oriented applications are often embedded in dynamic contexts, where requirements, environment assumptions, and usage profiles continuously change. Ergo, a key requirement for software is becoming the capability to adapt its behavior dynamically, in order to keep providing the required quality of service (QoS). Without adaptation, an application is prone to degrade performance because of faulty components, messages lost between services or delays due to an increasing number of users. Using adaptation, the application can change, for example, some of the services it uses or its overall service composition [2,3,9]. However, guaranteeing software adaptability can influence other quality attributes such as performance, reliability or maintainability and in the worst case, improving the adaptability of the system could decrease other quality attributes. A key challenge for the software engineering community is therefore how to efficiently and effectively manage such dynamic service compositions while guaranteeing QoS. Within this context, software metrics to quantify the adaptability of a business process[1] in orchestrating distributed services are needed in conjunction with techniques for evaluating other system quality attributes, like availability, reliability, performance, cost, etc. In [11], a set of software adaptability metrics are defined at the architectural level of a service-oriented software application to quantify the adaptability of a static assembly (or architecture) of service-oriented components. An approach for evaluating tradeoffs between the system adaptability and other system quality attributes, is also presented to fulfill also global QoS.

This paper introduces a new set of metrics that complement the previous ones defined in [11] in order to quantify the adaptability of a service-oriented application when services are composed dynamically trough a business process. Besides the metrics that enable comparison of process-based service compositions, we also studied a possible relationship between the business process adaptability and the satisfiability of a given quality requirement. If such relationship exists, then service compositions offering best trade-off, between adaptability and the target requirement, can be chosen. This approach allow us to evaluate different concrete business processes in order to select the one that best fits the quality requirements. In this paper, we present the results of such a study by considering availability as target quality. The architecture of a supporting tool and a case study are also presented to exemplify the overall approach.

The remainder of this paper is organized as follows. Section 2 proposes a set of metrics for quantifying SaaS adaptability at the business process level. Section 3 presents our approach for relating adaptability and a single quality attribute. Section 4 presents an example of service-oriented application used to exemplify the proposed approach. Section 5 describes a a tool to automate metrics calculation. Section 6 reviews the works related to our approach. Finally, Section 7 concludes the paper.

---

[1] Hereafter, we use the term "process adaptability" to denote the variability degree of a process in selecting concrete services. This vision is different from the broader concept of process adaptability in the context of self-adaptive systems [4,6,13].

2   Business Process Adaptability Quantification

This section defines a set of metrics to quantify the adaptability of a business process and its constituents. We adopt the OASIS BPEL (Business Process Execution Language)[2] as the de facto standard to specify business processes and realize them concretely. We assume the reader is familiar with BPEL constructs.

2.1   Process Activity Tree

For defining and computing metrics, we first introduce a tree-structure representing a BPEL process. Let p be the business process for a compound service. We define the *Process Activity Tree* of p as the structure $T_p = (V_p, E_p)$ where V_p is the set of nodes representing the BPEL activities of p and E_p is the set of edges representing the nesting relationships among the BPEL activities. Specifically, an internal node represents a BPEL structured activity in the set $\{sequence, switch, while, flow, pick\}$. Similarly, a leaf node is associated to a BPEL atomic action in the set $\{invoke, assignment, receive, reply\}$.

Let n be the number of different elementary services $s_i | i = 1, ..., n$ orchestrated by a process p. For each invocation of an elementary service s_i (i.e., an *invoke* leaf node), either in an asynchronous or synchronous manner, several *concrete services* (or *service instances*) that have been defined as partners may exist that match the description of s_i. We assume that all the instances available for a service s_i are functionally compliant with it, i.e., each instance provides at least all the capabilities provided by s_i and require at most all the capabilities required by s_i. Instances of the same service may differ for QoS values (such as cost and availability characteristics).

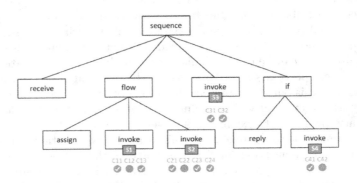

Fig. 1. Example of a BPEL activity tree

Figure 1 shows an example of BPEL tree for a compound service realized by the orchestration of four elementary software services ($n = 4$). The activity tree

---

[2] http://www.oasis-open.org/committees/tc_home.php?wg_abbrev=wsbpel

also shows the service instances available for each service invoked. We assume the existence of n sets of "used" service instances UC_i in the process p, where service instances in each set UC_i are the ones that provide s_i ($UC_1 = \{C11, C12\}$, $UC_2 = \{C21, C23\}$, $UC_3 = \{C31, C32, C34\}$ and $UC_4 = \{C41\}$, in Fig. 1); the existence of n sets of service instances C_i, each C_i includes the instances that can provide s_i ($C_1 = UC_1$, $C_2 = UC_2 \cup \{C22\}$, $C_3 = UC_3 \cup \{C32\}$ and $C_4 = UC_4 \cup \{C42\}$ in Fig. 1).

2.2 Process Adaptability Index

The proposed metric measures the adaptability of a business process in terms of the average number of service choices made per each activity. We make the assumption that the services orchestrated by the process are stateless. We postpone as future work the extension of such a metric for stateful services.

Process Adaptability Index (PAI). is a metric that quantifies the degree of adaptability of a BPEL process definition. It measures the adaptability of a process by relating the number of service instances used to make up the process with the number of service instances that the most adaptable process would use:

$$PAI \in \mathbb{Q}\{0..1\} \mid PAI_p = \frac{EAI_{root(T_p)}}{EAI_{root(T_{map})}}$$

where $EAI_{root(T_p)}$ and $EAI_{root(T_{map})}$ are, respectively, the **Element Adaptability Index (EAI)** for the root of T_p and the one for the root of the activity tree T_{map} of the most adaptable process map.

The value of the metric PAI ranges between zero and one. A value of one means that the process is using all existing instances for each service, and then its adaptability is already to the maximum. A value close to zero means that the market offers few choices to increase the process adaptability.

To complete the definition of the metric PAI, we define the adaptability index for the nodes of the process activity tree. Starting from the root node of a process activity tree, a recursive traversal calculates the EAI of every node depending on the node type and handles a leaf node (at the bottom) as the base case.

Node *invoke*. The EAI index of a leaf node *invoke* for a service s_i can be expressed mathematically as follow:

$$EAI \in \mathbb{N} \mid EAI_{invoke\ s_i} = |UC_i|$$

where $|UC_i|$ denotes the number of concrete service instances used to provide the service s_i. This index corresponds to the metric *Absolute adaptability of a service (AAS)* defined in [11] that uses a natural number to quantify how much adaptable a service is by counting the different alternatives to execute the service (1 no adaptable, >1 adaptable), where the service adaptability grows according to the number of concrete service instances able to provide it. Referring to the example in Fig. 1, we observe that $EAI_{invoke\ s_1} = 2$, $EAI_{invoke\ s_2} = 3$, $EAI_{invoke\ s_3} = 2$, and $EAI_{invoke\ s_4} = 1$.

Node n in $\{assignment, receive, reply\}$. $EAI_n = 0$

These node types are neutral w.r.t. the adaptability quantification. Referring to the example in Fig. 1: $EAI_{receive} = 0$, $EAI_{reply} = 0$, and $EAI_{assign} = 0$.

Node $flow$. The $flow$ construct provides a kind of parallelism of interaction activities. The EAI index of a node $flow$ can be expressed mathematically as follow:

$$EAI \in \mathbb{Q}^+ \mid EAI_{flow} = \frac{\sum_{j=1}^{m} EAI_{a_j}}{m}$$

where m is the number of child nodes and $a_j | j = 1, ..., m$ denotes the j-th child activity within the scope of the flow node. Referring to the example in Fig. 1:

$$EAI_{flow} = \frac{EAI_{assign} + EAI_{invoke\ s2} + EAI_{invoke\ s3}}{3} = \frac{0+2+3}{3} = 1.67.$$

Node $switch$. The $switch$ construct expresses conditional behavior. The EAI index of a node $switch$ can be expressed as:

$$EAI \in \mathbb{Q}^+ \mid EAI_{switch} = \sum_{j=1}^{m} p_j \cdot EAI_{a_j}$$

where m is the number of child nodes, $a_j | j = 1, ..., m$ denotes the j-th activity in a conditional branch of the switch construct, and p_j is the probability of executing the activity a_j. In our view, adaptability of interaction within a switch construct is related to the probability of the occurrence of each of its conditions. Thus, the EAI of a switch construct is calculated as the summation of the probability of each condition occurrence multiplied with the EAI of the interaction activity within that condition. At design time, we assume that the probability of execution for branches is equivalent: $p_j = \frac{1}{m}$. It must hold: $p_j \geq 0$ for all $j = 1 \ldots m$ and $\sum_{j=1}^{m} p_j = 1$. At runtime, the probability of execution for every single conditional branch may differ from the other branches. These probabilities can be estimated from the *operational profile*[3] [10].

A node *if-else* is considered equivalent to a node $switch$ with two conditional branches. Referring to the example in Fig. 1, we observe at design time:

$$EAI_{if-else} = 0.5 \cdot EAI_{reply} + 0.5 \cdot EAI_{invoke\ s4} = 0.5 \cdot 0 + 0.5 \cdot 1 = 0.5$$

Node $pick$. The construct $pick$ is used to wait for the occurrence of one of a set of events (message events or alarm events) and then perform an activity associated with the event. The semantics of a $pick$ construct is similar to that of a $switch$. The EAI index of a node $pick$ is therefore:

$$EAI \in \mathbb{Q}^+ \mid EAI_{pick} = \sum_{j=1}^{m} p_j \cdot EAI_{a_j}$$

---

[3] Environmental data about the business process collected from domain experts.

where m is the number of child nodes, $a_j | j = 1, ..., m$ denotes the j-th activity associated with an event e_j (a message event or an alarm event), and p_j is the probability that event e_j occurs. Also in this case, at design time, we assume $p_j = \frac{1}{m}$ as for a *switch* construct.

Node *while.* The EAI index of a node *while* is:

$$EAI \in \mathbb{Q}^+ \quad | \quad EAI_{while} = \frac{N \cdot \Sigma_{j=1}^{m} EAI_{a_j}}{m}$$

where m is the number of child nodes, $a_j | j = 1, ..., m$ denotes the j-th child activity, and N is the number of loop iterations. At design time, we are not able to calculate N exactly, however, it can be estimated with the aid of an operational profile.

Node *sequence.* The *sequence* construct is used to define activities that need to be performed in a sequential order. The EAI index of a node *sequence* is:

$$EAI \in \mathbb{Q}^+ \quad | \quad EAI_{sequence} = \frac{\Sigma_{j=1}^{m} EAI_{a_j}}{m}$$

where m is the number of child nodes, $a_j | j = 1, ..., m$ denotes the j-th child activity executed sequentially within the sequence node.
Referring to the example in Fig. 1:

$EAI_{sequence} = \frac{EAI_{receive} \cdot EAI_{flow} \cdot EAI_{invoke\ s3} \cdot EAI_{if-else}}{4} = \frac{0+1.67+2+0.5}{4} = 1.04.$

Note that the sequence node in Fig. 1 is also the root of T_p. Therefore, it results: $EAI_{root(T_p)} = EAI_{sequence} = 1.04$. The EAI of the root of T_{map} is calculated in the same way by considering for each service s_i all available service instances $|C_i|$. Referring to Fig. 1, $EAI_{root(T_{map})} = 1,33$, and therefore:

$$PAI_p = \frac{EAI_{root(T_p)}}{EAI_{root(T_{map})}} = \frac{1.04}{1.33} = 0.78$$

3 Relating Adaptability with a Quality of Service Attribute

Software quality attributes can rarely be achieved in isolation. Most often, the achievement of a quality attribute has an effect, positive or negative, on the achievement of others [1]. Process adaptability is not an exception, and it can influence quality attributes such as performance, reliability or maintainability. Therefore, an increment in the process adaptability can cause an improvement in some of them, but also a damage.

For example, given a performance response time requirement, it may happen that more adaptability produces better performance, since the expected fastest service instance can be chosen at each invocation moment. However, it can also happen that all service instances are always fast, and then the time necessary to compute decision of which service instance to use creates a delay that results in a lower performance than a non-adaptive system.

The same happens for the probability of an execution of the business process to succeed. Although at first sight it may seem that having more alternative service instances to execute a concrete service will always improve its probability to succeed, we can also argue that the implementation of the required adaptation manager adds a complexity in the software, then it creates an additional point of failure and can damage the overall process quality.

From these examples, as in [11], we cannot assume that a certain quality attribute is always in the same type of relationship with the adaptability, hence it is needed a system analysis to identify their type of relation.

Quality Computation: In this work we focus on the quality attribute of "probability of a process execution to succeed its execution", called $Qual$ in the following. For computing $Qual$ value in a given process, we use basic formula of availability evaluation.

We assume that leaf nodes in the process activity tree of type *assignment, receive, reply* never fail their execution, then their $Qual$ is 1. We assume as known the $Qual$ value of service instances Cij, called $Qual_{Cij}$.

Then, the $Qual$ of a leaf node *invoke* is the probability of any of the service instances that receive such invocation to succeed an execution, whose formula is: $Qual_{invoke\ s_i} = 1 - \prod_{j=1}^{j=EAI_{invoke\ s_i}} (1 - Qual_{Cij})$

The quality of nodes *switch, pick*, is calculated as:

$$Qual_n = \sum_{j=1}^{m} p_j \cdot Qual_j \quad \forall n \in \{switch, pick\}$$

while, the quality of nodes *flow, sequence* and *while* is calculated as:

$$Qual_n = \prod_{j=1}^{m} Qual_j^{N_j} \quad \forall n \in \{flow, sequence, while\}$$

where m is the number of child nodes and $a_j | j = 1, ..., m$ denotes the j-th child activity within the scope of the node; p_j is the probability of executing child node j; and N_j is the number of times that child node j is executed in iteration (it is straightforward to see that this value is higher than 1 for nodes of type *while* and equal to 1 for the rest of types).

Therefore, system $Qual$ is recursively computed in the process activity tree and it is equivalent to the quality value calculated for its root node $Qual_{root}$.

4   A Case Study: The University Student Enrollment

This section presents a more realistic example to illustrate the proposed metrics. The example is a web service application used by students to register for an

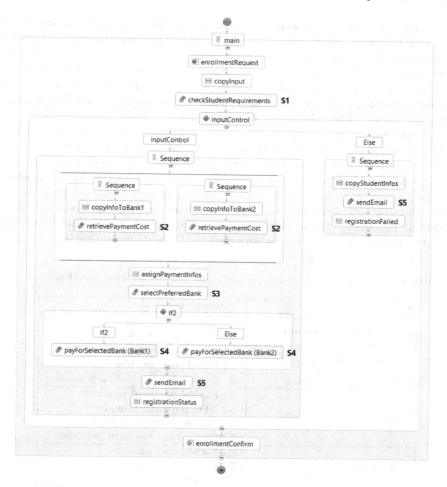

Fig. 2. Student enrollment BPEL process

academic year in the University. Figure 2 sketches the BPEL process for student enrollment as modeled through the Eclipse BPEL Designer plug-in[4].

At first, a student registers and introduces his/her proposal (a list of courses to take) in the web system. Then, the proposal is sent to a web service (an application logic layer) to check if it fulfills the University rules. In case of reject, the registration process interacts with a mail web service to send an email to the student with information about the registration failure. If, instead, the proposal fulfills the University rules, the process interacts with two bank web services (known at design time) to proceed with the payment. To this purpose, the process asynchronously calls back the student with the bank transaction costs, thus

---

[4] Eclipse BPEL Designer Plug-in: http://www.eclipse.org/bpel/

allowing the student to choose the bank service with the lowest costs. Once the bank has been selected by the student, and the bank payment has been predisposed, the process invokes a web mail service (not known at design time) to send an email to the student with the information of the successful registration. For both proposals approve or reject cases, a presentation layer with a web-GUI and mechanisms to interact with the student sends a message back to student with information about the registration outcome.

For the student enrollment BPEL process, Table 1 relates the abstract services (ID and description) invoked by the process with the corresponding concrete service instances (ID and description) available as internal or external service components. Figure 3 shows a possible process activity tree for the student enrollment process. This process configuration has been obtained by selecting some concrete service instances. The activity tree of the corresponding most adaptable process for the student enrollment example is similar and takes into account all the service instances reported in Table 1. Note that labels n_k in Fig. 3 enumerate the internal nodes.

Table 1. Abstract and concrete services for the student enrollment process

Service	Concrete service
s_1 Check student requirements	C11 Application Logic 1 C12 Application Logic 2
s_2 Retrieve payment cost	C21 Mobile cost provider C22 Email cost provider
s_3 Select preferred bank	C31 Bank selection (callback handler)
s_4 Pay for selected bank	C41 PayPal payment provider C42 NFC payment provider C43 Mobile payment provider C44 Credit card payment provider
s_5 Send email	C51 Local email provider C52 Email provider 1 C53 Email provider 2

Table 2 shows the value of the metrics (the EAI values for the internal nodes and the final PAI) for the process configuration in Fig. 3. The given process configuration exhibits a good adaptability since it differs from the most adaptable one by 7%.

Adaptability and Quality Measures at Work. At present, the student enrollment process invokes service instance $C11$ for $s1$. With the information returned it has been observed that only 2.5% of students do not satisfy the University requirements and an email rejection is sent by $C51$. The interaction with $s2$ of the two different banking web services is done by invoking service instance $C21$. The interaction with the bank payment process is done by the invocation of one of the service instances $C41$, $C42$, $C43$ or $C44$. The final interaction with email service is carried out again by $C51$. The observed quality

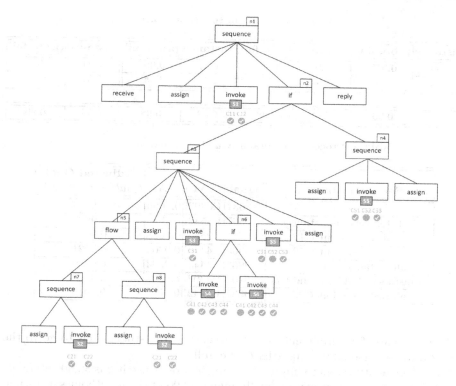

Fig. 3. A process activity tree for the student enrollment process

Table 2. The metrics values for the given process configuration

Activity tree T_p	Activity tree T_{map}
$EAI_{n_7} = \frac{0+2}{2} = 1$	$EAI_{n_7} = \frac{0+2}{2} = 1$
$EAI_{n_8} = \frac{0+2}{2} = 1$	$EAI_{n_8} = \frac{0+2}{2} = 1$
$EAI_{n_5} = \frac{1+1}{2} = 1$	$EAI_{n_5} = \frac{1+1}{2} = 1$
$EAI_{n_6} = 0.5 \cdot 3 + 0.5 \cdot 3 = 3$	$EAI_{n_6} = 0.5 \cdot 4 + 0.5 \cdot 4 = 4$
$EAI_{n_3} = \frac{1+0+1+3+2+0}{6} = 1.17$	$EAI_{n_3} = \frac{1+0+1+4+3+0}{6} = 1.5$
$EAI_{n_4} = \frac{0+2+0}{3} = 0.67$	$EAI_{n_4} = \frac{0+3+0}{3} = 1$
$EAI_{n_2} = 0.5 \cdot 1.17 + 0.5 \cdot 0.67 = 0.92$	$EAI_{n_2} = 0.5 \cdot 1.5 + 0.5 \cdot 1 = 1.25$
$EAI_{n_1} = \frac{0+0+2+0.92+0}{5} = 0.58$	$EAI_{n_1} = \frac{0+0+2+1.25+0}{5} = 0.65$
$PAI_p = \frac{EAI_{root(T_p)}}{EAI_{root(T_{map})}} = \frac{0.58}{0.65} = 0.89$	

of these service instances in terms of the probability of executing a request to
their offered service without errors is shown in the higher part of Table 3. We
assume that the rest of nodes in the process activity tree that are not of *invoke*
type can never fail. Therefore, the calculated quality of this process in terms
of the probability of executing a complete request for enrollment without errors
(*Qual*) is computed according to formulas presented in Section 3 and is 0.86377.

Table 3. Quality of service instance

Instance	prob. fail	Instance	prob. fail	Instance	prob. fail	Instance	prob. fail
$C11$	0.975	$C21$	0.95	$C31$	0.999	$C41$	0.9
$C42$	0.8	$C43$	0.7	$C44$	0.99	$C51$	0.98

$C12$	0.99	$C22$	0.98	$C52$	0.98	$C53$	0.99

Table 4. Processes adaptability and expected quality values

Service instances	Qual	EAI	PAI	Adjusted Qual $Qual \cdot f(EAI, 0.01)$
Initial process	0.8637	1.0303	0.7066	0.8635
ALL ten service instances	0.9967	1.4582	1	0.9921
all instances but $C12$	0.9721	1.2582	0.8628	0.9695
all instances but $C52$	0.9965	1.4443	0.9904	0.9921
all instances but $C53$	0.9963	1.4443	0.9904	0.9919
all instances but $C52$ and $C53$	0.9768	1.4303	0.9808	0.9726
all instances but $C22$	0.9037	1.2442	0.8532	0.9015

When a request for enrollment fails its execution, the student has to go to the secretariat to personally request his/her enrollment.

The University wants to improve the application, since it has 30,000 students but the secretary service can manually manage 200 of them without saturating. Then, it is required a $Qual \geq 29700/30000 = 0.99$. The IT service has considered the local deployment of a new service instance (called $C12$) that has been recently developed and offers an alternative for the execution of the application logic. For $s2$, it would be possible to use a service instance $C22$. Regarding the email service, the University considers the utilization of two other relays (called $C52$ and $C53$) to use in the moment when the local relay is not working properly (e.g., unreachable or saturated being rejecting connections). The quality of these existing service instances is shown in the lower part of Table 3.

Therefore, the current business process can use service instances $C11$, $C21$, $C31$, $C41$, $C42$, $C43$, $C44$ and $C51$; while the most adaptable process would be able to use also services $C12$, $C22$, $C52$ and $C53$. The implementation of an adaptive service-oriented application through composition of heterogeneous services – even if they provide the same functionality – will require some programming effort from the IT department to make interoperable their interfaces; i.e., the service invocation is not completely seamless in this case. For this reason, the IT department would like to know the business process that provides enough $Qual$ and uses the lowest level of adaptation. For calculating $Qual$ we use the formulae in Section 3 while the proposed EAI metrics are used for calculating the quantity of adaptability of each candidate business process. Using EAI metric and an estimation of the bug inclusion rate when implementing autonomic manager of adaptive processes, we can estimate the expected quality of the resulting adaptive process. The more adaptive a node in the BPEL process is, the higher its likelihood to include a bug created during its implementation. The estimated bug inclusion rate is 0.01, meaning that for each service instance that adds adaptability, the probability of failure during instance decision process increases by 1%. We do not go in detail calculation of the success rate of the autonomic manager execution and we call it $f(EAI, 0.01)$, just assuming that it is a non increasing function for EAI. By calculating the PAI of each candidate process, we can give an evaluation of the mean adaptability of each element in the process with respect to the most adaptable one and, in consequence, an insight of the relative implementation effort that the IT department saves by not deciding directly in favor of the most adaptable business process.

Table 4 shows the results of the metrics EAI, PAI, $Qual$ and $Adjusted\ Qual$ for some of the evaluated processes. Among the processes that satisfy the execution success requirement, the one composed by all service instances but $C53$ is the one that showed highest $Ajusted\ Qual$ lowest EAI value.

5   Implementation and Tool Support

To automatically calculate the proposed metrics, we adopted SOLAR [14] (SOftware quaLities and Adaptability Relationships), a tool developed in [11] for adaptability quantification of a software architecture. We extended SOLAR to include the new metrics defined at the business process level and validate it on the case study presented previously. The implementation units of this SOLAR extension, called B-SOLAR (Business SOLAR) are shown in Fig. 4.

First (*phase 1* in Fig. 4), the user must provide manually an input file settings.xml containing the names of two XML input files used by SOLAR. One input XML file is the conventional input read by SOLAR through the software module Components and services Parser (see *phase 2* in Fig. 4). This input file contains the description of the software architecture comprising components and connectors. This same input is also used by B-SOLAR (see *phase 3* in Fig. 4) to determine the relation between abstract services and concrete service instances. This information is stored in an hash table for a faster access during the metric computation.

The second input file is read by B-SOLAR trough the Business Process Parser (see *phase 4* in Fig. 4). This file is the BPEL XML file containing (among other things) the description of the considered business process. From this file a process activity tree is created (phase 5 in Fig. 4). Through a combinatorial algorithm, the various combinations that can be taken of the service concrete instances of a particular service type are generated (*phase 6* in Fig. 4). Each combination generated is then associated with the process activity tree and the metrics PAI and EAI are then computed according to the approach presented in Sect. 2 (*phase 7* in Fig. 4). The results of such evaluation are finally saved (*phase 8* in Fig. 4) in an output XML file through the module Output writer.

In order to enable the B-SOLAR tool in a cloud context, we added to B-SOLAR a further parser (*phase 2'* in Fig. 4) that is able to accept as input a TOSCA-based[5] description of a cloud-based software application (the SaaS layer only) and transforms it into the internal C&C view description used by SOLAR for representing software architectures. For the dynamic aspects, namely the TOSCA plans defined as process models, TOSCA specification relies on existing languages like BPMN or BPEL. We assume, therefore, TOSCA plans are provided using BPEL as supported by B-SOLAR.

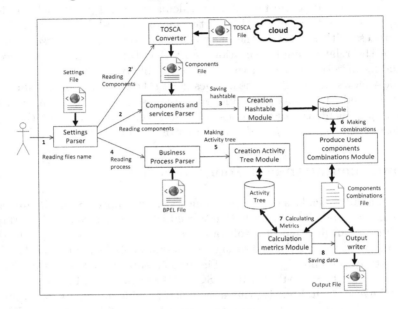

Fig. 4. B-SOLAR tool architecture

6   Related Work

In the following we briefly review papers dealing with metrics and approaches for adaptability and evolution of business processes. An extensive related work about metrics for system adaptability applicable at architectural level can be found in [11].

In software engineering, many approaches have been proposed to support the adaptability and evolution of business processes (such as [12], [7], to name a few). In these approaches process adaptability is conceived differently from the vision we take in this paper. Indeed, we quantify the variability degree of BPEL processes to adapt their bindings to concrete service instances during their life cycles. Instead, in the works mentioned above, process adaptability is intended in the broadest sense of self-adaptive systems [4,6,13]. They assume that business

---

[5] The OASIS Topology and Orchestration Specification for Cloud Applications. http://docs.oasis-open.org/tosca/TOSCA/v1.0/os/TOSCA-v1.0-os.html

process specification languages are extended with special constructs and self-adaptation plug-ins (e.g., for monitoring or diagnosis so that the plug-in can decide if the adaptation is needed though a feedback adaptation control loop) that allow the business process specification to change at runtime without the need to redeploy it and lose the ongoing transactions.

In [8], the authors propose an approach for quantifying the degree of structural adaptability of BPMN business processes using software metrics. They aim at quantifying how easily a process can be adapted to a different form by replacing combinations of BPMN constructs with other ones having the same runtime semantics. Such a degree can be helpful for quality assessment during development or decision support during migration. In such a work, yet process adaptability is conceived differently from our vision. The author considers adaptability as sub-characteristic of the portability quality, i.e. the degree to which a process can be adapted in order to be executed in a different execution platform.

7   Conclusions and Future Work

BPEL processes are workflow-oriented service compositions for creating service-oriented applications. Rapidly changing environmental and market conditions require flexible BPEL processes that adapt their bindings to concrete services during their life cycles.

In this paper, we have extended the set of metrics presented in [11] that quantify the software adaptability at architectural level with metrics that quantify the software adaptability at the business process level. These metrics allow us to quantitatively evaluate and compare different service-oriented applications in terms of architectural and behavioral adaptability and quality requirements. The approach can help software architects to find architectures and business processes satisfying all system quality requirements. The software architect may applies the approach when changes in the execution context force to change the service instances of the business process for satisfying quality requirements. To automate the analysis we have extended the SOLAR tool.

At present we are working on testing the B-SOLAR tool by designing several experiments from with real-size service-oriented applications. In particular, we are looking for a test-bed in a cloud computing scenario. We are also working to overcome some limitations. One limitation is that it is not possible to list and program all variability of service instances at design time. The generation of all possible process activity trees (or process configurations) for an input business process should, instead, carried out at run-time through a web service discovery mechanism.

References

1. Bass, L., Clements, P., Kazman, R.: Software Architecture in Practice. SEI Series in Software Engineering. Addison-Wesley (2005)
2. Calinescu, R., Grunske, L., Kwiatkowska, M.Z., Mirandola, R., Tamburrelli, G.: Dynamic qos management and optimization in service-based systems. IEEE Trans. Software Eng. **37**(3), 387–409 (2011)
3. Cardellini, V., Casalicchio, E., Grassi, V., Lo Presti, F., Mirandola, R.: Qos-driven runtime adaptation of service oriented architectures. In: Proceedings of the the 7th joint meeting ESEC/FSE, pp. 131–140. ACM, New York (2009)
4. Cheng, B.H., et al.: Software engineering for self-adaptive systems: A research roadmap **5525**, 1–26 (2009)
5. Cognini, R., Corradini, F., Gnesi, S., Polini, A., Re, B.: Research challenges in business process adaptability. In: Symposium on Applied Computing, SAC 2014, Gyeongju, Republic of Korea, March 24–28, 2014, pp. 1049–1054 (2014)
6. de Lemos, R., et al.: Software engineering for self-adaptive systems: a second research roadmap. In: de Lemos, R., Giese, H., Müller, H.A., Shaw, M. (eds.) Software Engineering for Self-Adaptive Systems. LNCS, vol. 7475, pp. 1–32. Springer, Heidelberg (2013)
7. Hermosillo, G., Seinturier, L., Duchien, L.: Using complex event processing for dynamic business process adaptation. In: IEEE Int. Conf. on Services Computing, SCC 2010, pp. 466–473 (2010)
8. Lenhard, J.: Towards quantifying the adaptability of executable BPMN processes. In: Proceedings of the 6th Central-European Workshop on Services and their Composition, ZEUS 2014, pp. 34–41 (2014)
9. Mirandola, R., Potena, P., Scandurra, P.: Adaptation space exploration for service-oriented applications. Science of Computer Programming **80**, 356–384 (2014)
10. Musa, J.: Operational profiles in software-reliability engineering. Software, IEEE **10**(2), 14–32 (1993)
11. Perez-Palacin, D., Mirandola, R., Merseguer, J.: On the relationships between QoS and software adaptability at the architectural level. Journal of Systems and Software **87**, 1–17 (2014)
12. Sabatucci, L., Lodato, C., Lopes, S., Cossentino, M.: Towards self-adaptation and evolution in business process. Proceedings of the Workshop AI Meets Business Processes **2013**, 1–10 (2013)
13. Salehie, M., Tahvildari, L.: Self-adaptive software: Landscape and research challenges. ACM Trans. Auton. Adapt. Syst. **4**(2), 1–42 (2009)
14. SOLAR (2011). http://webdiis.unizar.es/GISED/?q=tool/solar. Universidad de Zaragoza

Formal Verification of Service Level Agreements Through Distributed Monitoring

Behrooz Nobakht[1,2]($\boxtimes$), Stijn de Gouw[2,3], and Frank S. de Boer[1,3]

[1] Leiden Advanced Institute of Computer Science,
Leiden University, Leiden, Netherlands
bnobakht@liacs.nl
[2] SDL Fredhopper, London, UK
{bnobakht,sgouw}@sdl.com
[3] Centrum Wiskunde En Informatica, Amsterdam, Netherlands
{frb,cdegouw}@cwi.nl

Abstract. In this paper, we introduce a formal model of the availability, budget compliance and sustainability of istributed services, where service sustainability is a new concept which arises as the composition of service availability and budget compliance. The model formalizes a distributed platform for monitoring the above service characteristics in terms of a parallel composition of task automata, where dynamically generated tasks model asynchronous events with deadlines. The main result of this paper is a formal model to optimize and reason about service characteristics through monitoring. In particular, we use schedulability analysis of the underlying timed automata to optimize and guarantee service sustainability.

Keywords: Runtime monitoring · Service availability · Budget compliance · Service sustainability · Distributed architecture · Cloud computing · Service Level Agreement

1 Introduction

Cloud computing provides the elastic technologies for virtualization. Through virtualization, software itself can be offered as a service (Software as a Service, SaaS). One of the aims of SaaS is to allow service providers to offer reliable software services while scaling up and down allocated resources based on their availability, budget, service throughput and the Service Level Agreements (SLA). Thus, it becomes essential that virtualization technologies facilitate elasticity in a way that enables business owners to *rapidly* evolve their systems to meet their customer requirements and expectations.

The fundamental technical challenge to a SaaS offering is maintaining the quality of service (QoS) promised by its SLA. In SaaS, providers must ensure a

This paper is funded by the EU project FP7-610582 ENVISAGE: Engineering Virtualized Services, http://www.envisage-project.eu.

S. Dustdar et al. (Eds.): ESOCC 2015, LNCS 9306, pp. 125–140, 2015.
DOI: 10.1007/978-3-319-24072-5_9

consistent QoS in a dynamic virtualized environment with variable usage patterns. Specifically, virtualized environments such as the cloud provide elasticity in resource allocation, but they often do not offer an SLA that can guarantee constant resource availability. As a result, SaaS providers are required to react to resource availability at runtime. Furthermore, by offering a 24/7 software service, SaaS providers must be able to react to certain service usage patterns, such as an increase in throughput to ensure the SLA is maintained.

Runtime monitoring [4, 20] is a dynamic analysis approach based on extracting relevant information about the execution. Runtime monitoring may be employed to collect statistics about the service usage over time, and to detect and react to service behavior. This latter ability is fundamental in the SaaS approach to guarantee the SLA of a service and is the focus of this paper.

The monitoring model that is presented in this paper is designed to *observe* in real-time certain service characteristics and *react* to them to ensure the evolution of the system towards its SLA. Asynchronous communication is an essential feature of a monitoring model in a distributed context. Asynchronous communication accomplishes non-intrusive observations of the service runtime. Further, the monitoring model is expected to operate according to certain real-time constraints specified by the SLA of the service. Satisfying the real-time constraints is the main challenge in a distributed monitoring model.

In this paper, we formalize service availability and budget compliance in a distributed deployment environment. This formalization is based on high-level task automata models [1, 9, 13]. The automata capture the real-time evolution of the resources provided by a distributed deployment platform and the above two main service characteristics. These task automata represent the real-time generation of the asynchronous events extended with deadlines [3, 22] by the monitoring platform for managing resources (i.e. allocation or deallocation). The main result of this paper is a formal model to optimize and reason about the above service characteristics through monitoring. In particular, the *schedulability* of the underlying timed automata implies service availability and budget compliance. Furthermore, we introduce a composition of service availability and budget compliance which captures service sustainability. We show that service sustainability presents a multi-objective optimization problem.

2   Related Work

Vast research work present different aspects of runtime monitoring. We focus on those that present a line of research for distributed deployment of services.

MONINA [12] is a DSL with a monitoring architecture which supports certain mathematical optimization techniques. A prototype implementation is available. Accurately capturing the behavior of an in-production legacy system coded in a conventional language seems challenging: it requires developing MONINA components, which generate events at a specified fixed rate, there are no control structures (if-else, loops), the data types that can be used in events are predefined, and there are no OO-features. We use ABS [15], an executable modeling language that supports all of these features and offers a wide range of tool-supported analyses [5, 25]. The mapping from ABS to timed automata [1] allows to exploit the state-of-the-art tools for timed automata, in particular for reasoning about real-time properties (and, as we show, SLAs using schedulability analysis [9]). MONINA offers *two pre-defined* parameters that can be used in monitoring to adapt the system: cost and capacity. Our service metric function generalizes this to *arbitrary user-defined* parameters, including cost and capacity.

Hogben and Pannetrat examine in [11] the challenges of defining and measuring availability to support real-world service comparison and dispute resolution through SLAs. They show how two examples of real-world SLAs would lead one service provider to report 0% availability while another would report 100% for the same system state history but using a different period of time. The transparency that the authors attempt to reach is addressed in our work by the concept of monitoring window and expectation tolerance in Section 4. Additionally, the authors take a continuous time approach contrasted with ours that uses discrete time advancements. Similarly, they model the property of availability using a two-state model.

The following research works provide a language or a framework that allows to formalize service level agreements (SLA). However, they do not study how such SLAs can be used to monitor the service and evolve it as necessary. WSLA [18] introduces a framework to define and break down customer agreements into a technical description of SLAs and terms to be monitored. In [21], a method is proposed to translate the specification of SLA into a technical domain directed in SLA@SOI EU project. In the same project, [8] defines terms such as availability, accessibility and throughput as notions of SLA, however, the formal semantics and properties of the notions are not investigated. In [6], authors describe how they introduce a function how to decompose SLA terms into measurable factors and how to profile them. Timed automata is used in [24] to detect violations of SLA and formalize them.

Johnsen [16] introduce "deployment components" using Real-Time ABS [3]. A deployment component enables an application to acquire and release resources on-demand based on a QoS specification of the application. A deployment component is a high level abstraction of a resource that promotes an application to a resource-aware level of programming. Our work is distinguished by the fact that we separate the monitors from the application (service) themselves. We argue that we aim to design the monitoring model to be as *non-intrusive* as possible to the service runtime. Thus, we do not deploy the monitors inside the service runtime.

In Quanticol EU project[1], authors in [7] and [10] use statistical approaches to observe and guarantee service level agreements for public transportation. We also present that service characteristics can be composed together. This means that evolving a system based on SLAs turns into a multi-object optimization problem. In addition, in COMPASS EU project[2], CML [26] defines a formal

---

[1] Quanticol EU project with no. 600708: http://quanticol.eu/

[2] COMPASS EU project with no. 287829: http://www.compass-research.eu/

language to model systems of systems and the contracts between them. CML studies certain properties of the model and their applications. CML is used in the context of a Robotics technology to model and ensure how emergency sensors should react and behave according to the SLAs defined for them. Our approach is similar to provide a generic model for service characteristics definition, however, we utilize timed and task automata.

3   SDL Fredhopper Cloud Services

In this section, we introduce a running example in the context of SDL Fredhopper. We use the example in different parts of the paper and also in the experiments.

SDL Fredhopper develops the Fredhopper Cloud Services to offer search and targeting facilities on a large product database to e-Commerce companies as services (SaaS) over the cloud computing infrastructure (IaaS). Fredhopper Cloud Services provides several SaaS offerings on the cloud. These services are exposed at endpoints. In practice these endpoints typically are implemented to accept connections over HTTP. For example, one of the services offered by these endpoints is the Fredhopper Query API, which allows users to query over their product catalog via full text search[3] and faceted navigation[4].

A customer of SDL Fredhopper using Query API owns a *single* HTTP endpoint to use for search and other operations. However, internally, a number of resources (virtual machines) are used to deliver Query API for the customer. The resources used for a customer are managed by a load balancer. In this model of deployment, each resource is launched to serve *one* instance of Query API; i.e. resources are *not* shared among customers.

When a customer signs a contract with SDL Fredhopper, there is a clause in the contract that describes the minimal QoS levels of the Query API. For example, we have a notion of query per second (QPS) that defines the number of completed queries per second for a customer. An agreement is a bound on the expected QPS and forms the basis of many decisions (technical or legal) thereafter. The agreement is used by the operations team to set up an environment for the customer which includes the necessary resources described above. The agreement is additionally used by the support team to manage communications with the customer during the lifetime of the service for the customer.

Maintaining the services for more than 250 customers on more than 1000 servers is not an easy operation task[5]. Thus, to ensure the agreements in a customer's contract:

- The operation team maintains a monitoring platform to get notifications on the current metrics.

---

[3] http://en.wikipedia.org/wiki/Full_text_search

[4] http://en.wikipedia.org/wiki/Faceted_navigation

[5] Figures are indication of complexity and scale. Detailed confidential information may be shared upon official request.

- The operation team performs *manual* intervention to ensure that sufficient resources are available for a customer (launching or terminating).
- The monitoring platform depends on *human* reaction.
- The cost that is spent for a customer on the basis of safety can be *optimized*.

In this paper, we use the notion of QPS as an example in the concepts that are presented in this research. We use the example here to demonstrate how the model that is proposed in this research can address the issues above and alleviate the *manual* work with *automation*. The manual life cycle depends on the domain-specific and contextual knowledge of the operations team for every customer service that is maintained in the deployment environment. This is labor-intensive as the operations team stands by 24×7. In such a manual approach, the business is forced to over-spend to ensure service level agreements for customers.

4 Distributed Monitoring Model

We introduce a distributed monitoring platform and its components and discuss some underlying assumptions and definitions. Further, we define the notion of service availability and service budget compliance. In the deployment environment (e.g., "the cloud"), every server from the IaaS provider is used for a *single* service of a customer, such as the Query Service API for a customer of SDL Fredhopper (c.f. Section 3). Typically, multiple servers are allocated to a single customer. The number of servers allocated for a customer is not visible to the customer. The customer uses a single endpoint - in the load balancer layer - to access all their services.

The ultimate goal is to maintain the environment in such a way that customers and their end users experience the delivered services up to their expectations while minimizing the cost of the system. The first objective can be addressed by adding resources; however, this conflicts with the second goal since it increases the cost of the environment for the customer. In this section, we formalize the above intuitive notions as *service availability* and *service budget compliance*.

We then develop a distributed monitoring platform that aims to optimize these service characteristics in a deployment environment. The monitoring platform works in two cyclic phases: *observation* and *reaction*. The observation phase takes measurements on services in the deployment environment. Subsequently, the corresponding levels of the service characteristics are calculated. In the reaction phase, if needed, a platform API is utilized to make the necessary changes to the deployment environment (e.g. adjust the number of allocated resources) to optimize the service characteristics. The monitoring platform builds on top of a real-time extension of the actor-based language ABS [15]. To ensure non-intrusiveness of the monitor with the running service, each monitor is an active object (actor) running on a separate resource from that which runs the service itself, and the components of the monitoring platform communicate through *asynchronous messages* with deadlines [16].

Below, we discuss assumptions and basic oncepts that will be used in the analysis of the formal properties of the monitoring platform and corresponding theorems. We assume that the external infrastructure provider has an *unlimited* number of resources. Further, we assume that all resources are of the *same type*; i.e. they have the same computing power, memory, and IO capacity. Finally, we assume that every resource is initialized within at most t_i amount of time.

In our framework time T is a universally shared clock based on the NTP[6] that is used by all elements of the system in the same way. T is discrete. We fix that the unit of time is *milliseconds*. This level of granularity of time unit means that between two consecutive milliseconds, the system is not observable. For example, we use the UTC time standard for all services, monitors and platform API. We refer to the current time by t_c.

We denote by r a resource which provides computational power and storage and by s a general abstraction of a service in the deployment environment. A service exposes an API that is accessible through a delivery layer, such as HTTP. In our example, a service is the Query API (c.f. Section 3) that is accessible through a single HTTP endpoint.

In our framework, *monitoring platform* P is responsible for (de-)allocation of resources for computation or storage. We abstract from a specific implementation of the monitoring platform P through an API in Listing 1. There is only *one* instance of P available. In this paper, P internally uses an external infrastructure provisioning API to provide resources

Listing 1: Platform API

```
1  interface Platform {
2      void     allocate(Service s);
3      void     deallocate(Service s);
4      Number   getState(Service s);
5      boolean  verify_α(Service s);
6      boolean  verify_β(Service s);
7  }
```

(e.g. AWS EC2). The term "platform" is interchangeably used for monitoring in this paper. The platform provides a method `getState(Service s)` which returns the number of resources allocated to the given service s at time t_c.

We use monitoring to observe the external behavior of a service. We formalize the external behavior of a service with its service-level agreement (SLA). An SLA is a contract between the customer (service consumer) and the service provider which defines (among other things) the minimal quality of the offered service, and the compensation if this minimal level is not reached. To formally analyze an SLA, we introduce the notion of a service metric function. We make basic measurements of the service externally in a given monitoring window (a duration). The service metric function aggregates the basic measurements into a single number that indicates the quality of a certain service characteristic (higher numbers are better).

Basic measurement $\mu(s, r, t)$ is a function that produces a real number of a *single* monitoring check on a resource r allocated to service s at some time t.

---

[6] https://tools.ietf.org/html/rfc1305

For example, for SDL Fredhopper cloud services, a basic measurement is the number of completed queries at the current time.

Service Metric f_s is a function that aggregates a sequence of basic non-negative measurements to a single non-negative real value: $f_s : \bigcup_n \mathbb{R}^n \rightarrow \mathbb{R}$. For example, for SDL Fredhopper cloud services, the service metric function f_s calculates the average number of queries per second (QPS) given a list of basic measurements.

Monitoring Window is a duration of time τ throughout which basic measurements for a service are taken.

Monitoring Measurement is a function that aggregates the basic measurements for a service over its resources in the last monitoring window. The last monitoring window is defined as $[t_c - \tau, t_c]$. To produce the monitoring measurement, f_s is applied. Formally:

$$\mu(s, r, \tau) = f_s(\langle \mu_i(s, r, t) \rangle_{i=0}^{\infty}) \text{ where } t \in [t_c - \tau, t_c]$$

in which $\mu_i(s, r, t)$ is the i-th basic measurement of services s on resource r at time t where $t \in [t_c - \tau, t_c]$.

Definition 1 (Service Availability $\alpha(s, \tau, t_c)$). First, we need a few auxiliary definitions before we can define service availability.

Service Capacity $\kappa_\sigma(s, \tau) = \sum_{r \in \sigma(s)} \mu(s, r, \tau)$ denotes the capability of service s that is the aggregated monitoring measurements of its resources over the monitoring window τ and $\sigma(s)$ is the number of allocated resources to service s.

Agreement Expectation $E(s, \tau, t_c)$ is the minimum number of requests that a customer expects to complete in a monitoring window τ. The agreement expectation depends on the current time t_c because the expectation may change over time. For example, SDL Fredhopper customers expect a different QPS during Christmas.

We define the availability of a service $\alpha(s, \tau, t_c)$ in every monitoring window τ as:

$$\alpha(s, \tau, t_c) = \frac{\kappa_\sigma(s, \tau)}{E(s, \tau, t_c)}$$

Capacity Tolerance $\varepsilon_\alpha(s, \tau)) \in [0, 1]$ defines how much $\kappa_\sigma(s, \tau)$ can deviate from $E(s, \tau, t_c)$ in every time span of duration τ.

Service Guarantee Time t_G is the duration within which a customer expects service availability reaches an acceptable value after a violation. Typically, t_G is an input parameter from the customer's contract.

Example 1. Intuitively, $\alpha(s, \tau, t_c)$ presents the actual capability of a service s over a time period τ compared to the expectation on the service $E(s, \tau)$. For values $\alpha(s, \tau, t_c) \ll 1 - \varepsilon_\alpha(s, \tau))$, the resource for service s are at "under-capacity" while for values $\alpha(s, \tau, t_c) \gg 1 + \varepsilon_\alpha(s, \tau))$, there is "over-capacity". The goal is optimize $\alpha(s, \tau, t_c)$ towards a value of 1.

For example, we expect a query service to be able to complete 10 queries per second. We define the monitoring window $\tau = 5$ minutes; thus, $E(s, \tau, t_c) = 10 \times 60 \times 5 = 3000$. Suppose we allocate only one resource to the service, measure the service during a single monitoring window τ and find $\mu(s, r, \tau) = 2900$. Then $\alpha(s, \tau, t_c) = \frac{2900}{3000} = 0.966$. If we have $\varepsilon_\alpha(s, \tau)) = 0.03$, this means that service s is under-capacity because $\alpha(s, \tau, t_c) < 1 - \varepsilon_\alpha$.

Definition 2 (Budget Compliance $\beta(s, \tau)$). We first provide a few auxiliary definitions.

Resource Cost $\mathcal{C}(r, \tau) \in \mathbb{R}^+$ is the cost of resource r in a monitoring window τ which is determined by a fixed resource cost per time unit.

Service Cost $\mathcal{C}_\sigma(s, \tau) \in \mathbb{R}^+$ is the cost of a service s in a monitoring window τ and defined as $\mathcal{C}_\sigma(s, \tau) = \sum_{r \in \sigma(s)} \mathcal{C}(r, \tau)$.

Service Budget $B(s, \tau)$ specifies an upper bound of the expected cost of a service in the time span τ. Intuitively $B(s, \tau)$ is the allowed budget that can be spent for service s over the time span τ. The service budget is typically chosen to be fixed over any time span τ.

We are now ready to define service budget compliance $\beta(s, \tau)$ that, intuitively, represents how a service complies with its allocated budget:

$$\beta(s, \tau) = \frac{\mathcal{C}_\sigma(s, \tau)}{B(s, \tau)}$$

Budget Tolerance $\varepsilon_\beta(s, \tau) \in [0, 1]$ specifies how much the service cost $\mathcal{C}(s, \tau)$ can deviate from $B(s, \tau)$ in every time span of duration τ.

Service Guarantee Time t_G is similar to that defined for service availability.

Example 2. Assume every resource on the environment costs 1 (e.g. $\mathcal{C}$) per hour. Suppose we set a budget of 1.5 per hour for every service, allocate *one* resource to the service and define a monitoring window of $\tau = 5$ minutes. Every hour has 12 monitoring windows. This means that each resource costs $\mathcal{C}(r, \tau) = \frac{1}{12} \approx 0.08$ per monitoring window. Since there is only one resource, the service cost is $\mathcal{C}(s, \tau) = \sum_{r \in \sigma(s)} \mathcal{C}(s, \tau) \approx 0.08$ per monitoring window. On the other hand, if we calculate the budget for one monitoring window, we have $B(s, \tau) = \frac{1.5}{12} = 0.125$ per monitoring window. This yields budget compliance as $\beta(s, \tau) = \frac{0.08}{0.125} = 0.64$.

The formal definitions of service availability and budget compliance provide a rigorous basis for automatic deployment of resource-aware services with an appropriate quality of service, taking costs into account. This in particular includes automated scaling up or down of the service with the help of monitoring checks that are installed for the service. The fundamental challenge in ensuring service availability and budget compliance is that they have *conflicting* objectives:

$$\alpha(s, \tau, t_c) \uparrow \iff \beta(s, \tau) \downarrow$$

Intuitively, if more resources are used to ensure the availability of a service; then $\alpha(s, \tau, t_c)$ increases. However, at the same time, the service costs more; i.e. budget compliance $\beta(s, \tau)$ decreases.

5   Service Characteristics Verification

In this section, we use timed automata and task automata to model the behavior of a monitoring platform P, the deployment environment E, and the monitoring components for service availability $\alpha(s, \tau, t_c)$ and budget compliance $\beta(s, \tau)$. [13] defines a task automata as an extension of timed automata in which each task is a piece of executable program with (b, w, d): best/worst time and deadline of the task. A task automata uses a scheduler for the tasks to schedule each task with a location on a queue.

Modeling the elements of the monitoring platform is necessary to be able to study certain properties of the system. The most important goal of a monitoring platform is to enable the autonomous operation of a set of services according to their SLA. Thus, it is essential how to analyze that the monitoring platform can provide certain guarantees about the service and its SLA. In addition, it is important be able to verify the monitoring platform through model checking and schedulability analysis. Using timed automata and task automata facilitates model checking and verification through formal method tools such as UPPAAL [2] supporting advanced methods such as state-space reduction [19].

We use task automata as defined in [9,13,14]. Task automata are an extension of timed automata [1]. In addition, we design the automata for the monitoring platform using the real-time extension of task automata presented in [13] p. 92 in which the author presents a mapping from Real-Time ABS [16] to the equivalent task automata.

A task type is a piece of executable program/code represented by a tuple (b, w, d), where b and w respectively are the best-case and worst-case execution times and d is the deadline. In a task automata, there are two types of transitions: *delay* and *discrete*. A delay transition models the execution of a running task by idling for other tasks. A discrete transition corresponds to the arrival of a new task. When a new task is triggered, it is placed into a certain position in the queue based on a scheduling policy [22,23]. Examples of a scheduling policy are FIFO or EDF (earliest deadline first). The scheduling policy is modeled as a timed automaton Sch. Every task has its own stop watch. The scheduler also maintains a separate stop watch for each task to determine if a task misses its deadline. All stop watches work at the same clock speed specified by T.

We design separate automata for each service s characteristic: service availability $\alpha(s, \tau, t_c)$ by an automata M_{α_s} and service budget compliance $\beta(s, \tau)$, by an automata M_{β_s}. Each automaton is responsible for one goal: to optimize the service characteristic. M_{α_s} aims to improve $\alpha(s, \tau, t_c)$ whereas M_{β_s} aims to improve $\beta(s, \tau)$. M_{α_s} uses allocate to launch a new resource in the environment and improve the service s. In contrast, M_{β_s} uses deallocate to terminate a resource to decrease the cost of the service.

We use task automata to design M_{α_s}. Periodically, M_{α_s} checks whether the service availability is within the thresholds, taking tolerance into account (Definition 1). If the condition fails, M_{α_s} generates a task for monitoring platform P to allocate a new resource to service s with a deadline of τ. We define the period to be τ. We use the semantics of a task automata in [13] p. 92 in the transitions of the task automata. Figure Fig. 1a and Fig. 1b present M_{α_s} and M_{β_s}. Both M_{α_s} and M_{β_s} share state with the monitoring platform P. The state keeps the current number of resources for a service s that is denoted by $\sigma(s)$. All timed automata and task automata in the monitoring platform have shared access to $\sigma(s)$. In the automata, we use a conditional statement to check the service characteristics $\alpha(s, \tau, t_c)$ or $\beta(s, \tau)$. If the condition fails, M_{α_s} requests P to allocate a new resource to s and M_{β_s} requests P to deallocate a resource. In addition, M_{α_s} triggers a new task verify$_\alpha$ with deadline t_G. Intuitively, this means the service characteristic $\alpha(s, \tau, t_c)$ is verified to be within the expected thresholds after at most t_G time.

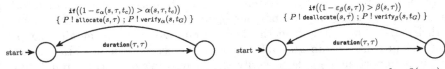

Fig. 1a: M_{α_s} task automata for $\alpha(s, \tau, t_c)$ **Fig. 1b:** M_{β_s} task automata for $\beta(s, \tau)$

We use a separate task automaton for each service characteristic to verify the SLA of the service after t_G time. Respectively, M_V^α and M_V^β execute tasks verify$_\alpha$ and verify$_\beta$ (Figures Fig. 2a and Fig. 2b). M_V^α uses await to ensure the condition of the SLA. In addition, the task is controlled by the scheduler using a deadline that is specified as t_G in the generated task verify$_\alpha(s, t_G)$ in M_{α_s}. If t_G passes before the guard statement in await statement holds, it leads to a *missed deadline*.

Fig. 2a: M_V^α to execute verify$_\alpha$ **Fig. 2b:** M_V^β to execute verify$_\beta$

Both M_{α_s} and M_{β_s} are specific to one particular service s. A generalized automaton for all services is obtained as their parallel composition: $M_\alpha = (\|_s M_{\alpha_s})$ and $M_\beta = (\|_s M_{\beta_s})$. The tasks generated by M_α and M_β (triggered by the calls to allocate and deallocate) are executed by the task automata for platform M_P.

We model monitoring platform P by a task automata M_P. The task types are $\{\text{A}(\text{allocate}), \text{D}(\text{deallocate})\}$. For task type A in M_P, we use $(b, w, d) = (t_i, \tau, \tau)$; i.e. the best-case execution time of a task is the resource initialization time, the worst-case is the length of the monitoring window, and the deadline is the length of the monitoring window. For task type D in M_P, we use $(b, w, d) = (0, \tau, \tau)$. We do not fix the scheduling policy Sch. The error state q_{err} in M_P is defined when either a deadline is missed or when the platform fails to provision a resource. Thus the monitoring platform P contains the following ingredients:

$$M_P = \langle M_A \| M_D \| M_V^\alpha \| M_V^\beta, \text{Sch}, \tau \rangle$$

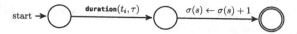

Fig. 3. M_{A_s}: Timed Automaton to execute task type `allocate` in M_P

We define M_{A_s} as the timed automata to execute the tasks of type `allocate` in M_P. We use the model semantics presented in [13] p. 92 to design M_{A_s}. The resulting automata is presented in Figure 3.

Then, we define M_A in M_P as: $M_\mathsf{A} = \|_s M_{\mathsf{A}_s}$; i.e. the composition of all timed automata to execute a task `allocate` for some service s. Similarly, we design M_{D_s} to execute task type `deallocate` in Figure 4. Therefore, we also have M_D in M_P as: $M_\mathsf{D} = \|_s M_{\mathsf{D}_s}$.

Fig. 4. M_{D_s}: Timed Automaton to execute task type `deallocate` in M_P

For a particular service s, its automaton M_{α_s} regularly measures the service characteristics and calculates $\alpha(s, \tau, t_c)$. When s is under-capacity, M_{α_s} requests to `allocate` a new resource for s through monitoring platform P. This generates a new task in M_P that is executed by M_{A_s}. When the task completes, the state of the service $\sigma(s)$ is updated; strictly increased. Thus, in isolation, the combination of M_{α_s} and M_{A_s} increase the value of service availability $\alpha(s, \tau, t_c)$ for service s over time. Similarly, in isolation, the combination of M_{β_s} and M_{D_s} increase the value of service budget compliance $\beta(s, \tau)$ for service s over time. Because in the latter, `deallocate` is used to decrease the cost of the service and as such increases $\beta(s, \tau)$.

In reality, resources might fail in the environment. The failure of a resource is not and cannot be controlled by the monitoring platform P. However, the failure of a resource affects the state of a service and its characteristics. Thus, we model the environment, including failures, as an additional timed automata, M_E. In M_E, in every monitoring window, there is a probability that some resources fail. For example, we present a particular instance of M_E in Figure 5. In this environment, in every monitoring, an unspecified constant (c) number of resources fail.

start $\rightarrow$ ◯ $\xrightarrow{\text{duration}(0, \tau)}$ ◯ $\xrightarrow{\sigma(s) \leftarrow \sigma(s) - c}$ ◯

Fig. 5. An example behavior for M_E

We define system automata [13] (p. 33, Definition 3.2.7) for each service characteristic; $\mathcal{S}_\alpha$ for $\alpha(s, \tau, t_c)$ and $\mathcal{S}_\beta$ for $\beta(s, \tau)$:

$$\mathcal{S}_\alpha = M_\alpha \parallel M_E \parallel M_P \qquad and \qquad \mathcal{S}_\beta = M_\beta \parallel M_E \parallel M_P$$

With the above automata that we designed for $\alpha(s, \tau, t_c)$ and $\beta(s, \tau)$, we are now ready to present the main results.

Theorem 1. If the SLA for service s on $\alpha(s, \tau, t_c)$ is violated, either:

- $\mathcal{S}_\alpha$ re-establishes the condition $\alpha(s, \tau, t_c) \geq 1 - \varepsilon_\alpha(s, \tau)$ (thereby satisfying the SLA) within t_G time, or,
- there exists at least one task verify$_\alpha$ in M_V^α with a missed deadline.

Proof. At any given time in T:

- If $\alpha(s, \tau, t_c) \geq 1 - \varepsilon_\alpha(s, \tau)$, then the SLA for service availability α is satisfied.
- If the above condition does not hold, on every monitoring window τ, M_α generates a new task allocate in M_A. In addition, a new task verify$_\alpha$ is generated with a deadline t_G. After a duration of t_G, the await statement allows M_V^α to complete the task verify$_\alpha$ only if the condition $\alpha(s, \tau, t_c) \geq 1 - \varepsilon_\alpha(s, \tau)$ holds. If this is not the case, since t_G has passed, the scheduler generates a missed deadline (moving to its error state). $\square$

Theorem 2. If the SLA for service s on $\beta(s, \tau)$ is violated, either:

- $\mathcal{S}_\beta$ re-establishes the condition $\beta(s, \tau) \geq 1 - \varepsilon_\beta(s, \tau)$ (thereby satisfying the SLA) within t_G time, or,
- there exists at least one task verify$_\beta$ in M_V^β with a missed deadline.

Proof. Similar to the proof of Theorem 1. $\square$

In practice, the guarantee of $\mathcal{S}_\alpha$ and $\mathcal{S}_\beta$ in isolation to eventually evolve the system to satisfy the SLA is not enough. In reality, a service provider tries ensure both simultaneously to reduce their cost of service delivery while ensuring the delivered service is of the expectations agreed upon with the customer. However, these goals conflict. When $\alpha(s, \tau, t_c)$ increases because of adding a new resource, it means that service s costs more, hence $\beta(s, \tau)$ decreases. The same applies in the other direction: increasing $\beta(s, \tau)$ negatively affects $\alpha(s, \tau, t_c)$.

To capture the combined behavior of service availability and budget compliance, we compose them. We define *service sustainability* $\gamma(s, \tau)$ as the composition of $\alpha(s, \tau, t_c)$ and $\beta(s, \tau)$. We present the composition by system automata $\mathcal{S}_\gamma$ as:

$$\mathcal{S}_\gamma = \mathcal{S}_\alpha \parallel \mathcal{S}_\beta$$

Authors in [9] define that a task automata is *schedulable* if there exists no task on the queue that misses its deadline. The next theorem presents the relationship between schedulability analysis of service sustainability and satisfying its SLA.

Theorem 3. If $\mathcal{S}_\gamma$ is *schedulable* given input parameters (τ, t_i, t_G), then the SLA for both service characteristics $\alpha(s, \tau, t_c)$ and $\beta(s, \tau)$ is satisfied within t_G time after a violation.

Proof. When a violation of the SLA occurs in $\mathcal{S}_\gamma$, either $\mathcal{S}_\alpha$ or $\mathcal{S}_\beta$ (or both) start to evolve the service based on Theorems 1 and 2. Therefore, there exists at least one task of verify$_\alpha$ or verify$_\beta$ with a deadline t_G. Hence, if $\mathcal{S}_\gamma$ is schedulable, then neither verify$_\alpha$ nor verify$_\beta$ miss their deadline. Thus, both $\mathcal{S}_\alpha$ and $\mathcal{S}_\beta$ are schedulable. This means that both verify$_\alpha$ and verify$_\beta$ complete successfully. Therefore, the SLA of the service is guaranteed within t_G after a violation in $\mathcal{S}_\gamma$.   □

Using the algorithm presented in Chapter 6 [13], we translate the above task automata into traditional timed automata. This allows to leverage well-established model checking techniques such as UPPAAL [2] to determine the schedulability of $\mathcal{S}_\gamma$. Moreover, the results of the schedulability analysis serves as a method to optimize the input parameters of the monitoring model including τ and t_G.

6   Evaluation of the Monitoring Model

In this section, we evaluate the implementation of the monitoring model.

We set up an environment to evaluate how the monitoring evolves a service according to its SLA. In the environment, a single instance of monitoring platform is present to provide new resources as necessary. Every resource hosts only one service. We define two customers in the environment. For both customers, we deploy the same service, Fredhopper Query API. For every resource that hosts a service, we set up a monitor that measures QPS and reports it to the platform. Both customers run with the same SLA: the QPS expectation is $E(s, \tau, t_c) = 10$ and $\varepsilon_\alpha(s, \tau, t_c) = 0.1$. We launch every customer service with only one resource. Monitors observe the customer service and calculate the service availability of every customer service $\alpha(s, \tau, t_c)$.

We run the environment setup for different monitoring windows $\tau \in \{1, 5, 10\}$ (seconds). We fix the initialization time of a resource to $t_i = 2.5$ seconds. We set $t_G = 300$ seconds; i.e. we verify the service after this time and evaluate if the service is guaranteed based on its SLA.

Figure 6 plots the service availability $\alpha(s, \tau, t_c)$ over time with the different monitoring windows. The following summarizes the behavior:

- As the monitoring window τ increases, the system converges with a slower pace towards the expected $\alpha(s, \tau, t_c)$.
- When the monitoring window is chosen such that $\tau < t_i$, the evolution of the system becomes *non-deterministic*.
- The setting $\tau < t_i$ causes a missed deadline in verify$_\alpha$ because after a duration of t_G the service availability has not yet reached the expected value.

Every monitoring measurement is performed in a monitoring window τ. Monitoring measurements are aggregated and calculated in every window and form the basis of reactions necessary to evolve the service to meet their SLA. Thus, selection of an appropriate monitoring window length τ is crucial, as we also discussed how schedulability analysis can be used to optimize it. The authors in [11] present that for the same

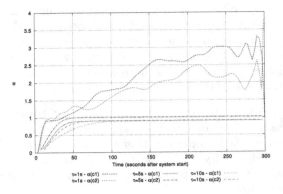

Fig. 6. Evolving $\alpha(s, \tau, t_c)$ with different τ

setup and deployment of services, measurements using different monitoring windows yield to very different understanding of service properties such as service availability. Therefore, it is essential to choose the value of τ such that monitoring measurements do not lead to *unrealistic* understanding and inappropriate reactions.

If $\tau < t_i$, Theorem 1 does not hold because every task allocate in M_A misses its deadline. Thus, it is essential that $\tau \geq t_i$. Analogously, choosing monitoring window as $\tau \gg 2 \times t_i$ also has a counter-productive effect on the service deployments. In a real setting, different services may use different types of resources. In such a setting, the monitoring window should be chosen as the largest t_i of any resource type that is available in the platform: $\tau \geq \max(t_i) \; \forall r \in P$.

7   Future work

We continue to generalize the notion of the distributed service characteristics and investigate how the composition of an arbitrary number of such properties can be formalized and reasoned about. In the context of the ENVISAGE project, industry partners define their service characteristics in this framework and monitor the service evolution. Moreover, the work will be extended to generate parts of the monitoring platform based on an input of different SLA formalizations such as SLA★ [17]. Currently, we are integrating our automated monitoring infrastructure into the in-production SDL Fredhopper cloud services (cf. Section 3).

References

1. Alur, R., Dill, D.L.: A theory of timed automata. Theoretical Computer Science **126**(2), 183–235 (1994)
2. Behrmann, G., David, A., Larsen, K.G.: A tutorial on UPPAAL. In: Bernardo, M., Corradini, F. (eds.) SFM-RT 2004. LNCS, vol. 3185, pp. 200–236. Springer, Heidelberg (2004)

3. Bjørk, J., de Boer, F.S., Johnsen, E.B., Schlatte, R., Tarifa, S.L.T.: User-defined schedulers for real-time concurrent objects. Innovations in Systems and Software Engineering 9(1), 29–43 (2013)
4. Bratanis, K., Dranidis, D., Simons, A.J.H.: Towards run-time monitoring of web services conformance to business-level agreements. In: Bottaci, L., Fraser, G. (eds.) TAIC PART 2010. LNCS, vol. 6303, pp. 203–206. Springer, Heidelberg (2010)
5. Bubel, R., Montoya, A.F., Hähnle, R.: Analysis of executable software models. In: Bernardo, M., Damiani, F., Hähnle, R., Johnsen, E.B., Schaefer, I. (eds.) SFM 2014. LNCS, vol. 8483, pp. 1–25. Springer, Heidelberg (2014)
6. Chen, Y., Iyer, S., Liu, X., Milojicic, D., Sahai, A.: SLA decomposition: translating service level objectives to system level thresholds. In: Fourth International Conference on Autonomic Computing, ICAC 2007, pp. 3–3. IEEE (2007)
7. Coles, A., Coles, A.J., Clark, A., Gilmore, S.: Cost-sensitive concurrent planning under duration uncertainty for service-level agreements. In: ICAPS (2011)
8. Comuzzi, M., Kotsokalis, C., Spanoudakis, G., Yahyapour, R.: Establishing and monitoring SLAs in complex service based systems. In: IEEE International Conference on Web Services, ICWS 2009, pp. 783–790. IEEE (2009)
9. Fersman, E., Krcal, P., Pettersson, P., Yi, W.: Task automata: Schedulability, decidability and undecidability. Information and Computation 205(8), 1149–1172 (2007)
10. Gilmore, S., Gönczy, L., Koch, N., Mayer, P., Tribastone, M., Varró, D.: Non-functional properties in the model-driven development of service-oriented systems. Software & Systems Modeling 10(3), 287–311 (2011)
11. Hogben, G., Pannetrat, A.: Mutant apples: a critical examination of cloud SLA availability definitions. In: 2013 IEEE 5th International Conference on Cloud Computing Technology and Science (Cloud-Com), vol. 1, pp. 379–386. IEEE (2013)
12. Christian, I., Waldemar, H., Benjamin, S., Philipp, L., Shahram, D.: Generic event-based monitoring and adaptation methodology for heterogeneous distributed systems. Software - Practice and Experience (2014)
13. Jaghoori, M.M.: Time at your service: schedulability analysis of real-time and distributed services. PhD thesis, Leiden University (2010)
14. Jaghoori, M.M.: Composing real-time concurrent objects refinement, compatibility and schedulability. In: Arbab, F., Sirjani, M. (eds.) FSEN 2011. LNCS, vol. 7141, pp. 96–111. Springer, Heidelberg (2012)
15. Johnsen, E.B., Hähnle, R., Schäfer, J., Schlatte, R., Steffen, M.: ABS: a core language for abstract behavioral specification. In: Aichernig, B.K., de Boer, F.S., Bonsangue, M.M. (eds.) FMCO 2010. LNCS, vol. 6957, pp. 142–164. Springer, Heidelberg (2011)
16. Johnsen, E.B., Schlatte, R., Tapia Tarifa, S.L.: Modeling resource-aware virtualized applications for the cloud in real-time ABS. In: Aoki, T., Taguchi, K. (eds.) ICFEM 2012. LNCS, vol. 7635, pp. 71–86. Springer, Heidelberg (2012)
17. Kearney, K.T., Torelli, F., Kotsokalis, C.: SLA⋆: an abstract syntax for service level agreements. In: 2010 11th IEEE/ACM International Conference on Grid Computing (GRID), pp. 217–224. IEEE (2010)
18. Keller, A., Ludwig, H.: The WSLA framework: Specifying and monitoring service level agreements for web services. Journal of Network and Systems Management 11(1), 57–81 (2003)
19. Larsen, K.G., Larsson, F., Pettersson, P., Yi, W.: Efficient verification of real-time systems: compact data structure and state-space reduction. In: The 18th IEEE Proceedings of the Real-Time Systems Symposium, 1997, pp. 14–24. IEEE (1997)

20. Logean, X., Dietrich, F., Karamyan, H., Koppenhöfer, S.: Run-time monitoring of distributed applications. In: Proceedings of the IFIP International Conference on Distributed Systems Platforms and Open Distributed Processing, Middleware 1998, pp. 459–474 (1998)
21. Mahbub, K., Spanoudakis, G., Tsigkritis, T.: Translation of SLAs into monitoring specifications. In: Service Level Agreements for Cloud Computing, pp. 79–101. Springer (2011)
22. Nobakht, B., de Boer, F.S., Jaghoori, M.M.: The future of a missed deadline. In: De Nicola, R., Julien, C. (eds.) COORDINATION 2013. LNCS, vol. 7890, pp. 181–195. Springer, Heidelberg (2013)
23. Nobakht, B., de Boer, F.S., Jaghoori, M.M., Schlatte, R.: Programming and deployment of active objects with application-level scheduling. In: Proceedings of the 27th Annual ACM Symposium on Applied Computing, SAC 2012, pp. 1883–1888. ACM (2012)
24. Raimondi, F., Skene, J., Emmerich, W.: Efficient online monitoring of web-service SLAs. In: Proceedings of the 16th ACM SIGSOFT International Symposium on Foundations of software engineering, pp. 170–180. ACM (2008)
25. Wong, P.Y.H., Bubel, R., de Boer, F.S., Gómez-Zamalloa, M., de Gouw, S., Hähnle, R., Meinke, K., Sindhu, M.A.: Testing abstract behavioral specifications. STTT **17**(1), 107–119 (2015)
26. Fitzgerald, J., Foster, S., Larsen, P.G., Woodcock, J., Cavalcanti, A.: Contracts in CML. In: Margaria, T., Steffen, B. (eds.) ISoLA 2014, Part II. LNCS, vol. 8803, pp. 54–73. Springer, Heidelberg (2014)

Dynamic Strategies for Query Constructing and Rank Merging from Multiple Search Engines

Kobkaew Opasjumruskit$^{(\boxtimes)}$, Birgitta König-Ries, and Jesús Expósito

Heinz-Nixdorf Chair for Distributed Information Systems, Institute for Computer Science, Friedrich-Schiller-University Jena, Jena, Germany
{kobkaew.opasjumruskit,birgitta.konig-ries,jesus.exposito}@uni-jena.de

Abstract. Heterogeneous search engines differ in the algorithms they use and the domains they cover, thus there is no single search engine that performs best in every circumstance. In order to obtain optimal search results, it often makes sense to use more than one search engine. However, appropriately merging results from different engines is challenging, i.e. combining results in such a way that they reflect the ranking of results the user would choose. In this paper, we propose an effective way to achieve this for web services search which can be extended to cloud services and be applied to big data. In contrast to "classical" search processed by conventional text-based search engines, a more elaborated search request is needed here. In addition to the result merging, we therefore present a method to create a structured request for this specific task. The evaluation of our proposed solution shows that it is satisfying in terms of both result quality and performance.

1 Introduction

Search engines have been around for a few decades and not only provide access to textual information, in other words digitalized data, but also to other types of information sources and to functionality offered online, e.g. smart objects, sensors and actuators around us. Moreover, the discoverable information can be presented either in plain text formats (like contents on web pages or text files) or in structured formats such as XML or RDF.

There is a plethora of search engines which differ in specialties and algorithms. Each search engine has its own benefits and drawbacks. Therefore, if a user wants to be sure to obtain the optimal result, he or she has to make multiple queries on several search engines and integrate the results manually. Additionally, the quality of the search results of a specific engine depends on keywords and their structures provided by the user.

As an example, consider the search for web services. We compared the quality of results from different search engines as depicted in Table 1. First, we prepared three different search queries (i.e. "camera price", "book price" and "city country hotel"). Secondly, we employed three different search engines specialized in web service searching (i.e., two variants of iSEM [10] and SeMa2 [18]) and one text-based search engine (i.e. ElasticSearch [1]). Thirdly, we measured the precision,

© IFIP International Federation for Information Processing 2015
S. Dustdar et al. (Eds.): ESOCC 2015, LNCS 9306, pp. 141–155, 2015.
DOI: 10.1007/978-3-319-24072-5_10

Table 1. Service matchers' performance depends on queries.

Query	camera price				book price				city country hotel			
	iSem (Cos, structured)	iSem (Cos)	SeMa2	ElasticSearch	iSem (Cos, structured)	iSem (Cos)	SeMa2	ElasticSearch	iSem (Cos, structured)	iSem (Cos)	SeMa2	ElasticSearch
Precision	0.50	**0.60**	0.40	0.40	**0.80**	0.80	0.40	0.90	0.30	0.30	**1.00**	1.00
Recall	0.71	**0.86**	0.57	0.57	**0.80**	0.80	0.40	0.64	1.00	1.00	**1.00**	0.59
F-measure	0.59	**0.71**	0.47	0.47	**0.80**	0.80	0.40	0.75	0.46	0.46	**1.00**	0.74
nDCG	0.91	**0.90**	0.82	0.73	**0.94**	0.87	0.74	0.83	1.00	1.00	**1.00**	0.62

recall, F-measure and nDCG (normalized Discounted Cumulative Gain) rates to compare the quality of search results of the search engines. Though "iSem text similarity (Cos, structured)" search engine performed best with the "camera price" query, the other search engines yielded better quality of results when we used other queries. Moreover, the overall quality of semantic search engines surpasses the text-based search engine. This advocates the need to use several search engines relying not only on a conventional text-based search.

There are several researches, e.g. [16] and [7], trying to take advantage of multiple search engines to improve the quality of search results. This way, one can always select the best result from all of them. One challenge in this approach is how to properly rank the results from search engines into one list. Assume that the search engines return match values between 0 and 1 for the individual services, where 1 means the services matches perfectly and 0 means the service does not match at all. In such a setting, for instance, results from a search engine A could be S1(0.9), S2(0.8), S3(0.75), and results from a search engine B could be S4(0.95), S1(0.8), S2(0.9); where Sn means an item of results, and a number in brackets is a similarity score between that item and the query. What would be the best way to integrate these results? Is S4 with 0.95 score from search engine B better than S1 with 0.9 score from search engine A?

Another challenge is how to convert a user's simple text input into a structured request, which is varied by different search engines. For example, the user is looking for a data in which containing "pricing" with in an attribute name "service", not in any other attribute. Search engine A may be able to search the data in XML format, while search engine B can search only for JSON format data. In order to use both search engines, this user needs to create two types of requests. This can take a great effort for the user to learn how to construct a request that conformed to different search engines. Therefore, we need to create a tool to help the user for these conversions.

Together with semantic technology, it is possible to improve the search process, where the search engine understands the meaning of keywords and can search not only "literally" but also "semantically".

As a tangible use case, we can apply the approaches of using multiple search engines and creating a structural request message to service discovery as proposed by [22]. Imagine that Brian needs to check whether a light in his study room is turned on or off. Since the light switch in this room is connected to the local network, he can check its status via a web service. But he does not know which one is belong to his study room. Fortunately, these devices are provided with standardized and machine-interpretable service descriptions which can be optionally extended by semantic annotations. Thus, instead of remembering all names of sensors in his house, he can input a simple keyword to the service discovery engine to look for the right sensor.

According to [3], there is currently no single global set of standards for the service descriptions, and in all likelihood never will be. This is also true for the service description language and service matching algorithm, since numerous of them have been developed and been widely in use for a while. They all have their own pros and cons; consequently, it is not deducible which one is the best for every circumstance. One optimal solution is to apply all prominent description languages and service matching algorithms together in one single discovery process as proposed in [22]. To realize such an approach, we need to compose a request which can be interpreted by service matching engines. Afterwards, a meaningful strategy to merge all outcomes is needed to create a single set of search results.

This paper is structured as follows: the technical background and related work will be reviewed in the next section. This also raises research questions which became requirements for our approach. Consequently, the solutions section will elaborate in technical detail how we fulfill the requirements. The evaluation section advocates the solutions we proposed, and finally, we conclude our work in this paper and plan for further development.

2   Literature Review

In this section, we provide an overview of existing techniques for result merging and discuss their respective advantages and drawbacks. We then focus on the specific type of search engine used for this evaluation, namely (semantic) web service search engines and the underlying service descriptions.

2.1   Result Merging

[16] and [7] discussed different methods of merging multiple search engines' results. These techniques can be categorized into three types: score-based, rank-based and content-based.

The *score-based method* is the simplest technique. Assuming all search engines have comparable similarity scores, then all the results can be merged by linear combination methods discussed in [25], which accumulate each item's normalised score from all search engines and reorder them to a final ranked list. However, this approach does not take into account that different search engines differ in their reliability. Thus, this does not work well in practice.

Content-based approaches like Search Result Records (SRRs), Top Document (TopD) and their successors are claimed to be the most effective [16]. However, they are rather heavy-weight since they need to download documents for analysis. Besides, the content-based algorithms are already used by search engines. Thus, there is no need to repeat the algorithm again in our approach.

The *Rank-based method*, which assigns each item a score corresponding to the rank in which it appears within each search result, is simple and versatile. It neglects the original scores from the search engines, on the other hand, assigns a new score to each item. This does not require document analysis, so it can save time and memory consumption. The simplest rank-based method is to consider the best rank from all search engines directly using voting systems as discussed in [23], like Borda's Positional method. Moreover, when taking the reliability of search engines into account, we can use an approach like weighted Borda-Fuse.

Borda count [23], a voting-based data fusion method, is also simple and effective in terms of quality and time consumption. In Borda count, each search engine represents a voter. Each voter ranks a fixed set of candidates according to preference. The top rank will gain the highest score. Consecutive ranks will get fewer scores. Finally, all scores of each candidate will be collected from all voters. The item which gets the highest sum of scores will be placed in the first rank and so on. In this work, Borda count is used for assigning scores to each item from search engines' results. Total scores will be arranged to provide the final result and also be used to calculate a weight value for each search engine. These technical details will be elaborated in the solution section.

2.2   Service Description

The service description plays a key role in the service discovery engine since we assume that all devices are available as web services which must be supplemented with basic information in WSDL (Web Services Description Language) [2], a recommendation by the World Wide Web Consortium.

For an automatic service discovery, the WSDL description alone is inadequate unless this description is enhanced with a semantic annotation. This problem is addressed by SAWSDL (Semantic Annotations for WSDL) [6], which allows the extension of WSDL descriptions with semantic annotations from arbitrary ontologies. As one example for a more heavy-weight semantic description language, we also cover OWL-S (Web Ontology Language for Web Services) [17] in our evaluation.

Based on these service descriptions, there are several promising matchmakers as reviewed by [21] and [29]. In order to evaluate all the techniques based on different description formalisms, there are competitions, e.g. the Semantic Web Services Challenge [5] and the S3 Contest [9]. According to the results of these contests, we collected some auspicious approaches like SAWSDL-iMatcher [30], iSEM, OWLS-MX [11–13], etc., and used those in our evaluation.

3   Our Solution

To assist a user in finding appropriate devices in dynamic situations, an environment-adaptive service discovery engine has been developed. This service discovery engine appears to users as a search engine. Consider that a request from a non-tech-savvy user would be simple keywords, e.g. 'my location', 'heart rate', etc.

Our first challenge is to construct a query with a specific format in order to be comparable with service descriptions. Secondly, when service descriptions contain synonyms instead of an exact term the user is looking for, we can apply semantic annotations to the query so search engines can discover them. Thirdly, to cope with different standards of description, we need a request converter. When the request is ready, then we deploy service matchers, which can be replaced by any matcher that complies with description standards.

Each service matcher can have their own algorithm in assigning a similarity score to each ranked result, thus we cannot compare similarity value between two ranks from different matchers directly. However, we need several matchers to boost the result quality. So a ranks merger, in other words, a result integrator must be able to calculate and formulate the final ranking with the best quality.

Therefore, our proposed service discovery engine is separated into four modules: a request constructor, a request converter, a service matcher and a result integrator as shown in Fig. 1.

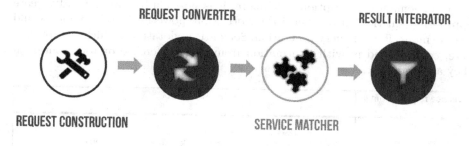

Fig. 1. A building block diagram for the service discovery.

3.1   Request Constructor

This module is responsible for constructing a meaningful query message out of the user inputs in free-text format. By using a semantic search engine, we can retrieve synonyms or relevant terms to enhance the search result. Afterwards, these terms will be separated into input, output and operational descriptions to be mapped with the predefined description format, which is WSDL in this work.

The number of irrelevant services is typically larger than the number of relevant services, therefore the keyword and synonyms are used to filter out irrelevant descriptions. This will save more time in the service matching process.

Additionally, service descriptions are either in XML or RDF structures, thus making them accessible to an attribute or value of node level. For example, if a user wants a service that provides him a price of a specific model of a camera, he will look for a service which contains "camera model" in input, "price" in output, and "find" in an operation description. It is more tangible to process this query by a structural search rather than a conventional text-based search, i.e. accessing the input, output, and operational attributes in each service description and comparing them with the user's query as exemplified in Fig. 2.

Furthermore, the user does not need to know how to construct these structural descriptions. The request constructor requires at least one simple keyword to create a structural request automatically.

3.2 Request Converter

As several service description languages exist, in order to find all relevant services, the request needs to be converted into appropriate input formats for search engines supporting these different languages. Therefore, the request converter is responsible for translating the previously constructed description into other formats such as OWL-S or SAWSDL. By using a mapping schema, we can convert a request from a user into different formats and this can be extended for other prominent formats, e.g. JSON, tagged-based description when they are available.

Fig. 2 shows the common placeholders where we can insert mandatory information in order to create a description in various formats. Please note that this only works because current search engines do not take advantage of the full power of semantic descriptions; therefore, it is possible to automatically create appropriate queries with rather little effort. More powerful search engines would require more effort in query generation. Semantic annotations, which are optional here, can be filled in with information from user preference or user context if they are available.

Service request from a user	SAWSDL

Input: GPS location
Output: Emergency Unit
Behavior: Find ambulance service
	`<wsdl:description ...> ...`
	    `<wsdl:input sawsdl:modelReference="http://.../protont.owl#Location" />`
	    `<wsdl:output sawsdl:modelReference="http://.../MedicalTransport.owl#Hospital"/>`
	    `...`
	`<wsdl:service name="FindAmbulanceService" >...</wsdl:service>`
	`</wsdl:description>`

	OWL-S

	`<rdf:RDF ...>`
	    `<service:Service rdf:ID="FindAmbulanceService"/>`
	    `<process:Input rdf:ID="Location">`
	        `<process:parameterType> http://.../protont.owl#Location</process:parameterType>`
	    `</process:Input>`
	    `<process:Output rdf:ID="Hospital">`
	        `<process:parameterType>http://.../ MedicalTransport.owl#Hospital </process:parameterType>`
	    `</process:Output> ...`
	`</rdf:RDF>`

Fig. 2. A user request and the resulting structured descriptions.

3.3   Service Matcher

For this part we rely on existing work. We use SAWSDL and OWL-S service matchers for a proof of concept. The different approaches and description formalisms of each matcher assure that all suitable services will be discovered. Each matcher operates independently, thus the time consumption in this process can be reduced by using multithreading. Still, since we need results from all of the matchers, the runtime of the slowest matcher determines the overall runtime.

3.4   Result Integrator

This work proposes a technique on how to retrieve the best quality result from multiple service matchers dynamically. First of all, results from search engines will be assigned scores based on their ranks by using Borda count as described in Section 2.1. With these scores, we can sort all search results into a list which will be compared with the original results from the search engines. Thereupon, the distance between the search results and the combined result will be calculated. The higher the distance value is, the less reliable that search engine will be. This reliability, i.e. weight, will be multiplied to the score computed by Borda count. Then, the merged list will be regenerated. This process will be iterated until there is no change in weight value between two consecutive iterations.

Consider that each matcher will return a set of results per query, which can be presented as an array, i.e. $[r_1, r_2, r_3, ...]$. Each element represents the unique ID of a service such as URI, and the similarity value of each result compared to the request. In our calculation, we apply several queries to measure average qualities. Therefore, each array from each query becomes a row of a matrix (R^k). Given that n = number of ranks, m = number of queries and k = number of matchers/search engines, the pseudo code depicted in Fig. 3 explains the result integrator's computation:

Result matrices (R^k) will be merged into a combined result matrix,
$$R^C = \begin{pmatrix} r_{q1,1} & \cdots & r_{q1,n} \\ \vdots & \ddots & \vdots \\ r_{qm,1} & \cdots & r_{qm,n} \end{pmatrix}, \text{ by the getCombinedResult function (line 13).}$$

Since not every matcher provides similarity scores, we estimate these scores from the result ranks. An element in the upper rank will get a higher score and vice versa. The formula for calculating the score, as shown in function getScore (line 32), is according to the normalized Discounted Cumulative Gain (nDCG). In addition, each matcher gets a reliability score, which is used as a multiplier to normalize the score with the other matchers. If there is no assigned weight, the integrator treats each matcher equally.

In function *getWeight* (line 38), a result matrix from each matcher, R^k, is compared with the combined result matrix R^C using the Euclidean distance method.

For testing the iteration condition, an *isWeightStable* function (line 50) compares weights between two consecutive rounds. When the difference converges to 0, indicating the stability of weight, the iteration will cease and the result from this round is supposed to yield the best quality.

```
1   FUNCTION resultIntegrator (ResultMatrices[k]):
2     SET weight[k] to [1/k, ... , 1/k]
3     SET CombinedMatrix to getCombinedResult(ResultMatrices, weight)
4     SET newWeight[k] to getWeight(CombinedMatrix, ResultMatrices)
5     WHILE ( !isWeightStable(weight, newWeight) ) DO
6       SET weight to newWeight
7       SET CombinedMatrix to getCombinedResult(ResultMatrices,weight)
8       SET newWeight to getWeight(CombinedMatrix, ResultMatrices)
9     END WHILE
10    RETURN CombinedMatrix
11  END.
12
13  FUNCTION getCombinedResult(ResultMatrices, weight):
14    DEFINE combinedResult[m][n]
15    FOR each i in queries
16      DEFINE rowResult[]
17      FOR each j in ranks
18        FOR each l in matchers
19          SET URI to ResultMatrices[i][j][l].URI
20          SET score to getScore(j, weight[l])
21          IF rowResult has URI THEN
22            add score to rowResult[URI].score
23          ELSE add URI and score to the rowResult as a new element
24        END FOR
25      END FOR
26      SET sortedRowResult[n] to n elements of the rowResult with the
              highest score sort
27      SET combinedResult[m] to sortedRowResult
28    END FOR
29   RETURN combinedResult
30  END.
31
32  FUNCTION getScore(a, b):
33    IF a = 1 THEN RETURN 1
34    ELSE RETURN b/log2(a)
35    END IF
36  END:
37
38  FUNCTION getWeight(combinedResult, ResultMatrices):
39    DEFINE distance[k]
40    DEFINE weight[k]
41    FOR each l in matchers
42      FOR each i in queries
43        increase distance[l] with Euclidean distance value
                between the combined matrix and the result matrices
44      END FOR
45      SET weight[l] to 1-(distance[l]/m)
46    END FOR
47    RETURN weight/sum(weight)
48  END.
49
50  FUNCTION isWeightStable(weight, newWeight):
51    SET i to index of maximum element in newWeight[]
52    IF (weight[i] - newWeight[i])/weight[i] < 0.05 THEN
53      RETURN true
54    ELSE RETURN false
55    END IF
56  END.
```

Fig. 3. The Result Integrator Algorithm

To exemplify the process flow, assume that we use three matchers (k1, k2 and k3) and two queries on a set of services (S1 to Sn) and consider the top five ranks of the result. Then, we will have 3 matrices with dimension $[2 \times 5]$. The three matchers might return: $R^{k1} = \left(\begin{smallmatrix} S2 & S4 & S3 & S7 & S1 \\ S6 & S9 & S1 & S2 & S5 \end{smallmatrix}\right)$, $R^{k2} = \left(\begin{smallmatrix} S2 & S4 & S3 & S7 & S1 \\ S6 & S9 & S1 & S2 & S5 \end{smallmatrix}\right)$, $R^{k3} = \left(\begin{smallmatrix} S2 & S3 & S4 & S8 & S6 \\ S9 & S6 & S1 & S7 & S3 \end{smallmatrix}\right)$. Next, the following steps will be executed:

1. Accumulating scores from each rank in each matcher (each element in R^k), e.g. service "S4" is ranked in the second place by matcher k1 and k2, while k3 ranks the service in the 3rd place, the total score for service "S4" is $\frac{1}{\log_2 2} + \frac{1}{\log_2 2} + \frac{1}{\log_2 3}$.

2. After finishing scoring all services for each query, the scores are sorted descending and the top 5 ranks are added to a row of the combined result matrix, i.e. $R^c = \left(\begin{smallmatrix} S2 & S4 & S3 & S7 & S1 \\ (3) & (2.63) & (2.26) & (1) & (0.86) \\ S6 & S9 & S1 & S2 & S5 \\ (3) & (3) & (1.89) & (1) & (0.86) \end{smallmatrix}\right)$.

3. The result matrices from the three matchers are compared with the combined result matrix to calculate the distances and the weights. The (average) Euclidean distances of the matchers are 0, 0, and 0.235. These figures will be used to calculate normalized weights, which become 0.34, 0.34 and 0.32.

4. The weight value of each matcher is multiplied to the original result matrix and the combined result matrix, R^C, is calculated again. From the previous step, the third matcher performs worse than the other matchers, thus the result from this matcher has fewer score than the rest.

5. The step 1-4 are iterated until the quality of returned results changes insignificantly, then the best combined result is completed.

From our previous experiment, a poor performance matcher weakened the overall quality of the final result. Thus, in Step 1 of each iteration, the matcher with the lowest weight below a threshold, $mean - 0.2(standard variation)$ of all matchers, is removed. The number 0.2 in the formula is adjustable; however, we chose this value based on results of our previous evaluation. When this number is too high, there is more possibility that no matcher will be removed, but if this number is too low, it is more likely that an average performance matcher will be eliminated.

4   Evaluation

To evaluate the idea proposed in the previous section, we adopted service descriptions from the S3 Contest [9]. As it provides pre-defined solution sets, we can measure the quality of the result from our work. The binary quality measurement is calculated by precision, recall and F-measure rates. Meanwhile, to measure the quality of rank, the nDCG is used.

4.1   Test Collections

The S3 Contest provides a sample set of service descriptions equally in SAWSDL and OWL-S formalisms. The total number of descriptions (for each formalism) is

1080. The contest also provides 42 service requests together with the ideal solution of the matching task. There are 2 types of solutions; a binary relevance and a grading relevance. The former states only "relevant" or "irrelevant". While a graded relevance provides more detail of relevancy level, i.e., highly relevant, relevant, partially relevant, and irrelevant.

4.2   Service Matchers

According to the test collections, we also adopted service matchers from S3 Contest for the evaluation. The two categories of service matchers we are using are OWL-S-based and SAWSDL-based which handle different description formalisms.

The OWL-S matchers used in this evaluation are: EMMA [4], iSeM, SeMa2, SPARQLent [26], OWLS-iMatcher [8], OWLS-SLR Lite [20], OWLS-MX1 [12], OWLS-MX2 [11], OWLS-MX3 [13].

The SAWSDL matchers used in this evaluation are: iSeM-SAWSDL [10], SAWSDL-MX1 [14], SAWSDL-MX2 [15], URBE [24], LOG4SWS.KOM [27], COV4SWS.KOM [28], SAWSDL-iMatcher.

To simplify the evaluation process, which is getting more complicated towards the end of the building block diagram, some matchers that have unsatisfactory performances are neglected.

4.3   Evaluation Results

The objective is to test whether the proposed technique can improve the quality of the service discovery process. The request construction and the request converter must be integrated to the whole process so that we can measure the quality of the result. It is unnecessary to evaluate the service matcher part since this was successfully done by efforts like [5] and [9]. Nevertheless, outcomes from the service matcher module are merged in a result integrator module.

Therefore, we focused in evaluating the result integrator in terms of result quality compared to an individual result of a single service matcher. Eventually, the overall time performance was measured and discussed in order to find a gap of improvement.

Result Integrator: By applying all descriptions from the test collections together with service matchers mentioned previously, the quality of a result integrator was compared with individual service matchers. Fig. 4 depicts a comparison in precision, recall, F-measure and nDCG between each SAWSDL matcher, a text-based search engine (Elasticsearch) and the outcome of the service integrator in each round. The weights of all matchers were calculated and illustrated in Fig. 6 (a).

In this experiment, the criteria to select a round that yield the best result was met in the fourth round. However, when we had a solution to compare with, the actual best result was from the third round. Since we cannot have the

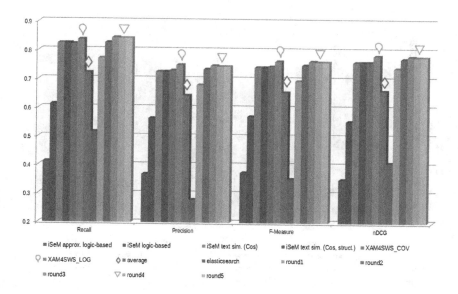

Fig. 4. Result integrator's quality in each iteration compare to each SAWSDL matcher.

Table 2. Evaluation result from the result integrator module

	Precision	Recall	F-measure	nDCG
Best SAWSDL Matcher	0.8377	0.7500	0.7638	0.7837
Average SAWSDL Matcher	0.7228	0.6444	0.6569	0.6624
This work on SAWSDL	**0.8421**	**0.7452**	**0.7613**	**0.7789**
Best OWL-S Matcher	0.9262	0.8167	0.8361	0.8539
Average OWL-S Matcher	0.6560	0.5762	0.5903	0.6101
This work on OWL-S	**0.9238**	**0.8143**	**0.8337**	**0.8673**

ground truth in the practical usage, plus, the difference between the third and fourth round were negligible, we can conclude that this technique produces a satisfactory result.

The same evaluation was applied to OWL-S matchers, see Fig. 5. From the weight measurement in Fig. 6 (b), the iteration stopped at round 7, which provided the best result.

From Table 2, our approach with SAWSDL matchers improved the recall rate compared to the best performing matcher by 0.5% while precision, F-measure and nDCG rates dropped by less than 0.7%. With OWL-S matchers, our approach boosted the nDCG by 1.57% whereas the other measurement declined by less than 0.3%. Nevertheless, comparing to the average performance of all matchers, our proposed solution outperformed them notably.

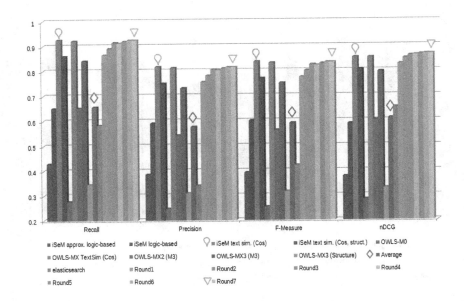

Fig. 5. Result integrator's quality in each iteration compare to each OWL-S matcher.

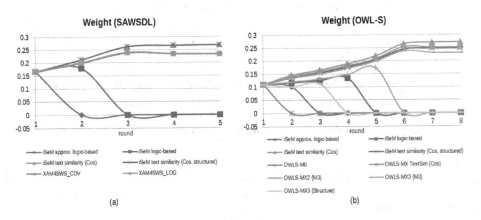

Fig. 6. Weight value of (a) SAWSDL and (b) OWL-S matchers calculated from each iteration.

Overall Performance: Up to now, we discussed how each component of a service discovery engine performs. Now we exhibit the overall run-time performance when everything is put together.

First, we set three different factors; type of query, number of service matchers and number of processing thread. There are two types of query for the service discovery engine; a simple keyword that has no structure and a user's request containing input, output and operational keywords. The second type is called a

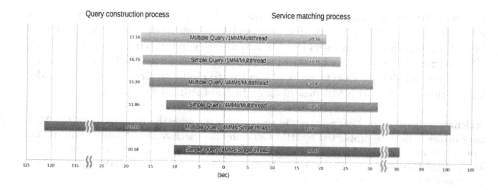

Fig. 7. Timing evaluation of a semantic search and service matcher modules.

multiple query since we need to query three times for semantic meanings. The more service matchers are used, the more time are consumed respectively. Thus, we deployed the multithreaded processing to the semantic search (in the query construction) and the service matcher modules, which consumed 95% of total time in service discovery.

According to Fig. 7, the time consumption for each semantic query were accumulated when using a single thread processing. The multithreading can dramatically reduce the query construction time though the multiple query generally takes more time than the simple query. This is due to waiting for the slowest query to finish.

On average, the number of queries has a small effect on the service matching's runtime. Multithreading can reduce the time usage significantly though not by 4 folds as expected due to waiting for all matchers to complete their tasks.

5   Conclusion and Future Plan

The evaluation in this paper proved that our proposed technique can dynamically retrieve the best set of results from multiple search engines. The outcome of the request constructor and converter is a service description that is compatible with prominent service matchers in OWL-S and SAWSDL standards. The bottleneck of the total time performance occurred in the semantic search process is caused by an HTTP request to a remote server.

The result integrator produces a single set of results from multiple search engines with conceivable ranks. Additionally, from automatically calculated weights, we can rate the reliability of each search engine. This value can be recorded and used for statistical analysis further on. The time performance of this module is negligible compared to the semantic search and service matcher modules.

Our ultimate goal is to implement a user-friendly tool to efficiently utilize the benefits of the Internet of Things (IOT) [19] and to support big data. In the near future, we aim to integrate this work as the service discovery engine in MERCURY [22], a platform for user-centric integration, and management of heterogeneous devices and services via a web-based interface. Since MERCURY offers a great interface, it is practical to evaluate a usability test there. Moreover, we can extend the use case from local services to cloud services. We also consider supporting JSON and XML descriptions in the future development as well.

Acknowledgments. This research is accomplished under the framework of the Mercury project and was supported by IBM Germany Research & Development GmbH. We would like to specially thank you to Prof. Martin Welsch, a Chief Technology Advisor at the IBM Germany and Dr. Andreas Nauerz, a Lead Architect at IBM Laboratories, Germany for all supports and advices.

References

1. Elasticsearch. https://www.elastic.co/products/elasticsearch (accessed 2015-10-07)
2. Christensen, E., Curbera, F., Meredith, G., Weerawarana, S.: Web services description language. http://www.w3.org/TR/wsdl (accessed 2015-10-07)
3. Fleisch, E.: What is the internet of things? an economic perspective. Auto-ID Labs White Paper WP-BIZAPP-053, Zürich (2010). http://www.im.ethz.ch/education/HS10/AUTOIDLABS-WP-BIZAPP-53.pdf
4. García, J.M., Ruiz, D., Ruiz-Cortés, A.: Improving semant. web services discovery using sparql-based repository filtering. Web Semant.: Science, Services & Agents on the World Wide Web **17**, 12–24 (2012)
5. Harth, A.M.D.: Semantic web challenge. http://challenge.semanticweb.org (accessed 2015-10-07)
6. Hobold, G., Siqueira, F.: Discovery of semant. web services compositions based on sawsdl annotations. In: IEEE 19th Int'l Conf. on Web Services, pp. 280–287 (2012)
7. Jadidoleslamy, H.: Search result merging & ranking strategies in meta-search engines: A survey. Int'l Journal of Comp. Sci. Issues (2012)
8. Kiefer, C., Bernstein, A.: The creation and evaluation of iSPARQL strategies for matchmaking. In: Bechhofer, S., Hauswirth, M., Hoffmann, J., Koubarakis, M. (eds.) ESWC 2008. LNCS, vol. 5021, pp. 463–477. Springer, Heidelberg (2008)
9. Klusch, M.: Semantic service selection (s3) contest. http://www-ags.dfki.uni-sb.de/klusch/s3/index.html (accessed 2015-07-10)
10. Klusch, M., Kapahnke, P.: isem: approx. reasoning for adaptive hybrid selection of sem. services. In: IEEE Int'l Conf. on Sem. Computing, pp. 184–191 (2010)
11. Klusch, M., Kapahnke, P., Fries, B.: Hybrid sem. web service retrieval: a case study with owls-mx. In: IEEE Int'l Conf. on Sem. Computing, pp. 323–330 (2008)
12. Klusch, M., Fries, B., Khalid, M.: Owls-mx: hybrid owl-s service matchmaking. In: Proc. of 1st Int'l AAAI Fall Symp. on Agents & the Semant. Web (2005)
13. Klusch, M., Kapahnke, P.: Adaptive signature-based semantic selection of services with OWLS-MX3. Multiagent and Grid Systems **8**(1), 69–82 (2012)
14. Klusch, M., Kapahnke, P., Zinnikus, I.: Hybrid adaptive web service selection with SAWSDL-MX and WSDL-analyzer. In: Aroyo, L., Traverso, P., Ciravegna, F., Cimiano, P., Heath, T., Hyvönen, E., Mizoguchi, R., Oren, E., Sabou, M., Simperl, E. (eds.) ESWC 2009. LNCS, vol. 5554, pp. 550–564. Springer, Heidelberg (2009)

15. Klusch, M., Kapahnke, P., Zinnikus, I.: Sawsdl-mx2: a machine-learning approach for integrating semant. web service matchmaking variants. 7th IEEE Int'l Conf. on Web Services (ICWS), pp. 335–342. IEEE Press, L.A. (2009)
16. Lu, Y., Meng, W., Shu, L., Yu, C., Liu, K.-L.: Evaluation of result merging strategies for metasearch engines. In: Ngu, A.H.H., Kitsuregawa, M., Neuhold, E.J., Chung, J.-Y., Sheng, Q.Z. (eds.) WISE 2005. LNCS, vol. 3806, pp. 53–66. Springer, Heidelberg (2005)
17. Martin, D., Paolucci, M., McIlraith, S.A., Burstein, M., McDermott, D., McGuinness, D.L., Parsia, B., Payne, T.R., Sabou, M., Solanki, M., Srinivasan, N., Sycara, K.: Bringing semantics to web services: the OWL-S approach. In: Cardoso, J., Sheth, A.P. (eds.) SWSWPC 2004. LNCS, vol. 3387, pp. 26–42. Springer, Heidelberg (2005)
18. Masuch, N., Hirsch, B., Burkhardt, M., Heßler, A., Albayrak, S.: Sema2: a hybrid semantic service matching approach. In: Semantic Web Services, pp. 35–47. Springer (2012)
19. Mattern, F., Floerkemeier, C.: From the internet of computers to the internet of things. In: Sachs, K., Petrov, I., Guerrero, P. (eds.) Buchmann Festschrift. LNCS, vol. 6462, pp. 242–259. Springer, Heidelberg (2010)
20. Meditskos, G., Bassiliades, N.: Structural & role-oriented web service discovery with taxonomies in owl-s. IEEE Trans. on Knowledge & Data Eng. $22(2)$, 278–290 (2010)
21. Ngan, L.D., Kirchberg, M., Kanagasabai, R.: Review of semantic web service discovery methods. In: 6th World Congress on Services, pp. 176–177 (2010)
22. Opasjumruskit, K., Expósito, J., König-Ries, B., Nauerz, A., Welsch, M.: Service discovery with personal awareness in smart env. In: Creating Personal, Social, & Urban Awareness through Pervasive Computing, pp. 86–107. IGI Global (2014)
23. Pacuit, E.: Voting methods. In: The Stanford Encyclopedia of Philosophy (2012). http://plato.stanford.edu/archives/win2012/entries/voting-methods/
24. Plebani, P., Pernici, B.: Urbe: Web service retrieval based on similarity evaluation. IEEE Trans. on Knowledge and Data Eng. $21(11)$, 1629–1642 (2009)
25. Renda, M.E., Straccia, U.: Web metasearch: rank vs. score based rank aggregation methods. In: Proc. of the ACM Symp. on Applied Computing, pp. 841–846 (2003)
26. Sbodio, M.: Sparqlent: a sparql based intelligent agent performing service matchmaking. In: Semantic Web Services, pp. 83–105. Springer, Heidelberg (2012)
27. Schulte, S., Lampe, U., Eckert, J., Steinmetz, R.: Log4sws.kom: self-adapting sem. web service discovery for sawsdl. In: 6th World Congress on Services, pp. 511–518 (2010)
28. Schulte, S., Lampe, U., Klusch, M., Steinmetz, R.: COV4SWS.KOM: information quality-aware matchmaking for semantic services. In: Simperl, E., Cimiano, P., Polleres, A., Corcho, O., Presutti, V. (eds.) ESWC 2012. LNCS, vol. 7295, pp. 499–513. Springer, Heidelberg (2012)
29. Talantikite, H.N., Aissani, D., Boudjlida, N.: Sem. annotations for web services discovery & composition. Computer Standards & Interfaces $31(6)$, 1108–1117 (2009)
30. Wei, D., Wang, T., Wang, J., Bernstein, A.: Sawsdl-imatcher: A customizable & effective semant. web service matchmaker. Web Semant. $9(4)$, 402–417 (2011)

Highly Customizable Service Composition and Orchestration

Luca Sabatucci[✉], Carmelo Lodato, Salvatore Lopes, and Massimo Cossentino

ICAR-CNR, Palermo, Italy
{sabatucci,c.lodato,s.lopes,cossentino}@pa.icar.cnr.it

Abstract. One of the current challenges of Service Oriented Engineering is to provide instruments for dealing with dynamic and unpredictable user requirements and environment. Traditional approaches based on workflow for orchestrating services provide little support for configuring at run-time the flow of activities.

This paper presents a general approach for composing and orchestrating services in a self-organization fashion. User requirements are made explicit in the system by a goal specification language. These can be injected into the running orchestration system that is able to autonomously and contextually reason on them. Therefore, the system dynamically organizes its structure for addressing the result. A prototype of the system has been implemented in JASON, a language for programming multi agent systems. Some aggregate statistics of execution are reported and discussed.

Keywords: Service orchestration · Self-organization · Holonic system

1 Introduction

In the last years there has been an increasing interest on composing and orchestrating heterogeneous services from many parties. To date, BPEL is the de facto standard for implementing the orchestration of services. Even if greatly supported by industry and research, the classic workflow approach is not easy to extend for supporting some advanced features: 1) integrating user's preference into the flow of activities complicates much the model; 2) there is no a simple way to change the flow of activities as consequence of a change of the execution context; 3) introducing new services requires to revise the whole workflow model; 4) service failures may be included in the design but any unexpected situations make the process fails. It is a fact that researchers are also investigating on dynamic workflows and on techniques for generating a highly configurable system behavior, potentially adaptable to unexpected events [5,9].

The assumptions of this work are that: i) services are delivered over the internet by service providers; as usual, these are accessible through standards protocols (i.e. WSDL and SOAP); (ii) the orchestration system is a distributed and decentralized software, made of a number of autonomous agents, each able

© IFIP International Federation for Information Processing 2015
S. Dustdar et al. (Eds.): ESOCC 2015, LNCS 9306, pp. 156–170, 2015.
DOI: 10.1007/978-3-319-24072-5_11

to perceive the environment and act as broker for web-services (of which it knows address, end points and business logic); and (iii) holons are temporary assembly of agents generated ad-hoc for aggregating services.

In this paper we propose a middleware for conciliating goal-orientation [24] with holonic systems [11] with the aim of creating a highly customizable orchestration of web-services. Goal orientation is used for decoupling the specification of what the system has to do from how it will be done. The request for a service is based on a technique we called goal-injection: a goal is the high level specification of the kind of service desired by the user. Once it has been specified, the goal may be injected into the system at run-time, thus becoming a stimulus for the holons of the system that try to self-organize in an ad-hoc architecture for fulfilling the request.

On the other side, holons provide an elegant and scalable method to design and develop a distributed software system with a natural inclination for knowledge sharing, coordination of activities and robustness. The goal specification language is enough flexible to create complex requests that any available service may satisfy alone. However the developer has to code only simple interactions with basic services: service compositions must not be programmed. It is responsibility of the system that of aggregating basic services thus to obtain composed ones.

The paper is organized as follows: Section 2 provides an overview of the proposed middleware. Section 3 presents some preliminary definition by introducing the holonic approach. Section 4 provides details on how services are aggregated and orchestrated for addressing a set of user-goals. Section 5 illustrates the state of the art in service composition and orchestration, whereas Section 6 presents a critical analysis of the approach. Finally, Section 7 briefly summarizes the impact of the work.

2   Overview: The MUSA Approach

This paper presents MUSA (Middleware for User-driven Service Adaptation) [1], a holonic multi-agent system for the composition and the orchestration of services in a distributed and open environment. The middleware aims at providing run-time modification of the flow of events, dynamic hierarchies of services and integration of user preferences together with a self-adaptive system for execution activities that is also able to monitor unexpected failures and to reschedule in order to optimize the flow.

The main feature of the system is to break the static constraints of a classic workflow model by decoupling the two dimensions: 'what to address' and 'how to address it' [21]. The core element of the approach is the use of *Goals* for explicitly representing user-preferences into the system (what to address). The injection of goals trigger for the re-organization of the agents of the system in hierarchical groups called holons. These self-adaptive structures allow for dealing with dynamic composition and orchestration of services.

---

[1] Website: http://aose.pa.icar.cnr.it/MUSA/

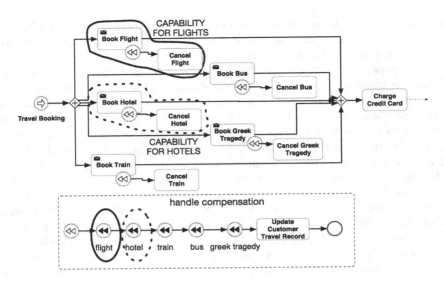

Fig. 1. An example of workflow for booking a set of related services for a travel The capability approach consists in identifying sub-parts to decompose for obtaining self-contained pieces of behavior of the system.

The Capability is the key for addressing the injected goals coming from the decomposing of standard workflow into a set of atomic and self-contained parts to connect in many different ways. An illustrative example is reported in Figure 1 that shows a portion of the BPEL for a travel reservation workflow. Tasks related to the flight reservation (search, booking, canceling) as well as those related to hotel reservation are highlighted.

As a running example we refer to the *smart travel system*, able to act as touristic tour operator in a geographical area. A scenario will help in clarifying variability and flexibility required in a service composition context.

Scenario: *Herbert from Munich wants to organize a vacation in Sicily for a week with his family. In seven days, Herbert desires: 1) to visit the city of Palermo; 2) to visit Agrigento and 3) to visit Syracuse and to attend the Greek tragedy performance. The smart_travel service suggests to flight to Palermo, stay there 3 days, than to visit Agrigento for 2 days, then to move to Syracuse (for the Greek tragedy) and finally to depart from the Catania airport. Herbert confirms the travel plan, and the smart_travel reserves flights and hotels and buys tickets for the trip.*

The MUSA middleware offers a suitable infrastructure for implementing the smart travel system. Figure 2 provides an overview of the customization of MUSA for the specific domain. The user will interact with the smart travel through a web page for specifying her preferences (dates, places to visit, events to assist, and other interests). The web page converts user-data into a set of goals in an ad-hoc language called GoalSPEC [22]. Goals are injected into the MUSA running system that interprets them and uses them as directives for a planning

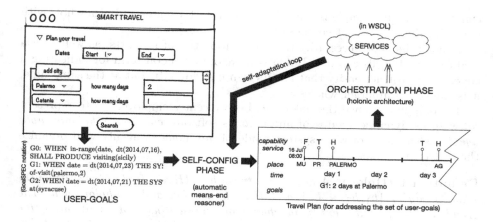

Fig. 2. An example of the MUSA approach to the case study of the smart travel.

phase. This algorithm, called automatic means-end reasoning [20], is responsible of discovering 0..n solutions for addressing the user-goals. A solution represents a collection of web-services and a semantic layer working as instructions for orchestrating them. Selecting one of these solutions triggers the organization of holonic architecture for orchestrating services and monitoring the state of interest. The system is able of identifying is some of the selected services fails. If this happens the self-adaptation mechanism calls again the planning algorithm for re-organize the architecture.

3 Preliminary Definitions

Holons provide an elegant and scalable method to guarantee knowledge sharing, distributed coordination and robustness.

3.1 A Brief Introduction to Holons

Holon is a Greek word for indicating something that is simultaneously a whole and a part [16]:

> A holon is a system (or phenomenon) that is an evolving self-organizing structure, consisting of other holons [15]. A holon has its own individuality, but at the same time, it is embedded in larger wholes (principle of duality or *Janus effect*).

Many concrete things in nature are organized as a holarchy (the recursive structure generated by holons and sub-holons). An example of concrete holon is an *organ* that is a part of an organism, but a whole with regard to the cells of which it is comprised. The human mind uses holarchies for organizing abstract concepts too. An example is a *word* that is part of a sentence, but a whole with regard to the letters that compose it.

A holon has not necessarily the same properties of its parts, as well as if a bird can fly, its cells can not. Holon is therefore a general term for indicating a concrete or abstract entity that has its own individuality, but at the same time, it is embedded in larger wholes.

In computer science the holon has been recently employed [8] to represent software as dynamic groups of autonomous software entities. A *holonic multi agent system* is a software system made of autonomous agents who organize themselves in holons.

Definition 1 (Holon). *A holon is a triple $h = \langle Head, Body, Commitments \rangle$ where $Body = \{h_1, h_2, \ldots h_n\}$ and $\forall i, h_i$ is a holon and sub-holon of h. The Head $\subseteq$ Body is the entity in charge of representing and coordinating the actions inside h and, finally, Commitments are relationships inside the holon that aggregate the parts h_i towards common objectives. The base for the recursion is the agent which represents a sort of atomic holon of the system (a holon that can not be further decomposed in sub-holons): if a is an agent of the system, $h_a = (\{a\}, \{a\}, \emptyset)$ is the corresponding atomic holon.*

In our approach we map 1) the distributed nature of services to agents of the system and 2) the composability of services to holons. Therefore each atomic holon is in charge of dealing with a single service, whereas higher level holons can handle compositions of services. Holons are not defined according design-time schema. They are able to generate super-holons for dealing with complex problems on demand.

3.2   Knowledge, Goals and Capabilities

Each holon of the system maintains a knowledge of the context of execution. We adopt a frame-based first order logic model of knowledge: (Bel h φ) specifies that the holon h believes φ is true, where φ is a first order fact.

In a holon, knowledge is maintained by the head adopting a structure called *State of World* and it is shared on request to sub-holons.

Definition 2 (State of the World). *A subjective state of the world, in a given time t, is a set $W^t \subset S$ where S is the set of all the (non-contradictory and non-negated) facts $(s_1, s_2 \ldots s_n)$ that can be asserted to describe a given domain.*

W^t describes a closed-world in which everything that is not explicitly declared is assumed to be false.

The peculiarity of this holonic system is that the commitment relationship (e.g. the glue that puts together a holon) is a run-time property called User-Goal. A goal is a specification of the expected behavior of the whole system.

Definition 3 (Goal). *A goal is a pair: $\langle tc, fs \rangle$ where tc and fs are logical formula indicating, respectively the trigger condition (i.e. when the goal may* *be actively pursued) and the final state (i.e. when the goal may be considered addressed). The truth table of these conditions is evaluated (by unification) through facts of the current state of the world.*

Goals can be used to specify the business logic of the desired service composition in terms of which outcome the user will receive. In MUSA the goal may be injected at run-time by using GoalSPEC see [22], a goal specification language that integrates a subset of natural language and first-order predicates. Examples of goals for the smart travel agency:

- G0: WHEN date IS BETWEEN dt(2014,07,16) AND dt(2014,07,23) THE SYSTEM SHALL PRODUCE visiting(sicily)
- G1: WHEN date IS dt(2014,07,23) THE SYSTEM SHALL PRODUCE day-of-visit(palermo,2)
- G2: WHEN date IS dt(2014,07,21) THE SYSTEM SHALL PRODUCE being-at(syracuse)
- G3: WHEN date IS dt(2014,07,21) THE SYSTEM SHALL PRODUCE enjoyed(greek-tragedy)

The WHEN reserved word is used for specifying an external event (in the example it introduces the goal triggering condition clause), whereas the SHALL PRODUCE reserved words specifies the final state of the world that is desired by the user. More details about this specification language are given in [22].

In the following we focus on illustrating that when the user defines and injects a set of goals, then the system generates a holonic architecture as response.

To this aim we need to introduce the concept of *Capability* as an atomic and self-contained action the agent knows to have and how to use it. A capability is a run-time property that holons may intentionally use to interact with a web-service.

In MUSA, a capability is concretely realized by two macro-components: (i) the abstract description that is a sort of 'manual' about the usage of the service, in a self-aware fashion, and (ii) the concrete implementation is the machine-code for invoking a specific web-service.

For what concerns the abstract description, the most significant properties are pre and post (conditions) to be uses in the orchestration phase, and the params and evolution to be used in the self-configuration phase for composing services thus to address complex problems that single services cannot afford.

The "pre-condition" must be true, when tested in the current state of the world ($pre(W^t) = true$), in order to execute the capability. The "post-condition" must be true, after the execution of the capability ($post(W^{t+1}) = true$), for assessing its correct execution. On the other side the "params" describes points of variability of the service for allowing self-configuration (see 4.1), whereas the "evolution" describes the endogenous effect of a capability in terms of changes of state of world ($W^t \rightarrow W^{t+1}$). Figure 3 shows an example of abstract description of the flight booking capability.

On the other side, the concrete implementation encapsulates the code for interacting with the real service by using SOAP and WSDL through the

Name	FLIGHT_BOOKING	Knowledge about:
Input	DptPlace : Airport, DptDate: Date, ArrPlace : Airport, PassNum : Integer	
Output	DptSchedule: Date, ArrSchedule: Date	data consumed in order to properly work, and data produced as result of the work
Constraints	$DptPlace \neq ArrPlace$ $DptSchedule > DptDate$ $ArrSchedule > DptSchedule$ $PassNumber > 1$	
Params	FlighId: String	how to customize the capability
Pre-Condition	$seat\_available(FlighId, DptSchedule, PassNum)$	when the capability may be executed and what to expect as result
Post-Condition	$flight\_booked(FlighId, DptSchedule, PassNum)$	
Evolution	$evo = \{remove(being\_at(DptPlace)),$ $add(being\_at(ArrPlace))\}$	how to change the state of the world

Fig. 3. An example of *abstract description* of a capability for dealing with flight booking web-service.

HTTP/ HTTPS protocol. The implementation of a capability is different for internal capability and webservice-capability. In particular the implementation of a web-services includes three parts: the *customize helper*, the *dispose service* and the *compensate service*. Figure 4 shows the three protocols used in the flight booking activity. They are detailed in the next section.

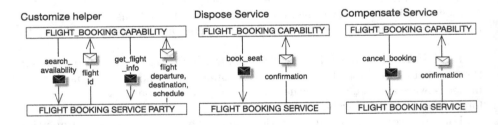

Fig. 4. The concrete implementation of a capability for dealing with flight booking activity.

4   Adaptive Composition and Orchestration of Services

This section assumes that MUSA has been instrumented with a set of capabilities for working in a specific problem domain. For instance, in the case of the smart travel, the capabilities may reserve flights, book hotels, buy ticket for a local event and so on.

When a user introduces a set of goals into MUSA for requesting the personalized execution of services, then the system will firstly discover i) how to compose its capabilities for addressing all the goals, and subsequently ii) it orchestrate the agents of the system thus to allow them properly using their capabilities.

4.1 Self-Configuration Phase

The Self-Configuration phase starts soon after that a set of goals is injected into the system. It aims at discovering a set of capabilities (among the available ones) which composition potentially leads to the achievement of all the goals. In particular, the problem is: given the current state of the world, a set of Goals and a set of Capabilities to produce a plan for addressing the goals. The procedure is called Proactive Means-End Reasoning [20].

A complete description of the algorithm is out of the scope of this paper. Conversely, an exemplar scenario of execution is reported for providing an intuition of the approach used for composing the capabilities. Supposing the current state of the world is:

$W_I = [at(palermo), it\_is(morning)]$:

1. simulate the use of the capability Visit_City_HalfDay:
   $[at(Place), visited(Place, X)] \rightarrow [at(Place), visited(Place, X + 0.5)]$
   for producing the new world:
   $W_1 = [at(palermo), it\_is(afternoon), visited(palermo, 0.5)]$
2. compare the previous result with the state of the world due to the use of a different capability: Book_Train:
   $[at(palermo), it\_is(morning)] \rightarrow [at(catania), it\_is(afternoon)]$
   that generates:
   $W_2 = [at(catania), it\_is(afternoon), visited(palermo, 0.5)]$
3. given that first path is more promising (with respect of the goal to visit Palermo for two days) then discard the second and proceeds from W_1
4. concatenate Visit_City_HalfDay with Reserve_Hotel:
   $[at(Place), it\_is(afternoon)] \rightarrow [at(Place), it\_is(morning)]$
   for obtaining
   $W_3 = [at(palermo), it\_is(morning), visited(palermo, 0.5)]$.
5. ...

In this context, the *customize helper* protocol of the involved capabilities is employed for exploring the range of possible impact that each individual capability may have towards the evolution of the state of the world. Indeed a capability may include, in its description, some parameters to configure for obtaining different results. For instance, the flight_booking capability may be customized by assigning a value to the flight_id param: FLIGHT_BOOKING[$flight\_id \leftarrow$ "AZ243"]. A different configuration for this parameter leads to different effects (departure/destination places, timetable, flight company and costs may be sensibly different).

During the Self-Configuration phase, the customize helper considers many parameters for a capability, in order to configure it for the specific context. This generally requires interacting with real web-services for querying the range of possible values for the parameters. For instance, the customize helper for the flight_booking searches for available flights that may be useful in the context of user's travel (existing flight from a destination to a target city, in a given date with available seats). It returns a list of possible Flight IDs that satisfy the input conditions: each item corresponds to a possible variant of the capability.

For a detailed description of the procedure, please refer to [20].

4.2 Service Orchestration Phase

The selection of a solution (for addressing a set of goals) triggers for a holon formation and it promotes the corresponding holon to become operative and to orchestrate all the embedded services for producing the compounded result. For instance, let us suppose the holon represented in Figure 5. It is made of four sub-holons: (H_{PA} able to address the goal G1, H_{SY} able to address the goals G2/G3 and H_{AG}, H_{CT} created for completing the travel).

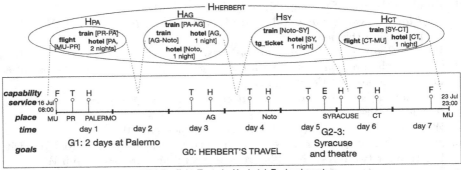

Fig. 5. In the topside: an instance of Holon ($H_{HERBERT}$) formed for addressing Herbert's travel specifications. It is composed of four sub-holons (H_{PA}, H_{AG}, H_{SY} and H_{CT}). Finally, atomic holons for simplicity are shown as the capability they offer (in bold text), followed by their params. Below: the corresponding travel plan showing the schedule and highlighting where Herbert's goals are satisfied.

When a holon becomes active, then (recursively) all its sub-holons become active. From the point of view of the atomic holon, this corresponds to execute the *dispose* protocols of service capabilities, as soon as the capability pre-conditions hold. It is worth noting that since agents are autonomous and distributed, all the dispose protocols will be executed by parallel threads. Figure 6 represents the corresponding flow of activities resulting from the holon orchestration of capabilities. In the case of the smart travel, the holon will book all necessary flights, hotels, ticket for the travel plan. In particular, the dispose protocol for the flight_booking service actually book the specified flight and produces a ticket for the user.

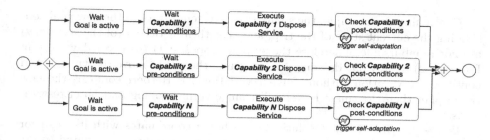

Fig. 6. The corresponding flow of activities resulting from the composition of three capabilities for addressing a goal.

In addition, when possible, holons will activate their monitoring capabilities for checking the real service execution. This detail is out of the scope of this paper. Just to provide an example, by interacting with Herbert's mobile applications the monitor agent may know his position, and interact with him for warning about delays or allowing to change details of the travel.

4.3 Self-Adaptation

The main purpose of monitoring the services is to look for failures or new goals that may affect the running holon. When something unexpected happens at run-time, it could be the case that some services that have been disposed are no more useful in the new plan. The proper way to proceed is to use the *compensate service* protocol in order to terminate the contract with a service. For instance, the compensate service for the flight_booking tries to cancel the user booking for a specified flight.

The holon in charge of addressing a goal is continuously updated about the state of the services and it is able to discover when something is going wrong by comparing perceptions with expected states of the world. When a service fails, or when a goal cannot be addressed then the head role of the corresponding sub-holon raises an event of failure (see Figure 6), which is the cause of an adaptation.

Let us consider the following variability scenario, concerning the smart travel system described in Section 3: *Herbert and his family are enjoying their vacation in Sicily. They are visiting Palermo and communicate to the smart_travel service their new desire to stay one day more in the city.*

In this example the user who modified her goals triggers the adaptation (by informing the system to change the travel plan). The adaptation is treated by the system as a reorganization of the holonic architecture. The reorganization produces a temporary disassembly of the holon and the re-execution of the Self-Configuration phase but considering the new situation (current state of the world, failures, service availability or new user goals) for generating a new solution.

Continuing the example, the smart travel system reacts to the new goal considering the current state of the trip, and that theater tickets (of the sixth day) are not reimbursable. Therefore the system proposes: 1) to stay 1 day more in Palermo, 2) to stay one day only at Agrigento, then 3) to move to Syracuse and continue the vacation without further variations. If Herbert confirms the new travel plan then the smart-travel will change train booking and hotel reservations.

Before starting the new solution, each holon coordinates with its head for deciding if executing the *compensate* protocols of capabilities associated to the services that are no more useful in the new solution. After that, the orchestration phase starts again.

5   Related Work

In last decade, researchers have been looking for alternative approaches to classic workflow models for describing service compositions. For instance, Laukkanen and Helin [17] illustrate a semantic type matching approach for creating or updating a workflow. Traverso et al. [6] show that an instance of the service choreography problem can be viewed as a STRIPS-style planning problem in which state descriptions are ambiguous and operator definitions are incomplete. Whereas approaches based on planning are NP-Complete, Doshi et al. [10] propose using Markov decision processes and Bayesian model learning to model workflow composition with a polynomial complexity. Buhler and Vidal [4] present an introductory work on adaptive workflow composition based on a multi-agent perspective. They suggest the utilization of standard workflow languages for multi-agent coordination.

SAPERE [25] (Self-Aware Pervasive Service Ecosystems), is a general framework for self-organizing distributed service ecosystems. Components of the system can inject Live Semantic Annotations that propagate to other components, while EcoLaws define how they interact in the ecosystem.

A-3 [1] is self-organizing distributed middleware aiming at dealing with high-volume and highly volatile distributed systems. It focuses on the coordination needs of complex systems, yet it also provides designers with a clear view of where they can include control loops, and how they can coordinate them for global management.

Blanchet et al. [2] view service orchestration as a conversation among intelligent agents, each one responsible for delivering the services of a participating organization. An agent also recognizes mismatches between own workflow model and the models of other agents.

Gomaa and Hashimoto, in the context of the SASSY research project [12], look into software adaptation patterns for Service-Oriented Applications. The goal is to dynamically adapt distributed transactions at run-time, separating the concerns of individual components of the architecture from concerns of dynamic adaptation, using a connector adaptation state-machine.

OSIRIS [23] is an Open Service Infrastructure for Reliable and Integrated process Support that consists of a peer-to-peer decentralized service execution engine and organizes services into a self-organizing ring topology.

Grassi et al. [13] propose a QoS-aware decentralized service assembly based on the 3 architectural layers. They concentrate their contributions on the middle layer (change management). A dynamic set of agents may enter/leave the system, each offering a specific service. In this context, producing fully resolved assemblies is complicated by dependencies among service. Plus, non-functional requirements and only the currently available services should be considered. Even further, all of this should be done using decentralized self-assembly (no external control, dynamic operation, no central control).

Hahn and Fischer, in [14] illustrate how a choreography model can easily be conceptually implemented through holons. Their approach is a design-to-code technique based on model-driven transformations which result is a holonic multi-agent system.

6   Discussion and Evaluation

The system[2] has been implemented by using JASON [3], an agent oriented platform based on AgentSpeak [18]. AgentSpeak is a programming language based on events and actions. The state of an agent together with its environment and eventual other agents represent its belief base. Desires are states that the agent wants to attain based on its perceptions and beliefs. When an agent adopts a plan it transforms a desire to an intention to be pursued. In JASON, the agent's knowledge is expressed by a symbolic representation by using beliefs, which are simple predicates that state what the agent thinks to be true.

Completeness and Complexity of the Approach. The current algorithm used for implementing the means-end reasoning is a variation of the depth-first search strategy. Indeed, at the worst case, it takes an exponential time to visit all the possible states.

We accepted this complexity because we observed that in a real situation rarely, given a state of the world, there are too much competing services that may solve a goal. Therefore we assumed to explore only a limited space of solutions 1) by filtering in advance capabilities that are impossible to compose (according to a preliminary evaluation of preconditions) and 2) by employing domain-specific utility functions to measure, step by step, the quality of the partial solutions.

We conducted an experiment in which we requested the smart travel system to organize available services for a 7 days vacation in Sicily. The algorithm has been executed 50 times with five different sets of user-goals in order to evaluate the number of steps necessary for discovering (at most) 5 travel plans; in all the cases the execution returned 5 solutions by exploring, in average, 73 states of world.

---

[2] Available at https://github.com/icar-aose/MUSA/archive/v0.2.zip (Jason 1.3.8 or higher is required).

We also compared the average branch factor with respect to a simple depth-first algorithm in which the number of capabilities (6 in the experiment) is equal to the branch factor. The resulting average branching factor is 2.65, therefore at each step more than 70% of the capabilities are discarded, thus reducing the space to explore.

Table 1. Aggregated statistics for the execution of the self-configuration phase for the smart travel. The algorithm has been executed 50 times with a range of 5 different configurations (changing the number and the type of user-goals from a minimum of 2 to a maximum of 5) but with a constant number of capabilities, set to 6.

First Solution	44,00 states
Total States of World	73,25 states
Max Depth	17,25 capabilities
Average Branch Factor	2,65 states
Max Number of Partial Solutions	76,75 part. solutions

Ontology Commitment and System Evolution. Another point of discussion concerns the degree of decoupling between Capabilities and Goals. These are specified in two independent languages, and injected into the system at run-time. In addition they can evolve during the time, thus making the whole system able to encapsulate new functionality on the fly. However the use of ontology is required for enabling a semantic compatibility between Capabilities and Goals. An ontology is the specification of a conceptualization made for the purpose of enabling knowledge sharing and reuse.

The Problem Ontology Diagram (POD) [8] may be used to provide a denotation to significant states of the world thus giving a precise semantics to goals and capabilities. A POD is a conceptual model [19] to create an ontological commitment between developers of capabilities and users who inject goals, i.e. the agreement to use a thesaurus of words in a way that is consistent with respect to the theory specified by ontology.

This artifact aims at producing a set of concepts, predicates and actions and at creating a semantic network in which these elements are related to one another. The representation is mainly human-oriented but it is particularly suitable for developing cognitive system that are able of storing, manipulating, reasoning on, and transferring knowledge data directly in first-order predicates [19].

Grounding goals and capability abstract description on the same ontology is fundamental to allow the system to adopt a proactive means-end reasoning to compose plans. By committing to the same ontology, capabilities and goals can be implemented and delivered by different development teams and at the same time enabling a semantic compatibility between them.

More details on the POD are in [8], whereas the link between goals and ontology is detailed in [19]. Finally we also provide GIMT (Goal Identification and Modeling Tool) a tool for supporting ontology building and goal modeling [7].

7 Conclusions

Holonic multi-agent systems provide a flexible and reconfigurable architecture to accommodate environment changes and user customization. This paper has presented a dynamic (re-) organization of the system by an autonomous and proactive collaboration of autonomous agents. The novelty of the proposed approach, with respect to the state of the art, is to encapsulate the desired service composition in run-time goal-models. Goals are injected into the system thus allowing holarchy to spontaneously emerge for orchestrating services that will address them.

Acknowledgments. The research was funded by the Autonomous Region of Sicily, Project OCCP (Open Cloud Computing Platform), within the Regional Operative Plans (PO-FESR) of the EU Community.

References

1. Baresi, L., Guinea, S.: A3: self-adaptation capabilities through groups and coordination. In: Proceedings of the 4th India Software Engineering Conference, pp. 11–20. ACM (2011)
2. Blanchet, W., Stroulia, E., Elio, R.: Supporting adaptive web-service orchestration with an agent conversation framework. In: Proceedings of the 2005 IEEE International Conference on Web Services. ICWS 2005. IEEE (2005)
3. Bordini, R., Hübner, J., Wooldridge, M.: Programming multi-agent systems in AgentSpeak using Jason, vol. 8. Wiley-Interscience (2007)
4. Buhler, P.A., Vidal, J.M.: Towards adaptive workflow enactment using multiagent systems. Information technology and management **6**(1), 61–87 (2005)
5. Buhler, P.A., Vidal, J.M., Verhagen, H.: Adaptive workflow = web services + agents. ICWS **3**, 131–137 (2003)
6. Carman, M., Serafini, L., Traverso, P.: Web service composition as planning. In: ICAPS 2003 Workshop on Planning for Web Services, pp. 1636–1642 (2003)
7. Cossentino, M., Dalle Nogare, D., Giancarlo, R., Lodato, C., Lopes, S., Ribino, P., Sabatucci, L., Seidita, V.: Gimt: a tool for ontology and goal modeling in bdi multi-agent design. In: Workshop "Dagli Oggetti agli Agenti" (2014)
8. Cossentino, M., Gaud, N., Hilaire, V., Galland, S., Koukam, A.: Aspecs: an agent-oriented software process for engineering complex systems. Autonomous Agents and Multi-Agent Systems **20**(2), 260–304 (2010)
9. Dixit, M., Casimiro, A., Lollini, P., Bondavalli, A., Verissimo, P.: Adaptare: Supporting automatic and dependable adaptation in dynamic environments. ACM Transactions on Autonomous and Adaptive Systems (TAAS) **7**(2), 18 (2012)
10. Doshi, P., Goodwin, R., Akkiraju, R., Verma, K.: Dynamic workflow composition using Markov decision processes. In: Proceedings of the IEEE International Conference on Web Services, 2004, pp. 576–582. IEEE (2004)
11. Ferber, J., Gutknecht, O., Michel, F.: From agents to organizations: an organizational view of multi-agent systems. In: Giorgini, P., Müller, J.P., Odell, J.J. (eds.) AOSE 2003. LNCS, vol. 2935, pp. 214–230. Springer, Heidelberg (2004)
12. Gomaa, H., Hashimoto, K.: Dynamic self-adaptation for distributed service-oriented transactions. In: 2012 ICSE Workshop on Software Engineering for Adaptive and Self-Managing Systems (SEAMS), pp. 11–20 (2012)

13. Grassi, V., Marzolla, M., Mirandola, R.: Qos-aware fully decentralized service assembly. In: Proceedings of the 8th International Symposium on Software Engineering for Adaptive and Self-Managing Systems, pp. 53–62. IEEE Press (2013)
14. Hahn, C., Fischer, K.: Service composition in holonic multiagent systems: model-driven choreography and orchestration. In: Mařík, V., Vyatkin, V., Colombo, A.W. (eds.) HoloMAS 2007. LNCS (LNAI), vol. 4659, pp. 47–58. Springer, Heidelberg (2007)
15. Kay, J.J., Boyle, M.: Self-organizing, holarchic, open systems (SOHOs). Columbia University Press, New York (2008)
16. Koestler, A.: The ghost in the machine. Hutchinson, London (1967)
17. Laukkanen, M., Helin, H.: Composing workflows of semantic web services. In: Extending Web Services Technologies, pp. 209–228. Springer (2004)
18. Rao, A.S.: AgentSpeak(L): BDI agents speak out in a logical computable language. In: Perram, J., Van de Velde, W. (eds.) MAAMAW 1996. LNCS, vol. 1038, pp. 42–55. Springer, Heidelberg (1996)
19. Ribino, P., Cossentino, M., Lodato, C., Lopes, S., Sabatucci, L., Seidita, V.: Ontology and goal model in designing BDI multi-agent systems. WOA@ AI* IA **66–72**, 2013 (1099)
20. Sabatucci, L., Cossentino, M.: From means-end analysis to proactive means-end reasoning. In: Proceedings of 10th International Symposium on Software Engineering for Adaptive and Self-Managing Systems, Florence, Italy, May 18–19, 2015
21. Sabatucci, L., Lodato, C., Lopes, S., Cossentino, M.: Towards self-adaptation and evolution in business process. In: AIBP@ AI* IA, pp. 1–10. Citeseer (2013)
22. Sabatucci, L., Ribino, P., Lodato, C., Lopes, S., Cossentino, M.: GoalSPEC: a goal specification language supporting adaptivity and evolution. In: Winikoff, M. (ed.) EMAS 2013. LNCS, vol. 8245, pp. 235–254. Springer, Heidelberg (2013)
23. Stojnic, N., Schuldt, H.: OSIRIS-SR: a safety ring for self-healing distributed composite service execution. In: 2012 ICSE Workshop on Software Engineering for Adaptive and Self-Managing Systems (SEAMS), pp. 21–26 (2012)
24. Yu, E., Mylopoulos, J.: Why goal-oriented requirements engineering. In: Proceedings of the 4th International Workshop on Requirements Engineering: Foundations of Software Quality, p. 15 (1998)
25. Zambonelli, F., Castelli, G., Mamei, M., Rosi, A.: Programming self-organizing pervasive applications with SAPERE. In: Intelligent Distributed Computing VII, pp. 93–102. Springer (2014)

Service Repository for Cloud Service Consumer Life Cycle Management

Hong Thai Tran[1(✉)] and George Feuerlicht[1,2,3]

[1] Faculty of Engineering and Information Technology, University of Technology,
Sydney, Ultimo, Australia
{hongthai.tran,george.feuerlicht}@uts.edu.au
[2] Unicorn College, V Kapslovně 2767/2, 130 00, Prague 3, Czech Republic
[3] Department of Information Technology, University of Economics, Prague,
W. Churchill Sq. 4, Prague 3, Czech Republic

Abstract. With rapid uptake of various types of cloud services many organizations are facing issues arising from their dependence on externally provided cloud services. In order to enable operation in this rapidly evolving environment, end user organizations need new methods and tools that support entire life-cycle of cloud services from the perspective of service consumers. Service repositories play a key role in supporting service consumer SDLC (Systems Development Life-Cycle) maintaining information that is used during the various life-cycle phases. In this paper we briefly describe service consumer SDLC and propose a design of service repository that supports information requirements throughout the service life-cycle.

Keywords: Service repository · Cloud services · Service life-cycle

1 Introduction

Cloud computing is a novel approach for implementing enterprise IT (Information Technology) solutions that has the promise of increased agility, flexibility, elasticity and cost savings. Rapid growth in the availability of various types of cloud services provides opportunities for the implementation of innovative enterprise applications, and organizations are increasingly relying on external cloud providers to deliver a significant part of their enterprise infrastructure and applications. Unlike in on-premise situations, in cloud computing environments service consumers and service providers are typically separate entities with different roles and responsibilities during the service life-cycle. Consequently, the traditional service life-cycle used in on-premise development is not suitable in situation where cloud services are implemented by external cloud service providers and deployed by service consumers in their enterprise applications [1]. More specifically, the primary role of cloud service consumers has changed from implementation of on-premise enterprise applications to integration and management of cloud services [2], with cloud service providers taking responsibility for IT infrastructure and a significant part of the application portfolio.

© IFIP International Federation for Information Processing 2015
S. Dustdar et al. (Eds): ESOCC 2015, LNCS 9306, pp. 171–180, 2015.
DOI: 10.1007/978-3-319-24072-5_12

The Programmable Web directory [4] currently lists almost fourteen thousand APIs (Application Programing Interfaces) for various types of services, making the identification of suitable services challenging for service consumers. In many cases, similar services are available from various cloud providers with different interfaces, protocols and Quality of Service (QoS) attributes [3]. The integration of such disparate cloud services with on-premise enterprise applications requires a significant effort. This emerging situation where enterprise applications utilize a large number of cloud services requires a new approach to service life-cycle management. A key architecture component needed to address these issues is the service repository that stores information about available services and related QoS attributes, providing a database of cloud services that are certified for use within the enterprise and can be shared among different projects.

In our earlier work [5], we have described the SDLC (Systems Development Life-Cycle) for cloud services as viewed from a service consumer perspective, and we have specified SDLC phases and described architectural components required to support life-cycle activities. This paper focuses on defining the structure and properties of the service repository. In the next section (section 2) we review research literature on service life-cycle management and service repositories. The following section (section 3) is a description of the proposed service repository structure for cloud service consumer life-cycle management, and section 4 contains our conclusions and proposals for future work.

2   Related Work

The life-cycle of a cloud services involves different stakeholders that include service providers and service consumers that participate in delivering cloud-based enterprise applications and ensuring runtime management of cloud services. Generally, service life-cycle management includes three types of activities: design time, runtime and change time activities. Although cloud service life-cycle is still a subject of extensive investigation, there is a general agreement in the literature about the individual life-cycle phases and the need for a service repository to support life-cycle activities.

In early research, Yelmo, et al. [6] describe user-centric service life-cycle management for telecom services. The authors focus on Service Lifecycle Manager and the Service Execution Environment modules of the OPUCE platform (Open Platform for User-centric service Creation and Execution). In OPUCE, a service repository is used to store service description including all related attributes e.g. service type, descriptions, and the terms and conditions of use. Services are specified using three sets of *facets* (i.e. description of a specific aspect of a service): Functional facets, Non-functional facets and Management facets. Vitharana and Jain [7] introduce a Knowledge Based Component Repository (KBCR) for enabling requirements analysis. The repository includes basic information about services (name, version, functionalities, and QoS attributes), facet information, business process templates, relationships among components, and provides support for a search capability. Yu, et al. [8] propose a semantically enhanced service repository for user-centric service discovery and management.

The repository consists of two main components: a service registry for storing and managing service metadata (i.e. service name, service version, provider and service descriptions) and a service discovery component that allows discovery of services. Lakshmi and Mohanty [9] describe the design of a scalable service repository implemented using a relational database supporting algebraic operators for service composition using Composition Search Trees. The database service includes five tables: Providers, Services, Parameters, Service Input and Service Output. Service providers are categorized by reputation (using categories Best, Good, Average and Below Average), and services are classified using QoS attributes. This information is used to search for services in the registry and to compose business process based on identified services.

Shetty and D'Mello [3] review service repository strategies and service discovery techniques with the aim to support diversity of cloud services. The cloud service discovery feature supports search and browsing of services based on functional and non-functional properties. Authors classify discovery methods according to different architectures of the cloud service repository into centralized architectures and distributed architectures. They also describe the various service discovery algorithms used in the literature for cloud service discovery such as functional description based methods: keyword (syntactic) based discovery, semantic based discovery and hybrid matching. Non-functional description method that includes *static and dynamic QoS* based methods. A method for managing integrated life-cycle of cloud services was proposed by Joshi, et al. [10]. The authors have identified performance metrics associated with each life-cycle phase that include data quality, cost, and security metrics based on SLA (Service Level Agreement) and consumer satisfaction, and they have proposed a service repository with a discovery capability for managing cloud services life-cycle [1]. The authors divide cloud services life-cycle into five phases: requirements specification, discovery, negotiation, composition, and consumption. During the service discovery phase, service consumers search for services using service description and provider policies in a simple services database. Service information is stored as a Request for Service (RFS) that contains functional specifications, technical specifications, human agent policy, security policy, and data quality policy.

Field, et al. [11] present a European Middleware Initiative (EMI) Registry that uses a decentralised architecture to support service discovery for both hierarchical and peering topologies. The objective of the EMI Registry is to provide robust and scalable service discovery that contains two components: Domain Service Registry (DSR) and Global Service Registry (GSR). Service discovery is based on service information stored in service records that contain mandatory attributes such as service name, type of service, service endpoint, service interface, and service expiry date. Vukojevic-Haupt, et al. [12] proposed a service selection method for on-demand provisioned services. Services are provided by a third party provider and service consumers have no knowledge about the implementation and the underlying infrastructure that supports the delivery of services. Authors develop an entity relationship diagram of the service registry that contains service information and metadata, including functional and non-functional properties, service configuration parameters, service provider information, functional description of the service, and QoS attributes. In a recent publication Bauer, et al. [13] present the design of an advanced SOA repository enriched with analysis capabilities.

The repository contains various types of services and their relationships. Authors propose a meta-model for repositories to analyse service dependency and the impact of changes.

Most of the research publications reviewed in this section focus on service selection and discovery. Our service repository design aims to cover the entire life-cycle of cloud services from the perspective of service consumers, and includes the phases: requirements specification, service identification, service integration, service monitoring and service optimization.

3 Repository Support for Service Consumer SDLC

As noted in our previous work [5], traditional SOA systems development methodologies do not explicitly differentiate between service provider and service consumer SDLC cycles. In the context of cloud computing, service providers and service consumers are separate entities that perform different tasks throughout their SDLC cycles. Service providers are responsible for the implementation and delivery of cloud services and service consumers are primarily involved in the selection and integration

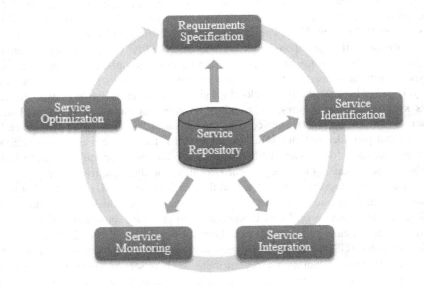

Fig. 1. Cloud service consumer life-cycle

of suitable cloud services into their enterprise applications. As illustrated in Figure 1, we identify five SDLC phases of the service consumer life-cycle: requirements specification, service identification, service integration, service monitoring and service optimization. These phases can be classified into design-time activities that include requirements specification, service identification and service integration, and run-time activities that involve service monitoring, and service optimization. The information held in the service repository is used to manage services and to define service compositions that are executed by the workflow engine at runtime. In the following sections we consider information requirements for the individual life-cycle phases and define the structure and properties of the service repository.

3.1   Requirements Specification

The service requirements specification phase involves description of functional and non-functional requirements that a given service needs to fulfil. Functional specifications of the service describe what functions the service should provide. While there are differences in the specification according to the type of service (e.g. application service, infrastructure service, etc.), typically the specification includes technical details of the service interface (e.g. WSDL interface) and may also include details of the technological environment (e.g. specific hardware platforms, programming languages, etc. in the case of infrastructure and platform services). The non-functional attributes include service availability, response time, and security requirements, and may also include requirements regarding data location, security certification and the maximum cost of the service. Once the service is fully described and classified, the service consumer creates a Request for Service (RFS) and records the information in the service repository [10].

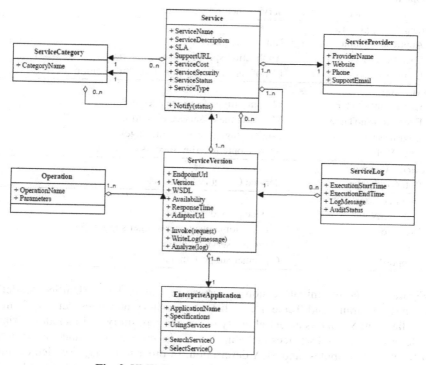

Fig. 2. UML diagram of the Service Repository

Table 1. List of repository attributes

Attribute	Description
Service	
ServiceName	The unique identifier of the service
ServiceDescription	Description of the service
SLA	Service level agreement
SupportUrl	URL of the support page of the service
ServiceCost	Cost usage plan of service
ServiceSecurity	Security characteristics of the service
ServiceStatus	Service status, e.g. online, offline or retired
ServiceType	The type of service (on-premise, cloud or composite)
Service version	
EnpointUrl	Network location of the service
Version	Service version number
WSDL	WSDL specification of the service
Availability	Service availability (estimated)
ResponseTime	Service response time (estimated)
AdaptorUrl	Network location of the service adaptor
Operation	
OperationName	Service method name
ServiceParamater	Service method parameters
EnterpriseApplication	
ApplicationName	Name of application
Specifications	Application specification requirements
UsingServices	List of services are using in this application
ServiceLog	
ExecutionStartTime	The start time of service execution
ExecutionEndTime	The end time of service execution
LogMessage	Log message (e.g. error message)
AuditStatus	Service outcome (i.e. success or failure)
ServiceCategory	
CategoryName	Service Category Name
ServiceProvider	
ProviderName	Service provider name
Website	Service home page or customer support page
Phone	Customer service hotline
SupportEmail	Customer support email

Figure 2 show the initial version of service repository UML (Unified Modelling Language) diagram, and Table 1 is a list of repository attributes derived from the UML diagram. *Service* is a central entity of service repository and includes attributes that describe registered services including service identification, a range of functional, non-functional attributes, and SLA description. In order to manage service evolution and keep track of changes of service functionality, information about *Service Versions* is stored in the repository. *Operation* is associated with service versions as it is possible for different versions of the service to have different operations when the service evolves. *Service Category* is used to categorize services according to service type resulting in a service type hierarchy illustrated in Figure 3. The concept of service substitution is represented by the *replaces* relationship that identifies services with same functionality (e.g. two payment services with identical functionality) that provide alternatives that can be used to improve service availability, or to replace services to reduce the cost and improve performance. Service substitution information is used at design time to support load balancing and failover features. *Service Provider* represents service providers and contains service provider attributes listed in Table 1. *Service Log* records runtime information that includes response time, results of service invocation, and other non-functional attributes collected at run-time and used for analysis of service performance. Each service can be used in a number of *Enterprise Applications*, and each enterprise application can use a number of registered services.

3.2   Service Identification

Service identification is constrained by the functional and non-functional requirements documented in the previous phase (requirements specification phase). Service identification phase uses service category hierarchy (Figure 3), and functional and non-functional attributes of the service identified during the service requirements phase. Service repository has a web-based user interface which allows consumers to

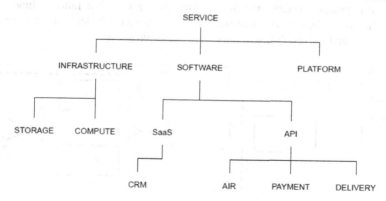

Fig. 3. Partial service category hierarchy

search for services based on their category and QoS information. Service identification phase begins by searching the service repository, attempting to match the requirements specified in the previous phase with services that are already registered in the repository and certified for use. If no existing service matches the requirements, the service consumer will need to search for the candidate services available from cloud service providers, or contact a preferred service provider directly to locate a suitable cloud service. In addition to selecting a suitable the service, the identification phase involves service testing and approval. Service approval is an internal certification process that certifies cloud services for use in enterprise applications within the organization. Given the large number of available cloud services, the selection of suitable services can be time consuming, in particular if this task is performed multiple times in the context of different projects that require similar services. Using the consumer service repository to store information about approved cloud services ensures that services are shared among different projects, and that service selection and approval process is not unnecessarily repeated. In some instances, the consumer may be able to negotiate details of the SLA with the service provider, although this will depend on the type and volume of services involved.

3.3   Service Integration

Following the service identification phase, cloud services need to be integrated into consumer enterprise applications. Following the registration of the enterprise application, relevant services are identified and composed to implement the desired business functionality using services that have been already certified and are recorded in the repository. The service substitution information is used to compose services. The design of a composite service involves searching for atomic services that match the requirements of enterprise applications and composing these services to define a suitable run-time execution sequence. For example, the online shopping process illustrated in Figure 4 includes a composite payment service composed of three different (atomic) payment services: PayPal, SecurePay and eWay. This composite payment service is used to load-balance the payment services, and at the same time provides a failover function that handles situations when a particular service becomes unavailable. This improves both the availability and the reliability of the enterprise application.

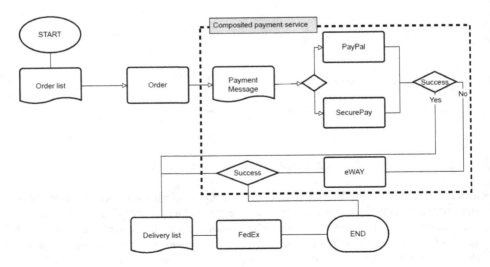

Fig. 4. Composite payment service for online shopping process

3.4   Service Monitoring

The service monitoring phase involves monitoring activities that take place at runtime and includes the management of service utilization. Typically, both the service provider and service consumer perform service monitoring independently, and both parties are responsible for resolving service quality issues that may arise. The service repository includes information that records runtime performance of services (i.e. response time, availability information, and various type of error messages) generated by the Notification Centre that records service status of cloud services in the runtime service log. This information is used by application administrators to monitor service utilization, plan maintenance activities, and to perform statistical analysis of response time and throughput for individual cloud services. Maintaining accurate QoS statistics in the service repository enables to compare the values of QoS attributes defined in the SLA against the actual (measured) QoS values.

3.5   Service Optimization

Service optimization phase is concerned with continuous service improvement. This can be done by replacing existing services with new versions when these become available, or by identifying substitute services from a different provider that have the same functionality. For example, the payment service PayPal could be replaced by the SecurePay service, based on information stored in the repository during the monitoring phase. Service repository supports the process of service optimization allowing service replacement without impacting on existing enterprise applications. In addition to optimizing individual services, entire business processes can be optimized by redesigning the constituent composite services.

4   Conclusion

The main difference between service provider SDLC (i.e. traditional service lifecycle as described in the literature) and service consumer SDLC is the focus on service integration and runtime management of services. Cloud service integration is a design-time activity that relies on accurate description of service interfaces and associated QoS attributes to allow service composition and definition of service execution sequences to implement specific business functions. Run-time activities include failover management and ensuring satisfactory levels of service quality to maintain continuity of operation. To achieve these objectives, designers must be able to match desired QoS attributes values against information stored in the repository and to define processing rules that determine the sequence of service execution at run-time [14].

Well-designed service repository is critical for the support the various activities throughout the consumer service life-cycle. In this paper, we have described the design of service repository that supports the information requirements of the life-cycle phases: requirement specifications, service identification, service integration, service monitoring and service optimization. Service repository structure includes both functional and non-functional attributes allowing a full description of the service for the purpose of creating RFS (Request for Service). Structuring service specification using service category hierarchy allows accurate matching of services based on service type and QoS attributes. During the service integration phase, service designers use this information to implement composite services with desired run-time properties (i.e. failover capability and load balancing).

In conclusion, our service repository design supports both design time and runtime activities throughout the service consumer SDLC. We are currently in the process of implementing the service repository using Microsoft SQL Server database and further enhancing the design of the repository.

References

1. Joshi, K.P., Yesha, Y., Finin, T.: Automating Cloud Services Life Cycle through Semantic Technologies. IEEE Transactions on Services Computing 7, 109–122 (2014)
2. Farrell, K.: Cloud Lifecycle Management: Managing Cloud Services from Request to Retirement. http://www.bmc.com/blogs/hybrid-cloud-delivery-managing-cloud-services-from-request-to-retirement
3. Shetty, J., D'Mello, D.A.: Repository design strategies and discovery techniques for cloud computing. In: 2013 International Conference on Green Computing, Communication and Conservation of Energy (ICGCE), pp. 761–766 (2013)
4. ProgrammableWeb: The World's Largest API Repository, Growing Daily. http://www.programmableweb.com/apis/directory
5. Feuerlicht, G., Tran, H.T.: Adapting service development life-cycle for cloud. In: The 17th International Conference on Enterprise Information Systems (ICEIS), Spain (2015)
6. Yelmo, J.C., Trapero, R., del Álamo, J.M., Sienel, J., Drewniok, M., Ordás, I., McCallum, K.: User-driven service lifecycle management – adopting internet paradigms in telecom services. In: Krämer, B.J., Lin, K.-J., Narasimhan, P. (eds.) ICSOC 2007. LNCS, vol. 4749, pp. 342–352. Springer, Heidelberg (2007)
7. Vitharana, P., Jain, H.: A Knowledge Based Component/Service Repository to Enhance Analysts' Domain Knowledge for Requirements Analysis. Information & Management 49, 24–35 (2012)
8. Yu, J., Sheng, Q.Z., Han, J., Wu, Y., Liu, C.: A Semantically Enhanced Service Repository for User-centric Service Discovery and Management. Data & Knowledge Engineering 72, 202–218 (2012)
9. Lakshmi, H., Mohanty, H.: RDBMS for service repository and composition. In: The 4th International Conference on Advanced Computing (ICoAC), pp. 13–15 (2012)
10. Joshi, K., Finin, T., Yesha, Y.: Integrated lifecycle of IT services in A cloud environment. In: The 3rd International Conference on the Virtual Computing Initiative (ICVCI), USA (2009)
11. Field, L., Memon, S., Márton, I., Szigeti, G.: The EMI Registry: Discovering Services in a Federated World. Journal of Grid Computing 12, 29–40 (2014)
12. Vukojevic-Haupt, K., Haupt, F., Karastoyanova, D., Leymann, F.: Service selection for on-demand provisioned services. In: The 18th International Enterprise Distributed Object Computing Conference (EDOC), Germany, pp. 120–127 (2014)
13. Bauer, T., Buchwald, S., Tiedeken, J., Reichert, M.: A SOA Repository with Advanced Analysis Capabilities-Improving the Maintenance and Flexibility of Service-Oriented Applications (2015)
14. Feuerlicht, G., Tran, H.T.: Service consumer framework: managing service evolution from a consumer perspective. In: The 16th International Conference on Enterprise Information Systems (ICEIS), Portugal (2014)

Cloud Detours: A Non-intrusive Approach for Automatic Software Adaptation to the Cloud

Michel Vasconcelos[1], Nabor C. Mendonça[1($\boxtimes$)], and Paulo Henrique M. Maia[2]

[1] Programa de Pós-Graduação em Informática Aplicada (PPGIA),
Universidade de Fortaleza (UNIFOR), Fortaleza, CE, Brazil
`michel.vasconcelos@gmail.com, nabor@unifor.br`
[2] Centro de Ciências e Tecnologia (CCT),
Universidade Estadual do Ceará (UECE), Fortaleza, CE, Brazil
`pauloh.maia@uece.br`

Abstract. A major challenge facing cloud migration is the need to change a legacy (on-premise) application's source code so that it can better benefit from the inherit cloud computing characteristics, such as resource elasticity and high scalability. When performed manually, those changes are error-prone and may require a great effort from application developers. This paper presents a novel approach to support organizations in automatically adapting their existing software applications to the cloud. The approach is based on the loosely-coupled implementation of non-intrusive code transformations, called *cloud detours*, which enable the automatic replacement of local services used by an application with similar or functionally-related services available in the cloud. To illustrate the approach, the paper reports on how an initial set of cloud detours, implemented using aspect-oriented programming and a generic cloud library, was used to seamlessly adapt an existing file-based Java application to save application data in a cloud-based storage service.

1 Introduction

Despite the several advantages commonly associated with the cloud computing paradigm, e.g, greater control over operational costs, the illusion of infinite resources, high scalability, and self-service on demand [3], in practice many organizations have found it difficult to use cloud-based solutions, particularly when faced with the need to migrate existing legacy applications to public cloud providers [14]. As opposed to cloud *adoption*, which means that an organization will use cloud resources and technologies to develop new cloud-native applications, the term cloud *migration* implies that the organization already has existing software that must somehow be adapted to better suit (or to better benefit from) the target cloud platform [11].

Cloud migration decisions are inherently complex since they are influenced by multiple, possibly conflicting factors, such as cost, performance, security and legal concerns [4]. In addition, applications developers must carefully consider possible technical restrictions that may hinder (or even prevent) the migration

© IFIP International Federation for Information Processing 2015
S. Dustdar et al. (Eds.): ESOCC 2015, LNCS 9306, pp. 181–195, 2015.
DOI: 10.1007/978-3-319-24072-5_13

process, such as when the legacy application relies on implementation technologies that violate environmental constraints imposed by the target cloud platform [7]. Another challenge consists of modifying or adapting the legacy application such that it can take advantage of available cloud services and resources, for instance, by replacing an on-premise relational database by a cloud-based NoSQL storage service, a form of adaptation commonly referred to as *cloudification* [2,13].

Although some recent work on automatic cloud conformance-checking [7] and the systematic classification of cloud migration types [10] and patterns [2,13] have started to partially address those challenges, there is still a lack of (semi) automated tools to support the cloud migration process [11]. This limitation implies in a more complex and error-prone migration effort, since the necessary source code changes have to be performed manually by the developer, requiring both a deep understanding of the software's internal structure as well as a detailed knowledge of the target cloud's libraries and APIs. Even in the cases in which the necessary software adaptations can be fully or partially automated, such as in the work described in [12], those are usually performed intrusively, by directly changing the legacy application's source code. As a consequence, the adaptation code becomes tightly coupled to the specific cloud resources and libraries used when performing the changes, making it harder for the developer to reuse the adaption code across different applications as well as to evolve the adapted application to use different cloud services and providers.

This paper presents a novel approach to support the automatic adaptation of legacy (on-premise) applications to the cloud. The proposed approach is based on the modular specification, implementation and reuse of non-intrusive code transformations, called *cloud detours*, which enable existing legacy applications to use existing cloud resources and services seamlessly, without the need to change their original source code directly. The approach is implemented by an event-based framework that decouples the adaptation mechanism that is non-intrusively injected into the application source code, from the cloud-specific libraries and APIs used to invoke the target cloud services. In this way, the chosen adaptation mechanism and cloud libraries can evolve independently, giving the developer more freedom to reuse the adaption code in other applications sharing the same development or execution environment as well as to experiment with different cloud technologies. This approach can be particularly useful during the early stages of the migration process, when comparing the services offered by different cloud providers may play a key role in helping individual and organizations in making informed cloud adoption decisions [4].

The remainder of the paper is organized as follows. Section 2 compares our approach with related work. Section 3 presents the main concepts behind the proposed approach, while Section 4 describes its supporting event-based framework. Section 5 illustrates the feasibility of the approach by reporting on the successful use of our framework to seamlessly adapt an existing file-based Java application to save application data in a cloud-based storage service. Finally, Section 6 provides some conclusions and directions for future work.

2   Related work

Jamshidi *et al.* have recently presented a systematic literature review where they discuss and compare several cloud migration strategies and techniques [10]. To this end, the authors introduce the *Cloud Reference Migration Model* (Cloud-RMM), which provides a conceptual basis to classify existing cloud migration approaches according to three main migration tasks, namely *planning, execution,* and *evaluation.* In addition, the authors consider complimentary approaches that address managerial issues, such as governance, effort estimation and risk analysis, as crosscutting concerns of the model. Our adaptation approach fits within the execution task of Cloud-RMM and addresses one of the main challenges identified by that study, which is to offer automated support for the cloud migration process [10].

Early works on cloud migration have focused on automatically detecting potential incompatibilities between the legacy application and the target cloud environment [6], on model-based transformation of legacy applications in to cloud services [14], and on providing high-level process support for cloud migration [4]. Another related work in this direction is an architecture-centric migration framework which includes pre-migration tasks and decisions, such as the development of a migration plan [1]. Our work on cloud detours can be seen as complementary to those works, as it provides a flexible, non-intrusive way to implement the necessary adaptations in the source code of the applications being migrated.

In another related research line, Andrikopoulos *et al.* have identified four migration types, namely, *replace, partial migration, migrate the whole execution stack,* and *cloudify,* according to the different application layers and adaptation levels required to make the migration possible [2]. In a similar fashion, Mendonça has identified two main migration strategies, namely *cloud hosting* and *cloudification,* with the former representing the case in which some (possibly modified) application components are hosted in the cloud and the latter the case in which those components are replaced by functionally-related cloud-based services [13]. In the context of those works, our adaptation approach follows the *cloudification* strategy, based on the *replace* migration type, since it non-intrusively transforms the original application source code to replace some of its original components with equivalente services in the cloud.

Finally, Kwon and Tilevich have propose the concept of *cloud refactorings* [12], which are code transformations used to automatically integrate on-premise applications to cloud-enabled services. The proposed code transformations are implemented by means of an IDE plugin and a recommendation tool based on static analysis and runtime monitoring of the application being migrated. Differently from our work, cloud refactorings follow a fully intrusive adaptation approach, since the refactoring tool changes the original application source code directly. As we have discussed previously, this approach makes it harder for the developer to experiment with different adaption mechanisms and cloud technologies, as those are hardcoded in the implementation of the cloud refactoring plugin.

3   Cloud Detours

Our cloud adaptation approach is based on the assumption that the change sets required to implement the desired software adaptions should be grouped into reusable assets called *cloud detours*. The idea is that developers could reuse these assets across different applications and execution environments, thus reducing the overall time and effort involved in the migration of existing (on-premise) applications to the cloud.

More specifically, a *cloud detour* is a non-intrusive reusable artifact containing source code change sets necessary to adapt applications to be hosted in a cloud environment or to use available cloud services. Developers may use cloud detours to automatically adapt on-premise applications, thus avoiding the risks and drawbacks involved when modifying the source code directly. Besides accelerating the migration process itself, cloud detours also can be useful to gradually adapt different parts of the application before fully migrating the whole application to the cloud.

Due to its non-intrusive design, a cloud detour needs to be aligned with the architecture and technologies of the local and target environments. In our work, we focus on cloud detours that are designed to adapt multi-layered software applications, by replacing services at a certain application layer with equivalent services in the cloud.

In a multi-layered application, each layer provides a set of services for the upper layers. This increases modularity and reduces the coupling between application components. Cloud detours benefit from this design by overriding local application services with services provided by the target cloud environment at execution time.

Cloud detours also can be defined in terms of elements that are external to the application. For instance, in a web application that is hosted by an application server that provides transaction control and persistence services, a cloud detour can be used to replace those services by similar ones in the cloud. In our work, we call such basic services and elements as *operating services*.

Figure 1 depicts the cloud detour architectural model. The dashed arrows highlight the different architectural levels at which a cloud detour can be used to adapt an application. Note that, depending on the chosen level, a cloud detour can be used to replace services that are either internal or external to the application being adapted. Choosing a proper adaptation level is important since each level restricts the suit of adaptation technologies as well as the context information available for implementing detours.

At the *application level*, a detour's adaptation logic can be implemented in terms of the components, patterns and technologies being used by the application itself. When defined at that level, a detour can access source code elements like units, classes, methods and parameters, and can be implemented using source or binary code instrumentation mechanisms, such as aspect oriented programming and meta-programming. As an example, we can cite a detour to adapt a Java application that initially accesses data through a certain (internal) local

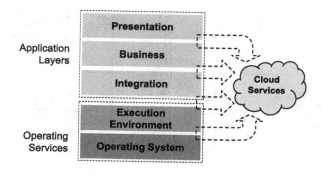

Fig. 1. Application architectural model and detour opportunities.

data service and, after adaption, replaces that service with a similar cloud-based storage service.

At the *operating level*, a detour's adaptation logic can be implemented in terms of elements belonging to the underlying execution environment or operating system (e.g., virtual machine or sandboxes APIs, low-level libraries). The context information available are system calls, libraries and environment variables. Implementing cloud detours at that level requires non-code based interception mechanisms like library overloading and function interposition.

Cloud detours are usually much easier to implement at the application level than at the operating level. This is because application level detours can be defined in terms of syntactic elements that are clearly visible in the application source code, while operating level detours require external system knowledge of the underlying execution platform that are not easily accessible to most application developers. On the other hand, application level detours tend to be less reusable as they rely on structural and contextual information that may be too specific to a given application.

Considering the same adaptation scenario described above, adapting a new Java application to use the same cloud-based storage service would require a new detour, as the implementation of the original detour would be too tightly coupled to the source code elements of the original Java application.

4 Cloud Detours Framework

The *Cloud Detours Framework* (CDF) provides a library of detours as well as the needed backbone to deploy them as part of the execution flow of existing legacy applications. This section describes the CDF design and its current implementation as a *proof-of-concept* for our cloud adaptation approach.

4.1 Domain Model

Figure 2 depicts the DCF's domain model.

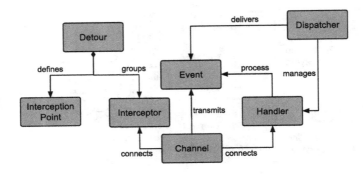

Fig. 2. Cloud Detours domain model

Detour, as described in the previous section, is the key entity that comprises the necessary change sets to adapt an application to interact with a cloud service. It can be extended according the category of services it replaces (e.g., I/O detour, database detour, messaging detour). Each detour defines a set of hot spots called *interception points* that describe the execution points where interceptors are expected to be injected into the application flow. *Interceptors* are responsible for catching the application execution flow and forwarding configured actions as events. Together, detours, interception points and interceptors comprise the code instrumentation mechanism provided by the CDF.

Event is the main entity responsible for interchanging data among the framework's front-end and back-end components. It can be extended according to the action types it encapsulates (e.g, I/O operation, database access). *Channels* interconnect interceptors and adapters and provide a safe path to send and receive events. *Adapters* connect the framework's back-end components to the target cloud and map the actions triggered in the application to available cloud service operations. Finally, *Dispatchers* manage the life cycle of adapters and distribute incoming events according to the tuple `<event, channel, adapter>`.

4.2   Architecture Overview

When adapting the system to interact with the cloud, the developer must consider different abstraction levels of services and features, such as modifying application source code, exception handling, resource allocation and bindings to external services. Although performing all those adaptations in a single element is possible, this would make it a into a high complex and poor maintainable software artifact. The CDF design addresses this issue by separating the concerns regarding application interception from those related with cloud interaction. To this end, the CDF relies on an event-based layered architecture to decouple those concerns and to allow different levels of abstraction to be softly handled.

Architectural Layers. The CDF architecture is organized in multiple layers to promote low coupling and high cohesion amongst its components, as well as to allow components of different levels of abstraction to evolve independently. The framework layers are described below:

Interception. The Interception layer interfaces with the on-premise application or the local environment to capture actions defined as interception points so that the application's original execution flow is detoured. Detours are "first-class citizens" of this layer and are implemented through instrumentation techniques like aspect-oriented programming and function interposition. Regarding the abstraction level, detours can be classified as (i) *abstract*, when they are generic and not bound to any particular application; or (ii) *concrete*, when they are tailored to specific applications or configured to catch particular actions. Besides instrumentation, detours also handle other concerns, such as binding code and exception handling, which are implemented through plain classes, units or other resources available in the local environment;

Transmission. This layer works as the central hub that connects the Interception and Adaptation layers. It provides event distribution, component mediation, location transparency, and mux/demux services. It also is responsible for physical and logical decoupling among the other layers such that they could be implemented and evolved using patterns and technologies that best suit their respective needs. Events and channels are key elements of this layer;

Adaptation. This layer provides access to cloud resources and services. Dispatchers and adapters, its main elements, are responsible for handling incoming events, mapping actions, and integrating with the target cloud. Adapters are components that execute incoming events as actions. They also collaborate with channels to provide a service abstraction to the Interception layer. Actually, this layer provides a service descriptor by supplying location (channels), data typing (events) and operation (adapters) to possible clients. A dispatcher accounts for components coordination in the Adaptation layer. It manages adapter life cycle, identifies incoming events and associates channels with respective adapters.

Build and Assembly. The elements of this layer cooperate with elements of the other layers to accelerate the configuration, building and deployment of the CDF components in the (local) application environment. The main elements of this layer are build tools, shell scripts and configuration files.

Event-Reactor Pattern. The Event-Reactor pattern is used in the CDF as a decoupled way to process events triggered by interceptors while preserving the latency and synchronism required by the adapted application [15]. This pattern is implemented through components of the Transmission and Adaptation layers.

4.3   Implementation Details

The CDF design enables the development of its internal components using programming languages and technologies that best suit their purpose. In its current version, interception components, detours and helper classes are implemented in AspectJ and Java. Transformation and building mechanisms are realized through Groovy and Gradle[1]. Cloud Detours back-end elements, adapters, dispatchers and execution infrastructure are implemented in Python. In the following we detail some CDF implementation decisions. The CDF source code, including its documentation, is publicly available at https://github.com/michelav/cloud-detours.

Abstract and Concrete Detours. Under the development perspective, detours are coarse-grained components that comprise aspects, helper classes (interceptors), general scripts and configuration files. Detours weave interceptors, implemented as plain Java classes, into the application through aspects. Each detour declares its own building and usage rules, therefore making them highly cohesive. This reduces the effort needed to extend the framework.

One important flexibility point of Cloud Detour resides on the relation of abstract and concrete detours. Abstract detours determine life cycle, interface usage and general behavior for all of its concrete detours. However, they cannot be instrumented alone since they lack interception points. Concrete detours cooperate with abstract ones by providing application-specific interception points and complementary behavior. Consequently, one must provide a suitable concrete detour in order to address a different on-premise application.

When instrumenting an application, the detours behave simultaneously as factories [8], by instantiating interceptors, and as a dependency injection mechanism [5], by injecting interceptors in the application seamlessly.

Figure 3 shows the source code for an excerpt of the IO detour provided by the framework. The abstract pointcut `outputStreamAP` defines the hotspot developers should configure in concrete detours. For instance, if someone needs to deviate all output actions incoming from `foo.bar` package, she should create a concrete detour and set it up as `pointcut outputStreamAP():within(foo.bar.*)`.

Cloud Detours Back-End. Events, channels and adapters are packaged together with the framework back-end. Events are implemented as plain Java classes and Python dictionaries.

Channels are developed as plain classes that provide send and receive primitives with the purpose of interconnect detours and adapters. Detours channels delegate low-level transmission procedures to *ZMQ* communication library. ZMQ provides asynchronous communication, concurrency control and several communication patterns (point-to-point, multipoint, pub/sub, broker, etc.) to its clients [9]. Each channel contains a *ZMQ Socket* that physically connects the application to the framework back-end.

Cloud Detours back-end may be deployed in a single **remote** area, accessible through local network and serving multiple applications at the same time, or in **local** one, executing in the operating system that hosts the application. The

---

[1] http://gradle.org

```
public abstract aspect AbstractIODetour {

  pointcut fileOutput(File f):
    call(public FileOutputStream.new(File)) && args(f);

  abstract pointcut outputStreamAP();

  FileOutputStream around(File f):
    outputStreamAP() && fileOutput(f) {
      DetFileOutputStream dfos = new DetFileOutputStream(f);
      dfos.configureChannel(channel);
      // Injecting new service
      return dfos;
  }
}
```

Fig. 3. Abstract IO Detour (code excerpt)

system architect must evaluate variables like quantity of application to be enable to cloud, solution complexity, event payload size and network latency in order to define the best deployment method to be used.

4.4 Adaptation Process

Cloud Detours adaptation process comprises stages that demand local system and target cloud evaluation, selection and extension of detours and reconstruction of previous application as a new binary artifact. Figure 4 draws the process that is described as the following steps:

(1) Evaluation. Adaptation scope is defined during this activity. Development team collects architectural information of the system, its logical (packages, components and classes) and physical organization (tiers, protocols, etc). Considering this information and the target cloud, developers select cloud services to be used and identify possible restrictions. The team defines which events will be intercepted and maps them to the available services. In case there is not a detour capable of intercepting an event, the developers may implement a new one. Finally, the development team decides the interception points and the application level of the detours.

(2) Extension. In this step, *Cloud Detours* is extended to instrument the on-premise application. Abstract detours are extended according to the category of events and interception points defined in previous activity. Detours building and assembly scripts are configured to execute in the local environment. At the end of this step, concrete detours are created and ready to be applied.

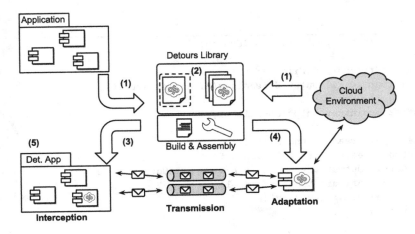

Fig. 4. CDF adaptation process

(3) Transformation. This step provides a new application binary to be deployed. One must use the building and assembly mechanism, configured earlier, to generate a new deployment asset corresponding to the on-premise application weaved by selected concrete detours.

(4) Configuration. *Cloud Detours* infrastructure is configured and loaded. At this moment, developers define the channels distribution and back-end deployment method as described in section 4.3. Channels must be created and assigned prior to deployment. At last, the adapters are configured (e.g.: endpoints definition, authentication and authorization issues, service addresses, etc) to work correctly with the target cloud.

(5) Deployment. The instrumented application is installed in the environment. The developers follow the normal directives to install the application in local environment.

The next section illustrates this process and shows an example of use describing how CDF can be applied in a third-party application.

5   Example of Use

In this example of use, we evaluate the *Cloud Detours* in a practical scenario of adaptation. During the process, we have also investigated the effects of the framework in the adapted application. For this, we have selected the IO detour available in the *Cloud Detours* framework and have measured its performance by comparing the time for executing IO operations before and after using the framework.

The remainder of this section details the tasks performed in the evaluation process and discuss the found results.

5.1   Tools Selection

The following tools have been selected to this example of use: JSpider[2] as the local application (the one that will be migrated), and Google Storage[3] as the cloud storage service.

JSpider: JSpider is a Java configurable engine to download and store web sites. It is commonly used to find errors and to perform structural analysis in web sites. Its architecture is designed as a set of plugins organized in layers that allow the creation of new tasks. Finally, JSpider makes available a embedded command line tool. In this example, we address the application components that save the web site files in the local storage area.

Google Storage: It provides an object-based storage area via Internet that offers high availability, data replication and protection using OAuth[4], an open authorization standard, as access control. The service users can organize their objects in containers, called *buckets*. An object is an data agglomerate submitted to Google Storage.

In our experiment, each file downloaded by JSpider is submitted as an object to the Google Storage. Although JSpider organizes its information as files and directories, Google Storage does not provide a file system abstraction. Hence, the framework adapter has to map the concepts.

5.2   Evaluation Method

To evaluate the performance of the solution, we have measured the necessary time for JSpider downloading two web sites that were locally hosted in order to eliminate the effects of the external network latency. The first one ($[S_1]$) is formed by several HTML pages containing links for internal and external pages, all of them summing up 55KB. The second one ($[S_2]$) is bigger (5MB) and has few HTML pages, but several text and binary files, varying from 500KB to 1000KB.

We can describe the scenarios evaluated in the experiment as:

- **Local application** ($[C_1]$): the selected application runs with no detours and stores all of its data in the local file system. This first scenario establishes a base line to be compared by the other tests;
- **Detoured application** ($[C_2]$): a new version of the application is generated after applying the *Cloud Detours* framework. However, we have used a special adapter that continues saving the application data in the local file system instead of sending them to the service in the cloud. This situation allows us to assess the cost of using *Cloud Detours*;

---

[2]   available at http://j-spider.sourceforge.net
[3]   available at https://cloud.google.com/storage
[4]   available at http://oauth.net

- **Adapted application** ($[C_3]$): a new version of the application is integrated to an adapter that uses the cloud storage services. This scenario allows us to assess how the application behaves after being adapted to the cloud.

The following measurements have been performed in the experiment:

- Tm_i, average scenario execution time $[C_i]$ for all iterations (excluding failures);
- Cd_i, detour cost for the web site $[S_i]$ calculated by $Tm_2 - Tm_1$; and
- L_i, cloud latency for the web site $[S_i]$ calculated by $Tm_3 - Tm_2$.

5.3   Experiment Details

Following the process described in the previous section, we have inspected JSpider's code and identified that the *DiskWriter* plugin is responsible by performing the application's local disk writing operations. It is implemented in the `DiskWriterPlugin` class and is based on the classic file-related classes `File` and `FileOutputStream` of the `java.io` package to store the files. This way, the `DiskWriterPlugin.writeFile(File, InputStream)` method has been defined as the interception point to be configured in the concrete cloud detour.

After the inspection, we use the IO abstract detour, contained in the *Cloud Detours* library, as the interception base element and generate a new concrete detour defining its coverage area according to the desired package, class and method. In the implementation of the concrete detour, we have chosen to use a buffer so the data of each file is sent only after its last update. This strategy aims at reducing (i) the complexity involved in syncing the memory-stored file and its respective cloud object; and (ii) the cost of sending the file data.

We have set up the cloud detour process to be executed locally and to be accessible via interprocess calls (ZMQ sockets). Thus, we not only reduced the solution complexity, but also eliminated the local network latency while the events were forwarded to the adapters.

To execute the tests, we have created a Python script that iterates for each test scenario and register its execution time in a CSV file.

5.4   Results

Figure 5a exhibits the experiment average execution time as the result of 30 iterations for each scenario. We can see that the average execution time of scenarios 1 and 2 were greater for web site 1 than web site 2, event though web site 1 is smaller. This happened due to the different configurations of each scenario. S_2 contains only a single HTML page to be processed, while S_1 has several ones. Therefore, this difference in time is caused by JSpider's own page processing mechanism.

The cloud latency for the second web site (L_1) was very small and the maximum value reached by one of the samples was 1,2 seconds. On the other hand, L_2

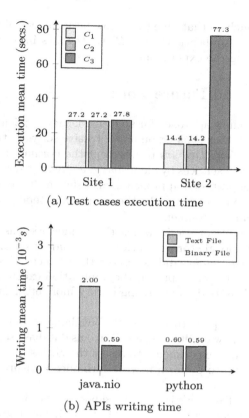

(a) Test cases execution time

(b) APIs writing time

Fig. 5. Experimental results

grows considerably due to the submission of S_2 bigger files. In both situations, the web sites integrity was preserved.

By assessing the detour costs (Cd_i), it was negligible for for C_1 and C_2 (both less than $1s$). We have also observed that in S_2 the average execution time of the detoured application is less than the one of the original application $(Cd_2 < 0)$. By analysing the values for each sample, we have verified that the ones in the set (C_1, S_2) had their execution time greater than $(C2, S_2)$, which means that the detoured application run faster than the original one. Regarding the second web site, we had (C_2, S_1) faster than (C_1, S_1) in 46% of the samples.

To figure this out, we performed a comparison among the writing operations of the Java IO (`java.io` and `java.nio`) and Python APIs . For this, we used those APIs to write both a binary and a text file in 30 iterations. The writing average time of the `java.io` API was 1,48 seconds for the text file and 1,47 seconds for the binary file. Both `java.nio` and Python I/O API performed significantly better than `java.io` as shown by Figure 5b.

Therefore, we conclude that, due to the low performance of the `java.io` API, the adaptation of the application using *Cloud Detours* improved the execution time of JSpider during the experiment.

6 Conclusion and Future work

This work proposes a new approach for adapting legacy applications to the cloud, called *Cloud Detours*, that is based on non-intrusive software transformations. It uses the concept of *Cloud Detours* to intercept the normal application flow and replace the its provided services by cloud-based equivalent services. A framework that implements the proposed approach is also shown. Its architecture uses the Layers and Reactor patterns to make the adaption independent of interception technology and cloud environment.

Through an example of use in which the framework was used to adapt an application that uses local storage service to a cloud-based one, it was possible to observe that *Cloud Detours* did not affect the correct execution of the application. Furthermore, it even improved the application execution time, since the adaptation mechanism used a file writing library more efficient than the original one.

As future work we plan to extend the available detours provided by the framework including new event categories, such as database services. In addition, we plan to conduct new experiments to assess the necessary effort to set up and use the framework and to perform new performance measures.

Acknowledgments. This work is partially supported by Brazil's National Council for Scientific and Technological Development (CNPq), under grants 311617/2011-5 and 487174/2012-7, and by a Microsoft Research's Software Engineering Innovation Foundation (SEIF) Award.

References

1. Ahmad, A., Babar, M.A.: A framework for architecture-driven migration of legacy systems to cloud-enabled software. In: Proceedings of the WICSA 2014 Companion. WICSA 2014 Companion, pp. 1–8. ACM (2014)
2. Andrikopoulos, V., et al.: How to adapt applications for the cloud environment - challenges and solutions in migrating applications to the cloud. Computing **95**(6), 493–535 (2013)
3. Armbrust, M., et al.: A view of cloud computing. CACM **53**(4), 50–58 (2010)
4. Beserra, P., et al.: Cloudstep: a step-by-step decision process to support legacy application migration to the cloud. In: Proc. IEEE 6th International Workshop on the Maintenance and Evolution of Service-Oriented and Cloud-Based Systems (MESOCA), pp. 7–16 (2012)
5. Fowler, M.: Inversion of control containers and the dependency injection pattern (January 2004). http://www.martinfowler.com/articles/injection.html
6. Frey, S., Hasselbring, W.: The cloudmig approach: Model-based migration of software systems to cloud-optimized applications. Int. J. Advances in Software **4**(3/4), 342–353 (2011)

7. Frey, S., et al.: Automatic conformance checking for migrating software systems to cloud infrastructures and platforms. J. Software: Evolution and Process **25**(10), 1089–1115 (2013)

8. Gamma, E., Helm, R., Johnson, R., Vlissides, J.: Design Patterns: Elements of Reusable Object-oriented Software. Addison-Wesley Longman Publishing Co., Inc., Boston (1995)

9. Hintjens, P.: ZeroMQ: The Guide. Internet draft (2010). http://zguide.zeromq.org/page:all

10. Jamshidi, P., et al.: Cloud migration research: A systematic review. IEEE Trans. Cloud Comp. **1**(2), 142–157 (2013)

11. Jamshidi, P., et al.: Cloud migration patterns: a multi-cloud service architecture perspective. In: Proc. 10th International Workshop on Engineering Service-Oriented Applications (WESOA) (2014)

12. Kwon, Y.W., Tilevich, E.: Cloud refactoring: Automated transitioning to cloud-based services. Automated Software Engineering **21**(3), 345–372 (2014)

13. Mendonça, N.C.: Architectural options for cloud migration. IEEE Computer **47**(8), 62–66 (2014)

14. Mohagheghi, P., Sæther, T.: Software engineering challenges for migration to the service cloud paradigm: ongoing work in the remics project. In: Proceedings of the 2011 IEEE World Congress on Services. SERVICES 2011, pp. 507–514. IEEE Computer Society (2011)

15. Schmidt, D.C., et al.: Pattern-Oriented Software Architecture: Patterns for Concurrent and Networked Objects, 2nd edn. John Wiley & Sons Inc, New York (2000)

Industry Track

Cloud Integration Patterns

Danny Merkel[1](✉), Filippos Santas[2], Andreas Heberle[3], and Tarmo Ploom[2]

[1] Julius Bär, Zürich, Switzerland
danny.merkel@julius-baer.com
[2] Credit Suisse, Zürich, Switzerland
{filippos.santas,tarmo.ploom}@credit-suisse.com
[3] Karlsruhe University of Applied Sciences, Karlsruhe, Germany
andreas.heberle@hs-karlsruhe.de

Abstract. Enterprises use the cloud for unlimited resource, scalability and elastic provisioning along with being able to use state of the art commodity or specialized solutions available in the cloud. The challenge of this vision is the proper and safe integration of on-premise IT-Landscapes with data and applications in the cloud. To find solutions for integration of classical and cloud environments two approaches, top-down and bottom-up, were used. In the top-down approach cloud integration patterns were specified based on scenarios. In the bottom-up approach cloud integration patterns were based on case study application requirements. Results of this paper are novel cloud integration patterns for various cloud integration scenarios.

Keywords: Cloud computing · SOA · Integration · Topology · Patterns · SaaS · Public cloud · Private cloud · Multi-cloud

1 Introduction

Cloud computing has emerged as one of the key technologies that are or will be heavily used by companies. According to a study of IDG Enterprises, 42% of the IT decision makers are planning to increase spending on cloud computing in 2015, making cloud computing projects the most important IT initiatives [2]. Enterprises with large application landscapes benefit from the availability of (potentially) unlimited resources and the elastic provisioning of cloud resources. The different service models are: Infrastructure as a Service (IaaS), Platform as a Service (PaaS); Software as a Service (SaaS). Together with the different deployment options (Public Cloud, Private Cloud and Hybrid Cloud) these allow for various integration options to optimize communication and deal with sensitive data. The hybrid cloud is one of the major areas where cloud integration is required and practiced with various levels of success. The question is: how to migrate existing enterprise application landscapes to a cloud computing environment? Existing enterprise application landscapes are usually based on heterogeneous technologies deployed on-premise with a high degree of tight coupling between applications in the form of point-to-point integration and sensitive data flows unconstrained within the application landscape. This makes the adoption of cloud computing challenging.

© IFIP International Federation for Information Processing 2015
S. Dustdar et al. (Eds): ESOCC 2015, LNCS 9306, pp. 199–213, 2015.
DOI: 10.1007/978-3-319-24072-5_14

Contribution: This paper examines how on-premise enterprise application landscapes can be integrated with private and multiple public clouds and with SaaS avoiding point-to-point integration. Various cloud integration scenarios and topologies are described and cloud integration patterns with required middleware are identified. Furthermore, we examine how cloud integration contributes to financial benefits.

This paper is organized as follows: Section 1 gives an overview on existing integration patterns; section 3 focuses on the integration problem in more detail; in section 4 we introduce the approach we used to find suitable integration patterns; section 5 shows our results. The last section concludes our work and discusses future research.

2   Integration Patterns and Related Work

Patterns represent the collective experience of software experts and allow for the cost effective implementation of software's non-functional requirements reducing development cost from 10%-35%, improving time to market up to 20%, and reducing maintenance costs by 15%-20% [5]. Proven message exchange patterns (MEP) patterns are used similarly in enterprise landscapes to integrate services and applications without harming system runtime (e.g. performance) and maintenance requirements. Services can communicate synchronously, or asynchronously and may consume bulk data asynchronously. The commonly accepted standard for MEPs is defined by the Web Service standard [9]. Baros, Dumas and Hofstede discuss interaction patterns for orchestrated web services with BPEL [1]. Hophe and Woolf describe general Enterprise Integration Patterns [3] like Message Routing, Message Transformations and error handling.

There is extensive literature on how to build a SOA and clouds using design patterns. T. Erl examines commonly applied SOA patterns [4], such as Enterprise Service Bus (ESB) including service broker, asynchronous messaging, etc., and Service Design Patterns for security, messaging, service implementation, etc. Cope, Erl et al. identified Cloud Computing Design Patterns to support scalability, reliability, or monitoring of cloud environments and applications deployed in a cloud [6], [17]. Fehling et-al introduce patterns for cloud offerings and design and management of cloud applications [14]. We observe that middleware patterns related to SOA are applicable to the cloud. We identified the following categories of patterns applicable in SOA and cloud architectures:

1. Patterns related to the Service Loose Coupling principle. These are implemented by the middleware messaging at the communication layer between services. Common implementations include the components of an Enterprise Service Bus.
2. Patterns related to the Service Autonomy principle. These involve storage and data replication and resource redundancy.
3. Patterns related to the Statelessness principle, which allows for a state repository for improving the availability and reliability of services.

Cloud usage in an existing enterprise landscape requires more topology-oriented patterns to integrate cloud capabilities with existing applications. Such topology patterns are not covered by the existing approaches.

3   Problem Statement

Enterprises invested vast amounts of money and resources in the last 40 years in building their own IT infrastructure, services and applications. With the advancement of the software industry many of these solutions are nowadays implemented by 3rd party providers in clouds and are available for reuse. The locally implemented CRM system or payments infrastructure that evolved over time and cost millions, no longer bring any competitive advantage and may become a cost factor that does not allow for prompt satisfaction of new business requirements. Using applications in the cloud is a way to increase organizational agility and reduce operational costs.

Multi-Cloud

Access to cloud implementations is constrained by regulations, company policies and billing policies. National laws may prescribe encryption for storage of data and disallow the replication of sensitive data to other countries. Other laws may prescribe that the operational data of a company related to a country lie within the borders of the country, even if the server hubs are in another country. SaaS offerings do not always guarantee confidentiality or controlled access for the data and where and how temporary state data is stored. Further, there are limitations in the products and policies of cloud providers, in particular billing.

Enterprises have the choice to use multiple cloud providers. The sensitive data may be hosted in one cloud (potentially private), the CRM system may be supported by a public (3rd-party) cloud provider, the payments by another public cloud provider and the archives may be hosted in a third cloud that has better prices for storage of large amounts of data, provides discovery and encryption, and guarantees storage within national borders. A fourth provider may provide data warehouse services with big data analysis for marketing purposes. Further, a provider may charge only for retrieval of data and not for the amount of data stored, while another provider charges only for storage of data but not for CPU consumption or file download. Assuming that everything else is equal, it is financially beneficial for an organization to use the former to store huge amounts of data and to use the latter to process data. In order to maintain decent operational costs and take advantage of the modern implementations of applications in the cloud, an international enterprise will decide to use different cloud providers for different applications.

Fig. 1. Potential Architecture

This distributed solution (Figure 1) is not an extreme scenario. Financial institutions, pharmaceutical companies, big travel agencies, almost all companies in developed countries face this dilemma. If they do not use technologies on the cloud they are confronted with high IT development and operational costs, while usage of these technologies from a single cloud provider will most probably result in legal issues, non-optimal operational costs and vendor locking costs. Statistical results are provided in [15]: the majority of the companies in the UK that use cloud purchased offerings from three vendors, although they prefer to use only one vendor.

Coupling in Enterprise Landscapes

Traditionally, the main implementations in the cloud involved single isolated applications with minimal dependencies to other applications; provisioning of market data; exchange rate calculations; auction systems; real estate databases; time plans; etc. Such systems are typically isolated from other applications, can be managed online, or fed asynchronously with data. Their migration to the cloud (or reuse of a SaaS offering) requires mainstream technologies and affordable effort.

But what happens if a single application is already integrated with several other applications that require a number of mandatory components to function properly? Migration of all dependent applications at once is associated with high risks and lack of any ROI (Return of Investment) in the first years after the project starts. A step-by-step migration reduces the risk and may show ROI shortly after each application has been migrated. This is however architecturally challenging.

The first step is the migration of internally hosted applications to a single cloud environment. This results in Single-Cloud Integration. Compared to Simple SaaS Integration, the integration effort is substantially higher. Due to dependencies, the externally hosted applications cannot operate without the depending internal systems. If more parts of this application ecosystem are deployed externally, reliable intra-cloud communication is necessary.

Multi-Cloud Integration

Services deployed and integrated in different clouds must be orchestrated so that they provide support for end-to-end business processes or for support of different kinds of processing. Credit applications may be created in a CRM system in one cloud; rated by experts in an in-house application with proprietary rating models; sent back to the CRM application; formalities and other documents are collected and archived in a third cloud; and the account opens in the private cloud.

These activities involve separate systems where each system does not know about the other. The CRM does not know the rating models, and the archive is agnostic to either of them. A separate orchestration mechanism must be available that allows for the flow of data and consistent state transition in the objects across the clouds. Notice that this orchestration manages long running transactions that tend to accumulate substantial state during their execution, including confidential data.

Access Control, Integrity, Confidentiality

Public access to the clouds and exchange of data across geographic locations introduce difficulties that must be resolved. The communication between CRM and an electronic archive of customer documents, or between CRM and payments systems, must have confidential customer info either stripped or encrypted, otherwise confidentiality may be compromised. Customer or transactional data can be patient data, the subjects of a medical experiment, the composition of a new substance, the client of a bank, etc.

Cross border constraints may further impose constraints on solutions. In several industries in the EU and the US, there are restrictions on the storage of customer data in other countries. For example medical data or certain formalities in the financial industry may not even leave the country from where they have been created.

Many organizations check security constraints only in the simple context of the applications that need to exchange data. Most organizations do not check security in solutions involving different applications in different clouds. In the cloud however, security requirements like authentication and authorization have to be implemented for the whole business process, i.e. over several clouds with different technical infrastructure.

4   Methodology

In this section we describe the process for identifying cloud integration patterns. The landscape is within Credit Suisse AG, a large organization in the financial services. The variety, variance and criticality of the requirements across domains in this industry allow us to examine a lot of useful and challenging use-cases involving the cloud. The analysis is done in three steps:

1.   current state analysis
2.   top-down analysis
3.   bottom-up analysis

Each analysis step includes the results of the previous step to improve the evaluation results. The following sections describe these steps in detail.

4.1   Current State Analysis

The current state analysis identifies the progress in cloud adoption in the enterprise. Internal information was collected by interviewing subject matter experts at Credit Suisse and combined with statistical data from a Federated Identity provider. Further, the current integration architecture of these solutions was analyzed.

The results are used to define suitable integration challenges in the top down analysis. The current state analysis reuses the results of different initiatives in the bank. Some of these analyze the potential of integrating applications in the private cloud, public cloud and multi-cloud to align these concepts with the IT strategy.

4.2   Top-Down Analysis

In the top-down analysis significant cloud integration challenges are identified and analyzed from a bird's eye view. The service and deployment models from the NIST [12] are used within the study. From the possible integration scenarios we selected those that clarify major aspects of multi-cloud integration.

The selected scenarios are: SaaS Integration, Public Cloud Integration and the Centralized and Decentralized Multi-Cloud Integration within Hybrid Clouds. The variations for PaaS or IaaS integration are not significant for the integration architecture at this level of abstraction. For simplicity in the presentation, without loss of accuracy, the private cloud is considered as a special case of the public cloud.

The common problem examined in all scenarios is how service integration challenges can be solved by integration patterns. Well-known integration patterns (see [3], [4]) are reused and combined together. Different combinations of patterns have different advantages and disadvantages and can solve an integration challenge in different ways. It is important that we select combinations that have a high score with respect to the quality requirements of the overall solution, including financial benefits. How do we rate such combinations? Each combined pattern (called a topology pattern) is rated by standardized evaluation criteria. As evaluation criteria we consider the system qualities [16], that are, non-functional such as Performance, Latency, Availability, Reliability, Extensibility, Maintainability, Security, Integrity, Scalability, and Portability across clouds. The SOA principles [4] contribute to the overall success of the architecture within an organization. It is imperative that the application of integration patterns respects these principles.

4.3   Bottom-Up Analysis: Two Applications

Different architectures are typically applied in different business domains or application areas. The one size fits all is associated with increased risks, high complexity and difficulty to obtain results in big organizations. In the bottom-up analysis the impact of different, real-life application types and architectures is analyzed. In our study we selected two application types that are as diverse as possible in order to identify the disparities in integrating cloud architectures in different contexts. One scenario focuses on a data intensive application and another on a computation intensive application.

As data intensive applications we consider applications that handle hundreds of terabytes of data, require data integrity and consistency and allow for discovery of information in very tight time constraints. As an example of a data intensive application we consider a large archive system in the ECM (Enterprise Content Management) domain, subject to tight regulatory conditions and able to satisfy requirements for investigations and litigation.

Computationally intensive applications must satisfy real time performance requirements, thousands of transactions per second and with very high availability and reliability. Business criticality of such applications increases the importance of these requirements. An example application that is also business critical for a financial institution is a trading system in the Securities domain.

The applications in these two distinct domains (ECM and Securities) help us to identify suitable patterns and combine them in an enterprise cloud architecture. The differences in these architectures are then compared against each other. New patterns are listed and put into context. Further, we examine the applications in these two domains in an orchestrated environment for providing end-to-end business processes.

5   Results

In this section we describe the patterns that have been identified in our three-step analysis. The results are obtained in the order defined in the methodology section, in several iterations within our big organization. It is not necessary to complete the state analysis in order to continue with the top-down and bottom-up analysis. We proceed to the next step with partial analysis results from the previous step.

5.1   Results from Current State Analysis

The internal research in the current state analysis indicated an ongoing and growing use of cloud service offerings even in a risk averse industry.

SaaS Integration

The SaaS integration has been the first integration challenge for our enterprise. The initial use of cloud services started with isolated mainstream SaaS applications for currency converters, legislation documentation (for the Legal and Compliance departments), registries of companies and business at national level (for checking the status of clients), intranet repositories, payments applications, Lombard credit rating models, price comparison data, financial instrument databases, etc. SaaS applications can be easily used and don't require long and expensive internal software provisioning processes. SaaS is often used for less critical software demands.

Initially, a SaaS application is designed to provide application functionality isolated from the enterprise network; we call this Simple SaaS Integration. The main concern for integrating the cloud applications with the applications of the internal environment was the accessibility and usability of the systems using strong authentication. Thus the integration effort was limited to SSO (Single Sign On) and PKI (Public Key Infrastructure) integration to enable implicit but secure login. In these cases, further integration into an existing application landscape was neither possible nor necessary. No major data flows were required from the applications in the private environment to the isolated SaaS in the public clouds. Data could be imported from the public SaaS, but there was no confidential out-going traffic, except for user credentials and certificates. This result is very intuitive and supports the problem statement of section 3.

As the functionality of this SaaS application is extended the integration effort increases. SaaS market leader Salesforce indicates this through several available service interfaces for their application [8]. We call Advanced SaaS Integration any SaaS integration that goes beyond isolated applications and targets the integration of a web of applications across organizations or across clouds. To enable usage of the entire functionality, these applications must be integrated with the services that are currently provided by the private enterprise landscape.

Complexity of Integration

Our current state analysis exposed the hard reality that integration in the SaaS context is almost always direct Point-to-Point Integration. This covers SaaS to SaaS integration as well as SaaS to enterprise environment integration. The Point-to-Point Integration is beneficial only if it is limited to a small number of nodes. In this case it may have a straightforward implementation and results in higher efficiency and availability due to the direct communication between the nodes. On the other hand, this pattern has disadvantages in SaaS service management and maintainability. Each node of the service communication is typically proprietary and involves transformations that are implemented redundantly in other nodes. The amount of transformations for each node has polynomial complexity. Without direct support from a centralized cloud infrastructure the result is increased management and maintenance effort (Figure 2).

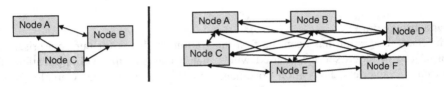

Fig. 2. Point-To-Point complexity for 3 and 6 Nodes

Overall, the current state analysis counted 23 simple and 2 Advanced SaaS Integration nodes. However, we expect that there are nodes hidden behind undocumented or external workflows and thus the number of integration nodes is higher in each category. A concept for standardizing the integration is needed at an architecture level in order to manage the high complexity of point-to-point integration.

5.2   Results from Top-Down Analysis

After concluding the current state analysis, a three step top-down analysis was performed. Each step examines the problem: How can the services communicate with each other and how do the solution topologies look like? During the analysis, we identified different patterns for each scenario. Due to space restrictions we present only selected patterns in more detail. These are SaaS Integration, Single-Cloud Integration, Centralized Multi-Cloud Integration and Decentralized Multi-Cloud Integration. The full description can be found in [13] along with information on the method we used for assessing the benefit of the patterns. In the following we examine each of these steps separately.

SaaS Integration

Problem: The integration of SaaS applications with applications in the private cloud results in Point-To-Point integrations with tight coupling and growing complexity.

Solution: With the SaaS Broker Integration (Figure 3) we introduce an intermediate layer in a cloud environment layer by applying the ESB (Enterprise Service Bus) pattern [10]. In this pattern the ESB is deployed to a public cloud. The ESB operates as a broker between the SaaS applications and the enterprise environment. It controls the communication between the applications in the different SaaS environments. No direct communication between the SaaS applications is allowed.

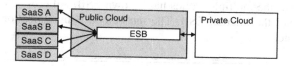

Fig. 3. SaaS Broker Integration Pattern

Consequences: The SaaS Broker Integration pattern enables centralized control of all SaaS communication and scales better compared to Point-to-Point integration. All service calls to the internal environment can be filtered or transformed to company standards. The single point of failure has negative impact on the availability, even though load balancing and failover may cover this risk. A drawback, especially for time critical services, is additional latency through transmission of the ESB. This effect can be significant if SaaS solutions are distributed in datacenters worldwide. If latency in transmission is critical, then direct communication should be preferred.

A similar solution using intermediate layers for integration among clouds is offered by several providers as Integration Platform as a Service (IPaaS) [7]. The difference between an IPaaS and the SaaS Broker Integration pattern is the self-hosted ESB in the Public Cloud versus a standardized IPaaS platform.

Single-Cloud Integration (Simple Hybrid Cloud)

Problem: A single public cloud is integrated with the private cloud. Services are deployed to both clouds and need to communicate with each other.

Solution: By applying the Distributed ESB pattern (Figure 4) we introduce two ESBs, one in each cloud. The intra-cloud communication is handled by the corresponding cloud ESB. Cross-cloud communication is steered over both ESBs.

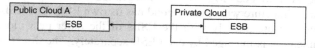

Fig. 4. Distributed ESB Pattern

Consequence: This pattern enables direct intra-cloud communication for each of the environments which has positive effects on the latency and availability of the overall topology compared to a single ESB in one of the environments This pattern shows advantages through the distribution of the ESB infrastructure which enables intra-cloud and cross-cloud communication. Further, this pattern allows for nodes to operate independently of the availability of other nodes. A disadvantage is the additional management effort for the ESB in the cloud.

Centralized Multi-Cloud Integration

Problem: Multiple Clouds need to be integrated in an enterprise network. Services are deployed to all environments and need to communicate with each other.

Solution: The Internal Cross-Cloud ESB is applied (Figure 5) resulting in an architecture where each of the multiple clouds has its own ESB. All cross-cloud communication is routed over the internal ESB. The intra-cloud communication is managed by each ESB separately.

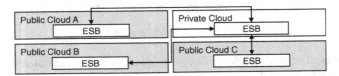

Fig. 5. Internal Cross-Cloud ESB

Consequence: This pattern supports integration of different platforms across cloud providers and decoupling within each cloud. Each cloud provider can select the appropriate brokerage and messaging platform that is available for all the services deployed within the cloud. The integration with the ESBs of each cloud provider is done by the organization's ESB in the private cloud, which manages the internal, private applications storing confidential data. This approach scales very well for different cloud providers; big organizations that take advantage of the platforms of each cloud provider. Another advantage of this topology is that is allows for centralized cross-cloud service communication management. The Internal Cross-Cloud ESB pattern is useful when the cross-cloud communication needs to be centrally controlled and restricted. Disadvantages are introduced through the additional transaction time through the cross-cloud communication.

Decentralized Multi-Cloud Integration

Problem: Same problem as in Centralized Multi-Cloud Integration where a centralized ESB is not possible or is not desired.

Solution: The Peer to Peer Multi-Cloud Integration Pattern (Figure 6) is applied, resulting in an architecture where each cloud has its own ESB. The ESB of each cloud is able to communicate directly with the ESBs of the other peer clouds. The intra-cloud communication is managed by each ESB separately. The direct communication between each cloud has positive impact on the latency of cross-cloud service communication in time critical cross-cloud communication and avoids the single point of failure in integration.

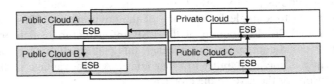

Fig. 6. Peer to Peer (P2P) Multi-Cloud Integration

Consequence: A disadvantage of this approach is that cloud providers with different platforms must implement broker functionality supporting all the format and protocol transformations required for the communication with other cloud providers. This introduces development and integration overhead. Further, it is very unlikely that cloud providers are able to support data model transformations required for the exchange of data across applications in different clouds. Additionally, high effort is necessary to manage this environment centrally. Monitoring of the communication requires additional components; this increases the complexity and results in additional development and maintenance effort.

This pattern can be implemented through a separate ESB management component. Alternatively an existing ESB is the master ESB and collects monitoring information from other ESBs.

5.3   Results from Bottom-Up Analysis

As mentioned in the Methodology section (4), the patterns identified by the top-down analysis have been applied in the bottom-up approach in the two domains. Nonfunctional requirements influence the architectural decisions; e.g. direct communication for increased performance vs. hub communication for reduction of costs and increased maintainability. Further enhancements include the support of mission critical integration aspects like authentication and authorization, monitoring (including load balancing, and usage monitoring) as well as reporting (including billing).

Topology Description

In all scenarios the topology consists of three environments. The private environment and two public clouds. The internal environment is necessary, because several applications cannot move to the public cloud. Two different public cloud environments are used to ensure the availability of the financial transaction system and to prevent any possible data loss and integrity issues in the archive system. Each important application layer is redundantly implemented. In the archive system (Figure 7) only the data layer is replicated over the clouds. The public cloud B runs as a secondary backup solution of the data layer in standby mode. Since business does not require very high availability for the online access of documents, the other layers are not replicated.

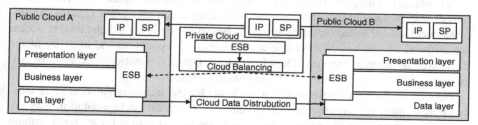

Fig. 7. Topology View Financial Transaction System

The financial transaction system must be fully replicated in two fully operational clouds for high availability (Figure 8). Eventual unavailability of one cloud solution is recognized by the cloud balancer which routes all service calls to the other cloud.

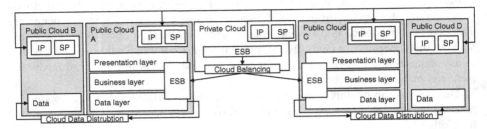

Fig. 8. Topology Archive System

Cloud Balancing and Cloud Data Distribution

We used the Distributed ESB pattern together with the Cloud Balancing pattern [6] for integrating different clouds with potentially different loads. Cloud balancing allows for IT resources to be load-balanced across multiple clouds and must not be confused with the cloud load balancing which distributes load in a cluster of servers within a single cloud. Cloud balancing requires all the mechanisms of the load balancing and workload distribution, along with the existence of redundant storage and servers in another cloud. Services can be cloud balanced if they have been provisioned in different clouds and user and service provisioning are supported across clouds.

In our implementation we are using clusters of servers (and hypervisors) within each cloud, but we are not clustering across clouds. When a service is load balanced to another cloud, then the temporary state of the service persists and can be migrated to the other cloud. Additionally, we are using Cloud Data Distribution to distribute queries on data across clouds. Data is distributed and replicated across clouds according to legal constraints along with requirements for performance and availability.

In the financial transaction system, the cloud balancer decides whether to use the service capabilities in public cloud A or public cloud B. The internal environment controls the cloud balancer and is not affected by the unavailability of either cloud.

In the archiving solution, all document searches and retrievals are balanced by the cloud balancer. Along with availability requirements, the documents of different customers may be located in different clouds due to legal and regulatory reasons. Appropriate mechanisms based on business and technical logic decide which cloud to access for different documents. Further, the archives require replication and integrity of the data layer in another location. Therefore Cloud Data Distribution mechanisms synchronize the data between different cloud environments.

Notice that the data distribution across clouds for the archiving solution must satisfy the data integrity requirements of the archive. A typical backup solution may periodically copy data from primary storage to secondary storage at binary level without knowledge of the objects represented by these bytes. But, if a document has been imported to the primary storage of the archive, and after that has been accidentally deleted, the backup to the secondary storage may not notice this import and deletion.

The cloud data replication includes checks and business rules that guarantee the integrity of the archive in all environments.

Security Topology Related Patterns
In order to establish the trust relation to externally hosted environments in a multi-cloud topology, we introduced authentication and authorization components in the top-down analysis. In the two applications analyzed in the bottom-up approach, all nodes use the same authentication and authorization mechanisms. In all clouds we had similar LDAP directories and PKI infrastructure and compatible authorization rule engines. The authentication and authorization data is synchronized across the external environments. This approach centralizes the management and control over the authentication and authorization system and improves the governance of security data. However, the synchronization requires some implementation effort. In the financial transaction system an identity and service provider is deployed to each cloud. In the archive system an identity and service provider is only deployed to the pubic cloud A.

The authentication and authorization system in each node must be connected with the internal master system and the synchronization jobs need to be configured and kept up to date. This cost is, negligible compared to the costs of maintaining different security mechanisms in each cloud and provisioning users separately in each cloud.

5.4   Important Insights from Bottom-Up and Top-Down Analysis

The examination of two real-life business scenarios in the bottom-up analysis gave us an interesting insight: Even with significant differences in the requirements, the resulting cloud architectures appeared to be very similar. The important layers were redundantly implemented; in the data archive the data layer and in the financial management system all layers were replicated. In both cases the Distributed ESB, Cloud Balancing and Cloud Data Distribution patterns have been applied. Both cases profit from the Cross-Cloud Monitoring and Cross-Cloud Security patterns. The former allows for performance and load control of the cloud services and the latter enables end-to-end security over different clouds. Currently, cross-cloud monitoring requires self-developed infrastructure because the monitoring capabilities of the different clouds are not (yet) standardized and the clouds use proprietary implementations.

6   Future Work

Our paper scratched the surface of cloud integration. Several aspects of cloud integration need further elaboration.

Security: Public clouds require significant effort in security measures. Beyond authentication and authorization topology patterns there are numerous other ways to secure public clouds like content encryption, key management, homomorphic encryption, data splitting, computing with encrypted functions, anonymization, data masking, encrypted virtual machines, etc. Future work may define combinations of security patterns to secure a public cloud for targeted trust level.

Cloud Middleware: Cloud middleware is emerging (Amazon, RedHat, Mule, etc.). To provide cloud elasticity there are slight shifts in cloud middleware. Our analysis showed that there is emphasis on asynchronous integration: push asynchronous integration is replaced with pull asynchronous integration, and there is higher emphasis on replication patterns. Further we saw emergence of completely new cloud middleware elements like Cross-Cloud Balancer, Cross-Cloud Data Distributor, etc.

To facilitate migration of existing IT landscapes to the cloud, a mapping of "old" on-premise integration patterns to "new" cloud integration patterns has to be worked out along with the definition of standards in balancing, distribution and monitoring.

Cross-Cloud Monitoring: Today, monitoring capabilities of clouds are limited to a single cloud. In a redundant implementation over different clouds, a cloud monitoring mechanism is necessary to control the load and performance of cloud services. As usual, the main challenge is the lack of standardization of monitoring capabilities, formats, and protocols, but also the lack of standard tools for this activity. A monitoring pattern requires a centralized management component which is linked with the surrounding environments. The monitoring must deliver reliable and agreed service quality during changing demands and be as cost effective as possible. Negative peaks and load throughputs must be addressed for checking cost savings. Scaling strategies are necessary based on application types (e.g., data intensive: transaction time minor relevance, computationally intensive: transaction time highly important).

Cloud Management: Cross-cloud management solutions enable the possibility of optimizing cloud usage and reduce the total cost for the multi-cloud environment based on billing information provided by the cloud providers. In combination with the service SLAs the service provisioning can be optimized to an optimal cost/value ratio. Currently, the cost models of the different cloud providers are not standardized and the prediction of the actual cost is hard and complex. Tools for cross-cloud monitoring and billing do not exist, but will be developed in the context of cross-cloud marketplaces, e.g. provided by Deutsche Börse Cloud Exchange [11].

Cloud Adoption: An adoption of cloud solutions into the enterprise landscape is driven by the offers of cloud providers and software companies. These offerings, especially in the SaaS market, enable the providers to highly standardize their software solution on the one hand and limit customization possibilities on the other. What cloud solutions can replace existing in-house solutions? What tangible steps are needed to migrate existing large-scale application landscapes to cloud based environments? We expect to see more work examining the degree to which Service Orientation and other methodologies need to be applied in order to migrate to the cloud and new patterns that combine SOA with cloud integration.

Multi-Cloud Offers: Enterprise cloud users won't limit their scope to a single cloud scenario. Our research indicated that vendors nowadays still focus on secure intra-cloud solution and don't offer capabilities for the cross-cloud integration. Reasons for the unavailability of cross-cloud support include the lack of advantage for the cloud provider and the fact that the cloud adoption process needs to progress further so that demands for such functionalities grow.

Very high availability requirements, which may not be supported by a single cloud provider, can be covered through redundant implementations over several clouds. Enabling this scenario through cloud middleware components will address new user groups whose cloud requirements aren't addressed with the existing cloud offerings.

Acknowledgments. This paper is based on a project between the University of Applied Sciences in Karlsruhe and Credit Suisse in Zurich. We thank Prof. Rainer Neumann and Robert Robinson for their feedback, Claus Hagen for his support and Roger Suess, Peter Schnorf and Alain Hsiung for sharing their cloud computing vision.

References

1. Barros, A., Dumas, M., ter Hofstede, A.H.M.: Service interaction patterns. In: 3rd Intl Conference on Business Process Management (BPM), Nancy, France. Springer (2005)
2. IDG Enterprise: Computerworld Forecast Study (2015). http://www.idgenterprise.com/report/computerworld-forecast-study-2015
3. Hohpe, G., Woolf, B.: Enterprise Integration Patterns: Designing, Building, and Deploying Messaging Solutions. Pearson Education (2004). ISBN 0-321-20068-3
4. Erl, T.: SOA Principles of Service Design. SOA Systems Inc. (2009). ISBN: 9780132344821
5. Buschmann, F., Henney, K.: Pattern-Oriented Software Architecture. Tutorial, OOP, Munich (2008). http://www.sigs.de/download/oop_08/Buschmann%20Mo2%20Patterns_OOP.pdf
6. Cope, R., Erl, T., Naserpour, A.: Cloud Computing Design Patterns. Prentice Hall/PearsonPTR, June 2015. http://cloudpatterns.org
7. Mulesoft: iPaaS: Integration for the Cloud. Cloud. https://www.mulesoft.com/resources/cloudhub/ipaas-integration-platform-as-a-service
8. Salesforce, Which API should I use? https://help.salesforce.com/HTViewHelpDoc?id=integrate_what_is_api.htm&language=en
9. W3C, Web Services Description Language (WSDL) Version 2.0 Part 2: Message Core Language (2007). http://www.w3.org/TR/2007/REC-wsdl20-20070626/
10. Erl, T., et al.: SOA Design Patterns. Prentice Hall (2009). ISBN: 9780136135166
11. Deutsche Börse Cloud Exchange. The marketplace for cloud resources (2015). http://cloud.exchange/en/wp-content/uploads/2015/02/20141112_DBCE_Factsheet_EN-1.pdf
12. Mell, P., Grance, T.: The NIST Definition of Cloud Computing (2011). http://csrc.nist.gov/publications/nistpubs/800-145/SP800-145.pdf
13. Merkel, D.: Cloud Integration Patterns. University of Applied Sciences, Karlsruhe (2014)
14. Fehling, C., Leymann, F., Retter, R., Schupeck, W., Arbitter, P.: Cloud Computing Patterns. Springer (2014)
15. Telstra research: Customer Centric Cloud: Hype or Hybrid? (March 2015). http://connect.telstraglobal.com/hybrid-customer-clouds.html
16. Bass, L., Clements, P., Kazmann, R.: Software Architecture in Practice. Addison-Wesley (2007)
17. Erl, T., Mahmood, Z., Puttini, R.: Cloud Computing: Concepts, Technology & Architecture. Prentice Hall (May 2013). ISBN: 9780133387520

Remote Collaboration, Decision Support, and On-Demand Medical Image Analysis for Acute Stroke Care

Renan Sales Barros[1]([✉]), Jordi Borst[1], Steven Kleynenberg[2], Céline Badr[3],
Rama-Rao Ganji[4], Hubrecht de Bliek[5], Landry-Stéphane Zeng-Eyindanga[6],
Henk van den Brink[7], Charles Majoie[1], Henk Marquering[1],
and Sílvia Delgado Olabarriaga[1]

[1] Academic Medical Center, University of Amsterdam, Amsterdam, The Netherlands
r.salesbarros@amc.uva.nl
[2] Sopheon, Maastricht, The Netherlands
[3] Prologue, Les Ulis, France
[4] ARTEMIS Department, Telecom SudParis, Evry, France
[5] Philips Healthcare, Eindhoven, The Netherlands
[6] Bull, Grenoble, France
[7] Technolution, Gouda, The Netherlands

Abstract. Acute stroke is the leading cause of disabilities and the fourth cause of death worldwide. The treatment of stroke patients often requires fast collaboration between medical experts and fast analysis and sharing of large amounts of medical data, especially image data. In this situation, cloud technologies provide a potentially cost-effective way to optimize management of stroke patients and, consequently, improve patient outcome. This paper presents a cloud-based platform for Medical Distributed Utilization of Services & Applications (MEDUSA). This platform aims at improving current acute care settings by allowing fast medical data exchange, advanced processing of medical image data, automated decision support, and remote collaboration between physicians in a secure and responsive virtual space. We describe a prototype implemented in the MEDUSA platform for supporting the treatment of acute stroke patients. As the initial evaluation illustrates, this prototype improves several aspects of current stroke care and has the potential to play an important role in the care management of acute stroke patients.

Keywords: Acute care · Cloud computing · Decision support · High performance computing · Medical image analysis · Remote collaboration · Stroke · Telemedicine

1 Introduction

Acute ischemic stroke is the leading cause of disability and fourth cause of death [1]. In acute ischemic stroke, a blood clot obstructs blood flow in the brain causing part of the brain to die due to the lack of blood supply. The amount of brain damage and the

© IFIP International Federation for Information Processing 2015
S. Dustdar et al. (Eds): ESOCC 2015, LNCS 9306, pp. 214–225, 2015.
DOI: 10.1007/978-3-319-24072-5_15

patient outcome is highly related to the duration of the lack of blood flow ("time is brain"). Therefore, fast diagnosis, decision making, and treatment are crucial in acute stroke management.

Medical data of a stroke patient is collected during the transport by ambulance to the hospital (e.g. vital signs, patient history, and medication). At arrival, various types of image data are acquired following protocols that involve opinions and decisions from various medical experts. Sometimes, a patient needs to be transferred to a specialized hospital and, in this case, it is important that all the data collected in the ambulance and at the referring hospital is available to the caregivers that will continue the treatment. Often, various medical specialists need to collaborate based on available information for determining the correct diagnosis and choosing the best treatment. Usually, this collaboration is based on tools that are not connected to each other and, because of that, they may not deliver the necessary information rapidly enough.

In addition to these challenges, the amount of patient medical data is growing fast [2]. This fast increase is especially observed in radiological image data, which is also a consequence of new medical imaging technologies [3, 4]. The management, sharing, and processing of medical image data is a great challenge for healthcare providers [3, 4] and they can be greatly improved by the usage of cloud technologies [5]. Cloud technologies also enable collaboration and data exchange between medical experts in a scalable, fast, and cost-effective way [5]. Mobile devices, remote collaboration tools, and on-demand computing models and data analysis tools supported by cloud technologies may play an important role to help in optimizing stroke treatment and, consequently, improve outcome of patients suffering from stroke.

In this paper, we present a cloud-based platform for Medical Distributed Utilization of Services & Applications (MEDUSA). This platform aims at improving current acute care settings by allowing fast medical data exchange, advanced processing of medical image data, automated decision support, and remote collaboration between physicians through a secure responsive virtual space. We discuss a case study implemented using the MEDUSA platform for supporting the treatment of acute stroke patients, presenting the technical details of the prototype implementation and commenting on its initial evaluation.

2 Related Work

The development of cloud-based platforms for collaboration and processing of medical data is a challenging task. Many authors [4, 5, 6, 7] put forward that these platforms hold the potential to define the future of healthcare services. Also, the analysis of medical data can be an important way to improve quality and efficiency in healthcare [8, 9].

The work presented in [10, 11] focuses on the development of a cloud-based solution aimed at only the storage and sharing of medical data. In other words, they propose solutions based on cloud infrastructures to facilitate medical image data exchange between hospitals, imaging centers, and physicians. A similar solution is presented in [12], however focusing on medical data sharing during emergency situations. A cloud-based system is presented in [13] for storage of medical data with an additional functionality that enables content-based retrieval of medical images. Still focusing on cloud-based data storage and sharing, [14] presents a solution to help managing medical resources for the prevention and treatment of chronic stroke patients.

In addition to storage and sharing, some studies also include the possibility of using the cloud infrastructure for processing of medical data. A simple cloud-based application is presented in [15] to monitor oxygenated hemoglobin and deoxygenated hemoglobin concentration changes in different tissues. Cloud computing is also used in [16] not only to support data storage and sharing, but also to visualize and render medical image data. In [17] the authors also propose a cloud application for rendering of 3D medical imaging data. This application additionally manages the cloud deployment by considering scalability, operational cost, and network quality.

Complete cloud-based systems for medical image analysis are presented in [18, 19, 20]. However, in these systems, image upload and download is manually performed by the user, while the system focuses on the remote processing, storage, and sharing of medical image data. The MEDUSA platform not only provides cloud-based storage, sharing, and processing of medical image data, but also real-time communication between medical experts, real-time collaborative interaction of the medical experts with the medical data, and a real-time decision support system that continuously processes patient data and displays relevant notifications about the patient condition.

The MEDUSA platform also includes a cloud management layer that coordinates the use of resources in the cloud infrastructure. Other studies also present some cloud management features. In [21] the authors propose a cloud architecture that reserves network and computing resources to avoid problems regarding load-balancing mechanisms of cloud infrastructures and to reduce the processing delays for the medical applications. Also, [2] proposes an algorithm to optimize the organization of medical image data and associated processing algorithms in cloud computing nodes to increase the computing performance. Finally, [3] presents a cloud-based multi-agent system for scalable management of large collections of medical image data.

The project presented in [22] tries to speed up current stroke care by integrating and sharing data from stroke patients using mobile networks. In this scenario, a hospital can, for instance, be prepared with the right resources before the arrival of the patient. This project also includes decision support, which suggests a predefined path through the emergency procedures according to the structure of mandatory and other supplementary healthcare protocols. However, differently from MEDUSA, this project does not include any image processing based feature.

3   Acute Stroke Care

Currently, treatment decision of stroke patients is increasingly driven by advanced imaging techniques. These imaging techniques consist of non-contrast computed tomography (ncCT), computed tomography angiography (CTA), and computed tomography perfusion (CTP). Because of the extensive usage of imaging techniques, it is common to produce gigabytes of image data per patient.

The primary treatment for patients with acute ischemic stroke is intravenous administration of alteplase (thrombolysis). Patients who are not eligible for treatment with alteplase or do not respond to the treatment can be treated by mechanical removal of the blood clot via the artery (thrombectomy). Thrombectomy is only available in specialized hospitals and often a patient must be transferred for treatment.

This transfer is arranged via telephone and imaging data created in the initial hospital is not available for the caregivers in the specialized hospital until the patient and imaging data arrive via the ambulance. On a regular basis it happens that the imaging data was wrongly interpreted in the initial hospital and that the patient is not eligible for thrombectomy. Also, often new imaging acquisitions have to be redone due to broken DVDs, wrong data, or insufficient quality. These problems result in futile transfers and loss of valuable time.

4   MEDUSA Platform

The MEDUSA platform was designed to support remote collaboration and high performance processing of medical data for multiple healthcare scenarios. The platform is accessible to final users through the MEDUSA Collaboration Framework (MCF), which is a web application that is compatible with any web browser that supports HTML5. The MCF is a special type of MEDUSA application that provides to the users an entry point to access other MEDUSA applications. A cloud management layer controls the deployment and execution of all MEDUSA applications in one or more cloud providers. Figure 1 illustrates the architectural design of the MEDUSA platform.

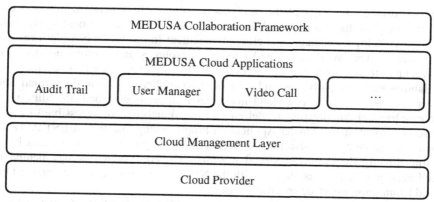

Fig. 1. The MEDUSA platform architecture.

4.1   MEDUSA Cloud Applications

The MEDUSA platform has a number of cloud applications that are available in all healthcare scenarios: Audit Trail, which reports the events generated by the other MEDUSA applications; User Manager, which allows assigning roles to users and defining which MEDUSA applications they can use; and Video Call, which allows communication between users of the MEDUSA platform.

The MEDUSA applications are started as part of a MEDUSA session. Multiple users in a session can interact with these applications, and these interactions are visible to all the users in the session. The handling of multiple user interactions is done by each MEDUSA application. The applications in the MEDUSA platform can be web applications or regular desktop applications. The desktop applications are integrated in the MEDUSA platform through a virtualization server that uses the technologies described in [23] and [24]. The multi-user interaction of the desktop applications is handled by the virtualization server.

4.2   Cloud Provider

The MEDUSA applications can be deployed in different cloud providers. Currently, these applications are being deployed in the High Performance Real-time Cloud for Computing (HiPeRT-Cloud) of Bull. The HiPeRT-Cloud is mainly designed for real-time computationally-intensive workloads. This solution is fully compatible with the Cloud Computing Reference Architecture of the National Institute of Standards and Technology (NIST) and provides infrastructure services under any cloud broker solution. The HiPeRT-Cloud is used in the MEDUSA platform because it provides solutions for handling complex applications in the field of real-time computational and data-intensive tasks in the cloud.

4.3   Cloud Management Layer

In order to take advantage of the on-demand, flexible, high-performance, and cost-effective options that cloud providers can offer, the cloud management layer, implemented by Prologue, manages the cloud deployment in the MEDUSA platform. This layer orchestrates the allocation and release of resources on the cloud provider's infrastructure. It also oversees the lifecycle of the deployed resources, ensures their availability and scalability, and links the desktop applications from the virtualization server back to the MCF. The cloud management layer is designed according to the Service-Oriented Architecture model and its functionalities are accessible through a Representational State Transfer Application Programming Interface (REST API). The cloud management layer also incorporates a monitoring service that operates by accessing directly the deployed virtual machines (VMs). The technology behind the cloud management layer is aligned with the NIST architecture and based on the Open Cloud Computing Interface specifications.

In the MEDUSA context, technical requirements for computing, storage, network, and security resources have been identified for each MEDUSA application to be deployed. All requirements are then translated into machine-readable code that is used to provision the cloud resources.

The components of the MEDUSA platform are hosted on the cloud through a security-aware, need-based provisioning process. By supporting on-demand hybrid and multi-cloud deployments, as well as monitoring, load balancing, and auto-scaling services through an agent embedded in each VM, the cloud management layer thus ensures a high resilience of the MEDUSA platform.

4.4   Security

The security of the MEDUSA platform is currently mainly based in the use of digital certificates, which are used to authenticate MEDUSA applications (VMs), to secure the data exchanges through the network, and to provide strong authentication of MEDUSA users.

The VMs containing the applications are deployed dynamically, and thus server certificates need to be created dynamically, during the deployment. A web service was developed to provide dynamic generation of server certificates for the different VMs in the MEDUSA platform. These server certificates must be created during the deployment of the VMs and there must be one certificate per application and VM (identified by the IP address).

Regarding the user authentication, an authentication module is called when a user opens a MEDUSA session. This module authenticates a user by checking the provided credentials against the user management component, which has access to a special internal directory containing the certificates used for strong authentication of MEDUSA users.

The MEDUSA platform also uses robust image watermarking and fingerprinting methods to prevent and detect unauthorized modification and leaking of medical images by authorized users by. However, due to legal regulations, an important requirement when dealing with medical images is the capability reconstructing the original image data. Because of this, reversible or semantic-sensitive techniques for watermarking and fingerprinting can be used in the MEDUSA platform. These techniques enable to completely recover the original image data or at least the recovery of the regions of these images that are relevant for the user or application.

5   MEDUSA Stroke Prototype

The MEDUSA platform was designed to support various medical scenarios. Here, we focus on a prototype for supporting acute stroke care. The MEDUSA Stroke Prototype (MSP) is built by combining the default MEDUSA applications with three applications specifically configured to support the treatment of stroke patients: Advanced Medical Image Processing, Decision Support System, and 3D Segmentation Renderer. All the applications of the MSP are executed in VMs running on the HiPeRT-Cloud. The cloud management layer is in charge of the deployment of these VMs.

5.1   Advanced Medical Image Processing

For supporting the assessment of the severity of a stroke, several medical image processing algorithms (MIPAs) have been developed. These algorithms perform quantitative analysis of the medical image data and the result of these analyses can be used to support the treatment decisions. The output of these algorithms are, for example, the segmentation of a hemorrhage in the brain [25], the segmentation of a blood clot [26], and the segmentation of the infarcted brain tissue [27]. The MIPAs are linked together into processing pipelines with well-defined input, output, and policies that control their execution. The execution of these pipelines is automatically orchestrated to deliver the lowest execution time based on a set of optimization strategies (e.g. task parallelism, data parallelism, and GPU computing).

The MIPAs are implemented as plugins for the IntelliSpace Discovery (ISD) platform, an enterprise solution for research, developed by Philips Healthcare. Figure 2 shows the output of the plugin for infarct volume calculation in the ISD. The collection of MIPAs specially developed to support acute stroke care that are included in the ISD constitutes the Advanced Medical Image Processing application of the MSP.

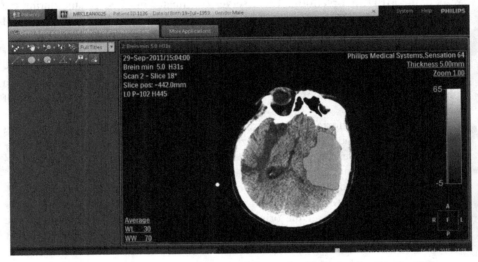

Fig. 2. Plugin for automated measurement of the cerebral infarct volume in the ISD.

The ISD is a Windows desktop application developed by using the .NET Framework. The development of the MIPAs is also based in the .NET Framework. For GPU-based computations, OpenCL 1.1 was used. OpenCL is a framework for the development and execution of programs across platforms consisting of different types of processors such as CPUs, GPUs, etc. OpenCL.NET was used to integrate OpenCL with the .NET. Framework.

The data generated by the MIPAs are exported to the DSS by using JavaScript Object Notation (JSON) files through WebSockets. (Anonymized) Patient information is sent to the MIPAs by using the tags of the medical image data used as input. The information about the current session is directly sent to the ISD and forwarded to the MIPAs.

5.2   Decision Support System

The Decision Support System (DSS) by Sopheon provides real-time process support to medical professionals collaborating on the stroke case. The DSS is rule-based: the rules specify the conditions under which actions are to be advised (delivered as notifications). The Decision Support rules are part of a medical protocol and thus defined and approved by medical professionals.

In the MSP, the DSS runs a set of rules specifically designed for dealing with stroke patients. It gathers real-time input from vital sign sensors and MIPAs. For instance, a rule could state that an infarct volume larger than 70 milliliters is associated with a poor outcome for the patient. When the DSS detects an infarct volume value of e.g. 80 milliliters, it will display the notification associated with this condition. The DSS also selects relevant information from the data generated by the MIPAs and forwards it to the audit trail and to the 3D Segmentation Renderer.

The DSS runs on Node.js, which is a platform built on Google Chrome's JavaScript runtime. The DSS is deployed on Fedora, which is an operating system based on the Linux kernel.

5.3   3D Segmentation Renderer

The 3D Segmentation Renderer by Sopheon is responsible for displaying 3D segmentations generated by the MIPAs. This application was developed by using the WebGL library, which enables to render 3D graphics in the browser without installing additional software. Figure 3 shows the GUI of this application rendering the segmentation of brain tissue (in green and blue) and the segmentation of the infarcted region (in red).

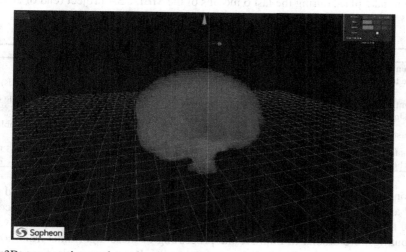

Fig. 3. 3D segmentation renderer showing the segmentation of brain tissue (green and blue) and the infarction in the brain (red).

6   Initial Evaluation

As this is an on-going project, the discussion presented below is based upon an evaluation of the first fully-integrated prototype.

The MSP integrates very heterogeneous applications, which run on different operational systems (Windows, Linux) and use different development technologies (Java, OpenCL, C#, C++). These applications are seamlessly available for the user from a single interface. Also, the deployment of the applications is transparently handled by the platform. This solution is provided in a smooth and transparent manner, hiding the complex details from the user.

In the MEDUSA platform, the data and user input need to cross several software layers, which might introduce overheads and decrease performance. However, such poor performance was not noticed in the initial MSP prototype. For instance, the Advanced Medical Image Processing application, which requires data exchange between different architectural components, was almost instantaneously ready for use without noticeable interaction delays.

The MSP implements a complete acute stroke use case, which has been demonstrated live in various occasions. Impressions have been collected informally to assess the potential value of this prototype system. Table 1 compares the current stroke care situation in the Netherlands versus the stroke care that could be supported by the MEDUSA platform based on the functionalities currently present in the MSP.

Because of its complexity, a detailed and quantitative evaluation of the MEDUSA platform involves several software components and requires a careful planning. The design of this evaluation was already defined in the first year of the project. It is scheduled to take place during the last 6 months of the MEDUSA project (end of 2015).

Table 1. Current stroke care vs. stroke care with MEDUSA.

	current	with MEDUSA
Data availability	images are not available	images are available online
Time to access data	transport by car of physical media (minutes to hours)	online data transfer (few seconds)
Potential value for decision	automated quantitative analysis not used yet for clinical decision	results of MIPAs readily available as decision parameters
Infrastructure	static, proprietary, fixed scale	pay-per-use, scalable, and portable to different cloud providers
Remote collaboration	by phone	by video-conference with access to the patient data

Concerning the image processing functionality, most of the MIPAs included in the MSP are too computationally expensive to be executed on a local machine according to the time constraints of an acute stroke patient. HPC capabilities delivered by cloud computing were crucial to improve the processing of these algorithms from hours to minutes, making them suitable for acute stroke care. For instance, the time to run the method used to reduce noise in CTP data was reduced from more than half an hour to less than 2 minutes [28].

7   Discussion and Conclusion

The development of the MEDUSA platform started in 2013. Back then, this kind of cloud-based solutions was not common. Today, however, there is a clear trend in the healthcare industry towards the usage of cloud computing, collaboration, and automated analyses of medical data. In addition, when dealing with processing of medical data constrained by the requirements of acute care situations, a lot of benefits can be derived from the use of cloud computing: scalability, pay-per-use model, high performance computing capabilities, remote access, etc.

There are innumerous technical challenges for enabling the execution and communication of software components in a platform like MEDUSA. Regarding stroke care, the software components execute in different computing devices (CPUs, GPUs, etc.) and based on different software platforms (web, Linux, Windows, etc.). In the MEDUSA platform these challenges are tackled using SOA approach and a virtualized infrastructure. Because of the variety of application types, a uniform way of establishing communication between the MEDUSA applications has not been developed yet. Nevertheless, the direct communication between applications based on the exchange of well-defined file formats through WebSockets was demonstrated to be effective, without a negative impact in the development and integration of these applications. The current functionalities present in the MSP have the potential to improve several aspects of current stroke care.

The MEDUSA platform is still under development. Thus, most of the components to implement security are still not completely integrated in the platform yet. Defining and developing the security aspects of a platform like MEDUSA is also a very challenging task, since it is necessary to cope with different legal constraints, in particular across countries. The development process of the MEDUSA platform includes the implementation and validation of the platform in three different hospitals. This validation is currently being carried out in one hospital. Preliminary evaluation of the platform indicates that the solution is promising and has potential large value for improving treatment of these patients.

Acknowledgments. This work has been funded by ITEA2 10004: MEDUSA.

References

1. Go, A.S., et al.: Heart disease and stroke statistics – 2013 update: a report from the American Heart Association. Circulation **127**(1), e1–e240 (2013)
2. Hallett, S., Parr, G., McClean, S., McConnell, A., Majeed, B.: Cloud-based healthcare: towards a SLA compliant network aware solution for medical image processing. In: Cloud Computing, pp. 219–223 (2012)
3. Alonso-Calvo, R., Crespo, J., Maojo, V., Muñoz, A., García-Remesal, M., Pérez-Rey, D.: Cloud computing service for managing large medical image data-sets using balanced collaborative agents. In: Advances on Practical Applications of Agents and Multiagent Systems, pp. 265–270 (2011)

4. Shini, S.G., Thomas, T., Chithraranjan, K.: Cloud based medical image exchange-security challenges. Procedia Engineering **38**, 3454–3461 (2012)
5. Kagadis, G.C., et al.: Cloud computing in medical imaging. Medical Physics **40**(7) (2013)
6. Jeyabalaraja, V., Josephine, M.S.: Cloud Computing in Medical Diagnosis for improving Health Care Environment. International Journal of Computing Algorithm **2**, 458–462 (2013)
7. Pino, C., Di Salvo, R.: A survey of cloud computing architecture and applications in health. In: ICCSEE (2013)
8. Jee, K., Kim, G.H.: Potentiality of big data in the medical sector: focus on how to reshape the healthcare system. Healthcare Informatics Research **19**(2), 79–85 (2013)
9. Murdoch, T.B., Detsky, A.S.: The inevitable application of big data to health care. Jama **309**(13), 1351–1352 (2013)
10. Kanagaraj, G., Sumathi, A.C.: Proposal of an open-source cloud computing system for exchanging medical images of a hospital information system. In: TISC, pp. 144–149 (2011)
11. Yang, C.T., Chen, L.T., Chou, W.L., Wang, K.C.: Implementation of a medical image file accessing system on cloud computing. In: CSE, pp. 321–326 (2010)
12. Koufi, V., Malamateniou, F., Vassilacopoulos, G.: Ubiquitous access to cloud emergency medical services. In: ITAB, pp. 1–4 (2010)
13. Zhuang, Y., Jiang, N., Wu, Z., Li, Q., Chiu, D.K., Hu, H.: Efficient and robust large medical image retrieval in mobile cloud computing environment. Information Sciences **263**, 60–86 (2014)
14. Hua, G., Lei, H., Bei, X.: A cloud computing based collaborative service pattern of medical association for stroke prevention and treatment. In: MID, pp. 345–349 (2014)
15. Sharieh, S., Franek, F., Ferworn, A.: Using cloud computing for medical applications. In: Proceedings of the 15th Communications and Networking Simulation Symposium, pp. 15:1–15:7 (2012)
16. Parsonson, L., Grimm, S., Bajwa, A., Bourn, L., Bai, L.: A cloud computing medical image analysis and collaboration platform. In: Cloud Computing and Services Science, pp. 207–224 (2012)
17. Dorn, K., Ukis, V., Friese, T.: A cloud-deployed 3D medical imaging system with dynamically optimized scalability and cloud costs. In: SEAA, pp. 155–158 (2011)
18. Chiang, W.C., Lin, H.H., Wu, T.S., Chen, C.F.: Bulding a cloud service for medical image processing based on service-orient architecture. BMEI **3**, 1459–1465 (2011)
19. Huang, Q., Ye, L., Yu, M., Wu, F., Liang, R.: Medical information integration based cloud computing. NCIS **1**, 79–83 (2011)
20. Ojog, I., Arias-Estrada, M., Gonzalez, J., Flores, B.: A cloud scalable platform for DICOM image analysis as a tool for remote medical support. In: eTELEMED, pp. 246–249 (2013)
21. Ahn, Y.W., Cheng, A.M.K.: Autonomic computing architecture for real-time medical application running on virtual private cloud infrastructures. ACM SIGBED Review **10**(2), 15 (2013)
22. Holtmann, C., Müller-Gorchs, M., Rashid, A., Weidenhaupt, K., Ziegler, V., Griewing, B., Weinhardt, C.: Medical opportunities by mobile IT usage–a case study in the stroke chain of survival. In: European Conf. eHealth (2007)
23. Joveski, B., Mitrea, M., Simoens, P., Marshall, I.J., Prêteux, F., Dhoedt, B.: Semantic multimedia remote display for mobile thin clients. Multimedia systems **19**(5), 455–474 (2013)
24. Joveski, B., Mitrea, M., Ganji, R. R.: MPEG-4 solutions for virtualizing RDP-based applications. In: IS&T/SPIE Electronic Imaging (2014)

25. Boers, A.M., Zijlstra, I.A., Gathier, C.S., van den Berg, R., Slump, C.H., Marquering, H.A., Majoie, C.B.: Automatic Quantification of Subarachnoid Hemorrhage on Noncontrast CT. American Journal of Neuroradiology **35**(12), 2279–2286 (2014)
26. Santos, E.M., et al.: Development and validation of intracranial thrombus segmentation on CT angiography in patients with acute ischemic stroke. PloS One **9**(7) (2014)
27. Boers, A.M., et al.: Automated cerebral infarct volume measurement in follow-up noncontrast CT scans of patients with acute ischemic stroke. American Journal of Neuroradiology **34**(8), 1522–1527 (2013)
28. Barros, R.S., et al.: High Performance Image Analysis of Compressed Dynamic CT Perfusion Data of Patients with Acute Ischemic Stroke. Submitted to MICCAI HPC Workshop (2015)

Hybrid Service Compositions:
When BPM Meets Dynamic Case Management

Konstantinos Traganos[✉] and Paul Grefen

School of Industrial Engineering, Eindhoven University of Technology,
Eindhoven, The Netherlands
kontrag@gmail.com, p.w.p.j.grefen@tue.nl

Abstract. In organizations' efforts to achieve process efficiency and agility, disciplines like business process management and case management have been used widely. While the former is a process-driven discipline which routes processes through specific activities, the latter advances through events based on the case data, characterizing it as event-driven and data-driven. However, these two apparently dissimilar approaches can be combined with the common goal to offer flexible service compositions in a service-dominant context. This paper proposes a way to do so through a business-engineering framework for service-dominant business. The structured approach for business design and the subsequent proposed implementation with IT systems will enable organizations, for instance in financial services sector, to leverage service automation. A working prototype for service management is developed as a proof-of-concept demonstrating that the realization of such a mixed approach is practically feasible.

Keywords: Service management · Service compositions · Service-dominance · Business process management · Dynamic Case Management

1 Introduction

Many business domains are currently transitioning towards a service-oriented business setting. Before the transition, the business value used to be in owning assets while in the new setting the business value is in using the services offered by these assets. Representative examples can be found in the goods logistics domain, in the entertainment industry and in the IT industry. In the personal mobility domain, a focus on providing cars (e.g. in lease constructs) is replaced by mobility services (for instance public transport card, flex offices, etc.) that enable users to arrive at the right place at the right time. This transition creates service-dominant business markets where their not-so-physical characteristics create a high level of dynamism. This places high demands on the agility of service providers operating in these markets.

A way to deal with this high level of dynamism is to not see the services delivered as monoliths that are completely produced in-house, but as flexible compositions of sub-services, part of which are produced in-house and part of which are produced by third parties in the market (which become partners for this reason). In other words,

© IFIP International Federation for Information Processing 2015
S. Dustdar et al. (Eds): ESOCC 2015, LNCS 9306, pp. 226–239, 2015.
DOI: 10.1007/978-3-319-24072-5_16

players in service-dominant markets typically engage into dynamic business networks in which parts of offered services can be delivered by business partners.

However, these providers find their agility heavily constrained by the IT platforms they use to deliver their services. This especially is problematic, as increasing dynamism in a market typically requires higher levels of efficiency in dealing with changes. These higher levels of efficiency require higher level of automation, which obviously are strongly dependent on the capabilities of the automated platforms available. Such automated platforms can be service management systems that facilitate the provisioning of services with the aim to achieve application and operational flexibility in a service-dominant world.

In this paper, we introduce a framework for service-dominant business design and focus mainly on service compositions as an agile way to cope with dynamism. The realization of these service compositions, depending on their characteristics, is done with the disciplines of Business Process Management (BPM) and Dynamic Case Management (DCM). While these two are different in their approach to compositions, their combination facilitates the implementation of a hybrid type of service compositions. Mainly, this combination is based on the fact that internal complexity requires structured business processes while customer-facing services require ad-hoc ones. The BPM and DCM disciplines together can support both complexity and customer orientation.

Regarding the related work, the essence of service compositions from a business point of view has already been identified in terms of service touch points and customer journeys [1], service encounters [2] and value constellation experiences [3]. Their support can be achieved with the business process management discipline, however, most of the approaches have been focused on how extensions [4], [5] or alternatives [6], [7] of WS-BPEL can provide automation of service compositions.

The lack of flexibility of workflow technologies has been addressed in [8] but does not refer to service compositions. The same goes for [9], where adaptive case management is presented as an extension to BPM 2.0 without discussing whether these two disciplines can work together.

We see therefore a need of an approach to support the business side of service compositions with both BPM and DCM characteristics. Our approach addresses this need by contributing a structured framework for hybrid BPM/DCM-oriented service composition. To show the feasibility of such a hybrid type of composition, we also present a prototype of a service management application in the financial services sector.

The rest of this paper is structured as follows. In Section 2, we briefly introduce BASE/X[1], a business engineering framework for service-dominant business, focusing on service compositions. In Section 3, we discuss the operationalization of service compositions, while in Section 4 we describe how BPM and DCM can provide automated support. Then, in Section 5, we present the prototype for service management and finally, we conclude the work in Section 6.

---

[1] BASE/X is the acronym for Business Agility through Service Engineering in a Cross-Organizational Setting.

2   The Three Faces of Service Compositions Through BASE/X

In the introduction, we have discussed the move from an asset-orientation to a service-orientation: customers recognize that business value is not in owning assets, but in using the services offered by assets (which they do not need to own). Before this transition, business settings used to be centered on the delivery of products or stand-alone services [10]. After the transition, they will be centered on the provisioning of solution-oriented, integrated services to customers (either business organizations or individual consumers) [11]. Services may require the deployment of products, but these products become part of the delivery channel of services, not the focal point themselves. The emphasis shifts from the value of the individual product or service to the value of the use of the product or service in an integrated context – the so-called value-in-use [12].

This transition though has consequences for the very basic characteristics of doing business [13]. First, customers expect coherent solutions, not stand-alone solution fragments. Second, customer-driven requirements to solution-oriented services will evolve much faster than requirements to the underlying products. Thus, managing agility in service delivery will be a key factor in the market position of a service provider. Third, managing service complexity and business agility requires a tight integration between the structure of business strategy and models on the one hand and the structure of business operation and information management on the other hand.

Performing the transition to service-dominant business and managing its consequences is a formidable task for any non-trivial business organization. Taking a traditional top-down, business-strategy-to-operations approach will be too slow in the current fast pace of market developments. Taking a quick-win, opportunity-driven, bottom-up approach will result in isolated implementations and chaos in integration efforts. A visionary, industry-strength approach is required that is completely tuned to the service-dominant transition and that has the very basics of service business at its core. BASE/X is such an approach, extending the well-known traditional pyramid which has been used for decades to distinguish the levels strategy, tactics, operations in business decision making.

BASE/X is a business engineering framework, a well-structured way to address the analysis and design of service-dominant business, i.e., business that puts service management at the forefront of its design and operation [13]. It covers the entire spectrum from high-level business strategy definition to business information system architecture design, including elements like business model conception, business service specification and business process modelling. We present here the main components of the framework, while more information can be found in the full documentation in [13].

2.1   Business Design in BASE/X

Business design in BASE/X is based on the observation that we need the distinction between business goals (the 'what' of business) and business operations (the 'how' of business) on the one hand and the distinction between the stable essence of an organization and its agile market offerings on the other hand. This leads to a model with four layers, as shown in Fig. 1.

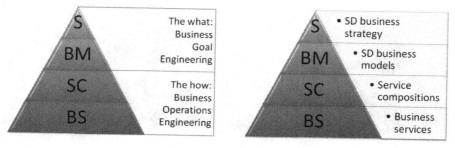

Fig. 1. BASE/X Business Pyramids

As shown in the left side of the figure, the top half of the pyramid covers business goal engineering. As shown in the right side of the figure, the top layer contains the service-dominant business strategy. This strategy describes the identity of an organization in a service-dominant market and is relatively stable over time. The second layer contains service-dominant business models. Each business model describes a market offering in the form of an integrated, solution-oriented complex service: they describe a concrete value-in-use. Business models follow fluid market dynamics and are agile.

The bottom half of the pyramid covers business operations engineering. The bottom layer contains business services, each of which contains a core service capability of the organization. These capabilities are related to the resources of the organization (covering both personnel and large-scale technical infrastructures). The third layer of the pyramid contains the service compositions. Each composition is a combination of business services to realize the service functionality required by a business model: they implement a concrete value-in-use. The combination includes business services from the organization's own set, but also business services of partner organizations in a business network. As service combinations follow business models, they are agile, meaning they revolve with their associated business models.

2.2   Organization and IT Platform Design in BASE/X

Organization design in BASE/X provides the organizational operationalization of the elements in the business pyramid discussed above. Organization design covers both automated organizational processes and manual processes. To obtain proper alignment between business and organization design, organization design follows the same four layers as business design. Proper co-engineering is achieved by mapping changes in a layer of the business pyramid to changes in the corresponding layer in the organization pyramid.

The design of the information technology platform in BASE/X provides the blueprint for the IT platforms that are required for the execution of the elements identified in the organization pyramid. For proper alignment, the platform design also follows the same four layers as the other two BASE/X pyramids.

The support of the business pyramid is shown in Fig. 2 below.

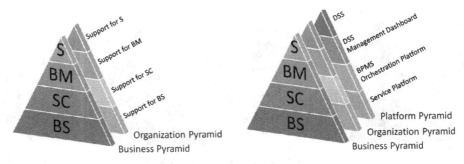

Fig. 2. Organization and Platform pyramids

2.3 Service Composition Layer in BASE/X

Focusing on the third layer of the pyramids of Fig. 2, we can say that the Organization Pyramid offers support for service compositions, i.e., design and execution of operational business processes. These can have the form of specifications of automatically executable processes or service mash-ups.

In turn, the Platform pyramid provides the automated support for efficient integrated service delivery. It contains business process management systems or other forms of service orchestration platforms.

The cross-cutting of the three pyramids in the Service Composition layer of BASE/X, as shown in Fig. 3, is the focus of this paper.

Fig. 3. The Service Composition layer

3   Operationalization of Service Compositions

The essence of service compositions is to make complex functionality available to a market by combining a set of simpler functionalities realized as services. The simpler business functionalities should be standardized within an organization (or even across its boundaries) as business services, such that these functionalities can be reused.

Service compositions exist in two basic types: the process type and the mash-up type. Hybrid types also exist, by combining the characteristics of both basic types. In this section we present the characteristics of the basic types of service compositions which will be later mixed for a hybrid type.

3.1   Service-Based Business Processes

The process type of service compositions is typically used for strictly sequenced business interactions in which the activities of multiple actors (business organizations and customers) need to be synchronized in time and information needs to be passed between these activities. Actors go through a well-defined sequence of steps: an explicit business process. A business process definition is required to make sure the individual actors remain well-synchronized in the execution of the composition. A definition is preferably described in a well-accepted business process specification language, such as BPMN.

In the process type, there is an explicitly managed (and possibly complex) state of a service delivery, where the management of the state is the responsibility (or even the added value) of the service orchestrator. Each defined service composition corresponds to a business process type. Each invocation of a service composition corresponds to a business process instance. The state of an individual service composition invocation is the state of that business process instance, which is typically managed automatically by a business process management system (third pyramid of BASE/X of Fig. 2), as we describe in Section 4.

Business processes are used to specify both customer-facing business processes, i.e. those who have meaning for a customer and change the state of the value-in-use defined by the business model and internal business processes, i.e. those who are encapsulated by a single customer-facing service and hence is invisible for the customer.

3.2   Service Mash-ups

The mash-up type is typically used for free-form business interactions in which a single actor invokes the functionalities of a number of other actors. Individual services of a composition are invoked at a single actor's own will, i.e., without a sequence predefined by the service provider. The composition execution is terminated when the actor uses a termination service.

In the mash-up type, there is an implicitly managed (and usually simple) state of a service delivery, where the management of the state is the responsibility of the service consumer. Comparable to the situation with process-based service compositions, each defined service composition corresponds to a mash-up type. Each invocation of a service composition corresponds to a mash-up instance. A mash-up instance is very light-weight from a provider point of view, as there is no state management by the provider (but the provider may want to be aware that a mash-up instance is active, e.g. for CRM purposes).

We consider service mash-ups as a suitable form of customer-facing business processes: those who have meaning for a customer and change the state of the value-in-use defined by the business model.

4   Realization of Service Compositions

According to the BASE/X framework, the Service Composition layer is supported by service orchestration platforms like business process management systems (BPMS) or service mash-up platforms in order to support the two kinds of business service composition that we have discussed in Section 1. In this section, we present the main characteristics of two disciplines, namely Business Process Management (BPM) and Dynamic Case Management (DCM), in order to show how they can be mixed and serve the role of realization of service compositions.

4.1   BPM

Business Process Management (BPM) is a field continuously growing, starting a few decades ago as a result of people's and organizations' efforts to redesign/reengineer boundary-crossing processes with the use of IT, aiming to improve customer services. Over these years, many definitions have been given for BPM. Examples are: "A customer-focused approach to the systematic management, measurement and improvement of all company processes through cross-functional teamwork and employee empowerment" [14], "Supporting business processes using methods, techniques, and software to design, enact, control, and analyze operational processes involving humans, organizations, applications, documents and other sources of information" [15]. From all these definitions, key observations can be made concluding in the following: BPM can be seen as a discipline that intersects knowledge from management and information technology and applies this to operational business processes. It covers all phases of these processes, from identification to discovery, diagnosis, planning, design, deployment, execution and control. Applying BPM in practice leads to consistency, lower operating costs, faster processes, enhanced flexibility and improved customer satisfaction translating into improved enterprise performance [16].

In this paper, we focus on BPM as a discipline to realize the concept of the Service Composition layer of the business pyramid of the BASE/X framework. This can be done by implementing a Business Process Management System (BPMS) which is an information system that coordinates automated business processes in such a way that all work is done at the right time by the right resource.

4.2   DCM

Case Management (or Case handling) is a paradigm for supporting flexible and knowledge-intensive business processes. Unlike workflow management, which uses predefined process control structures to determine what should be done during a workflow process, case management focuses on what can be done to achieve a business goal [17].

Case is the central notion, which can be seen as the coordination of multiple tasks (planned and unplanned) and associate content, towards a concrete objective. In case management, the knowledge worker in charge of a particular case is a cognitive worker who actively decides on how the goal of that case is reached, and the role of a case management system is assisting rather than guiding and restricting him in doing so.

The core features of case management are [17], [18]:

- avoid context tunneling by providing all information available (i.e., present the case as a whole rather than showing just bits and pieces),
- decide which activities are enabled on the basis of the information available rather than the activities already executed,
- separate work distribution from authorization and allow for additional types of roles, not just the execute role,
- allow workers to view and add/modify data before or after the corresponding activities have been executed (e.g., information can be registered the moment it becomes available).

In case management, the term "dynamic" refers to highly variable, unpredictable, loosely structured and subject to change cases and processes. It is related to flexibility and adaptability and the basic idea is to allow for changes at run-time, i.e. while work is being performed processes may be adapted [19].

A platform for service management with case management capabilities supports case workers to combine required knowledge, information and content in such a way that they either can solve the case or initiate the corresponding service(s), in compliance with rules, constraints and objectives.

4.3   BPM and DCM into a Hybrid System

Traditional workflow management focus on the complete definition and control of structured, repeated processes while case management works on an ad hoc basis to manage dynamic, unstructured processes. BPM is a process-driven discipline which routes processes through specific activities. On the other hand, DCM advances through events based on the case data, characterizing it as event-driven and data-driven. Also, DCM is better used in processes where many exceptions and deviations appear, since attempting to capture all of these scenarios with traditional BPM [20], results in complex models that are hard to manage and maintain.

Based on the Mintzberg's Five Organizational Structures [21], we can say that BPM is best applied in Machine bureaucracy structures, where the standardization of work processes is the prime coordinating mechanism, while DCM is most suitable for Professional bureaucracy organizations where standardization of skills is the dominant mechanism.

The approach we suggest in this paper is to combine these two disciplines into a hybrid service management platform in order to exploit all possible capabilities of both approaches. BPM can be used for the automation of the existing standardized and optimized business processes of an organization, while DCM can be used for the whole handling of cases that are associated to services.

With respect to the differentiation of business processes into customer-facing and internal ones, we consider BPM suitable for the orchestration of internal business processes, while DCM can be applied for the customer-facing business processes.

The hybrid type of service management can be achieved with a single suite where on the one hand services which are visible to the customer are handled with case management features and on the other hand internal workflows handle the execution and automation of building block services. Such a single platform is developed in a prototype of service management in the financial services sector, more specifically in the car leasing domain. The prototype is presented in the next section.

5   Service Management Prototype

A working prototype for service management was implemented to provide insight on how a hybrid service composition is realized. From a technical point of view, Service Oriented Architecture (SOA) techniques were applied in order to integrate services (mainly web services) from different information systems (internal or external to an organization). However, the interesting part is to show how a technical solution that combines both BPM and DCM capabilities is able to bridge business and technology in an agile way.

In the frames of a master thesis project [22], we applied our approach in an asset-based financial services company, and more specifically in its car leasing subsidiary. In this paper, we refer to this company using the fictitious name LeaseCar. After describing the service composition use case, its functionality and the underlying business process models, we present a few screenshots of the user interface.

5.1   Driver Desk use Case

LeaseCar offers a single point of contact for all questions regarding lease vehicles, called Driver Desk. Drivers can turn to the Driver Desk, with literally any type of request, from the moment that their vehicle is on the road, up and until it is being returned. Through several communication channels such as telephone, e-mail or internet portal, they communicate with LeaseCar in order to ask a service or a combination of them. Driver Desk supports drivers on topics like Fines / Fuel cards / Fuel management / Repair, maintenance, tires (RMT) / Damages / Returning vehicles / Replacement cars / Ordering progress (occasionally) / General complaints handling.

These services can be presented in a mash-up form where the driver is free to opt, adhering though to any constraints related to these services. When a driver contacts Driver Desk, he can have an inquiry for one or more of the offered services. This inquiry is handled as a case with the help of a Dynamic Case Management dashboard. The actual execution of each service is implemented as a traditional workflow with BPM techniques. An overview of the Driver Desk use case is shown in Fig. 4.

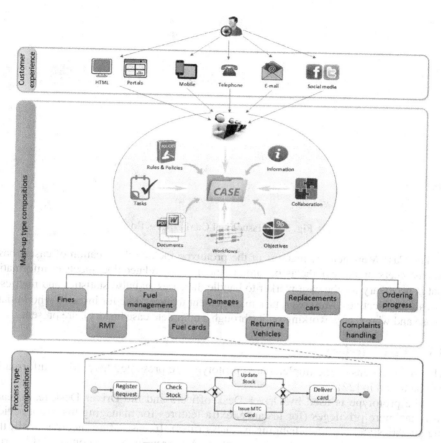

Fig. 4. Driver Desk overview

5.2   Business Processes Definition

The platform that facilitates our hybrid type of service compositions is based on the commercial Pega 7[2] tool, which combines both BPM and DCM capabilities. A cloud environment was used in order not to jeopardize information systems of LeaseCar company.

Pega 7 uses a stage-based approach to first define a high-level overview of the whole process. For each stage, steps are defined which in turn need to be specified into more detailed business process model.

Below, we present the internal business process (as a structured workflow) related to a corresponding service, the re-issue of a fuel card. The flow is rather straight-forward. We first have to cancel the existing fuel card and then issue a new one. Note here the existence of the "Cancel" sub-process which can be used also independently to run a card cancellation case. This flow is presented in Fig. 5.

---

[2] http://www.pega.com/products/pega-7, retrieved July 12th, 2015.

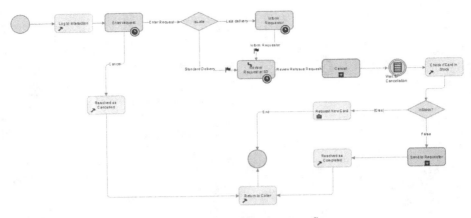

Fig. 5. Re-Issue Fuel Card process flow

The Case Management features of the prototype include the creation of cases (based on customers' inquiries), the association to them of any related documents or information that is necessary for the case worker to handle the cases and also statistics and metrics of cases and objectives. Moreover, task management features, like for instance who initiated a case and who is now working on it (through a complete case history), are present.

5.3   User Interface

The main screens of the implemented prototype are presented here. More information can be found in [22].

The prototype is used by Driver Desk officers and the Driver Desk team leader who has more privileges (for instance, extra features for managing his team, reviewing statistics and reports, changing business rules). In case of an incoming call, they look up the driver based on his license plate. After retrieving his contact, all the right information for the selected driver is presented in the screen below. This is the main dashboard which is the DCM part as presented in the overview of Fig. 4.

Fig. 6. Main screen for serving a driver

Information about driver's details, company's details in which he belongs, vehicle details and contract information are presented. A list with open cases for that specific driver and a list with past interactions are also available in order to allow the Driver Desk officer to serve the driver as efficiently as possible. After reviewing driver's data and getting his inquiry, a list of actions are available, corresponding to the services that Driver Desk can offer. This is available on the up left part of the dashboard and can be seen in Fig. 7.

Fig. 7. List of supported actions – services

Assuming for instance that the driver requests a list of fuel transactions on a predefined period, the corresponding service is executed as a number of workflow steps (not visible to the driver). As this is a service provided by an external partner, a web service is invoked to fetch the results as can been seen in Fig. 8.

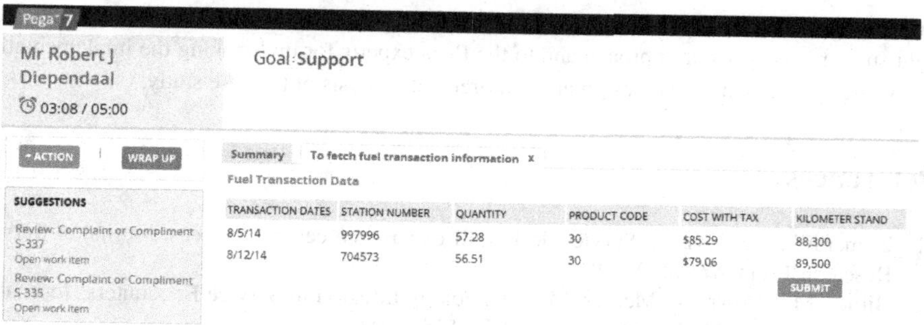

Fig. 8. Fuel Transactions results

6 Conclusion

Transitioning to a service-dominant world requires a major effort. Organizations need to engage into dynamic business networks with the aim to provide agile and flexible service compositions, as complete solutions to customer's problems. A well-structured framework for managing the complexity of service-dominant business is required. BASE/X is such an approach, consisting both of a conceptual and a tooling aspect for analysis and design.

The part of the BASE/X that we focus on our paper is the realization of service compositions, which is supported by automated service management systems. Business Process Management and Dynamic Case Management concepts and tooling, are already available to support the offering of service compositions. But since these two disciplines have inherently different characteristics, our approach is to combine them in such a way that capabilities of both are exploited. Thus, our contribution is both how to mix the two disciplines and also how to design such a mix based on a business-engineering framework.

However, this paper does not touch upon all aspects of BPM and DCM cycles. For instance, further research is needed on notations that can facilitate the modeling of the mixed service compositions.

To demonstrate the feasibility and usability of our approach, a prototype application for service management was built for the car leasing domain. A dashboard that handles drivers' inquiries on their lease cars is used for DCM purposes. On the other hand, BPM techniques are used for the invocation of services that are not visible to the customer. The combination of these two approaches offers the realization of service compositions, in accordance to BASE/X third layer of Fig. 3.

The prototype received positive feedback from professionals (enterprise architects and team managers who were involved in the project and could use such a tool) through discussions, as being suitable to facilitate flexible service compositions. Business people perceived it as an agile way to integrate various services as part of service compositions and make easily changes on business rules. To demonstrate more general applicability of our approach though, it has to be applied in other domains, like for example in healthcare, where the separation of business process types may not be so clear to allow for a hybrid type of service compositions.

Acknowledgements. Thanks go to the professionals of LeaseCar company who provided the right support to apply our approach and to the Pega experts for undertaking the implementation part while we focused on the design and requirement analysis of the case study.

References

1. Zomerdijk, L., Voss, C.: Service design for experience-centric services. Journal of Service Research **13**(1), 67–82 (2009)
2. Bitner, M., Brown, S., Meuter, M.: Technology Infusion in Service Encounters. Journal of the Academy of Marketing Science **28**(1), 138–149 (2000)

3. Patrício, L., Fisk, R., Falcão e Cunha, J., Cons, L.: Multilevel Service Design: From Customer Value Constellation to Service Experience Blueprinting. Journal of Service Research 14(2), 180–200 (2001)
4. Ezenwoye, O., Sadjadi, S.M.: TRAP/BPEL: a framework for dynamic adaptation of composite services. In: Proceedings of the International Conference on Web Information Systems and Technologies, Barcelona, Spain (2007)
5. Wu, Y., Doshi, P.: Making BPEL Flexible – Adapting in the Context of Coordination Constraints Using WS-BPEL. International Conference on Services Computing 1, 423–430 (2008)
6. Alexopoulou, N., Nikolaidou, M., Chamodrakas, Y., Martakos, D.: Enabling on-the-fly business process composition through an event-based approach. In: Proceedings of the 41st Annual International Conference on System Sciences, Hawaii, pp. 379–389 (2008)
7. Vanderfeesten, I.T., Reijers, H.A., van der Aalst, W.M.: Product based workflow support: dynamic workflow execution. In: Bellahsène, Z., Léonard, M. (eds.) CAiSE 2008. LNCS, vol. 5074, pp. 571–574. Springer, Heidelberg (2008)
8. van der Aalst, W.M.P., Adams, M., ter Hofstede, A.H.M., Pesic, M., Schonenberg, H.: Flexibility as a service. In: Chen, L., Liu, C., Liu, Q., Deng, K. (eds.) DASFAA 2009. LNCS, vol. 5667, pp. 319–333. Springer, Heidelberg (2009)
9. Herrmann, C., Kurz, M.: Adaptive case management: supporting knowledge intensive processes with IT. In: S-BPM ONE 2011, CCIS 213 (2011)
10. Lusch, R.F., Vargo, S.L.: The service-dominant mindset. In: Service Science, Management and Engineering Education for the 21st Century (2008)
11. Ostrom, A.L., et al.: Moving forward and making a difference: research priorities for the science of service. J. Serv. Res. 13 (2010)
12. Lusch, R.F.: Service-dominant logic: reactions, reflections and refinements. Mark. Theory (2006)
13. Grefen, P., Lüftenegger, E., Van der Linden, E., Weisleder, C.: BASE/X Business Agility through Cross-Organizational Service Engineering. Eindhoven University of Technology (2014)
14. Lee, R.G., Dale, B.G.: Business process management: a review and evaluation. Business Process Management Journal 4(3), 214–225 (1998)
15. Van der Aalst, W.M., ter Hofstede, A.H., Wesk, M.: Business process management: a survey. In: International Conference on Business Process Management (2003)
16. Hammer, M.: What is Business Process Management (2010)
17. Van der Aalst, W.M., Weske, M., Grünbauer, D.: Case Handling: A New Paradigm for Business Process Support. Data and Knowledge Engineering 53(2), 129–162 (2005)
18. Van der Aalst, W.M., Berens, P..: Beyond workflow management: product-driven case handling. In: Ellis, S., Rodden, T., Zigurs, I., (eds.) International ACM SIGGROUP Conference on Supporting Group Work, New York (2001)
19. Vanderfeesten, I., Reijers, H.A., Van der Aalst, W.M.: Product Based Workflow Design with Case Handling Systems (2007)
20. Strong, D.M., Miller, S.M.: Exceptions and exception handling in computerized information processes. ACM Transactions on Information Systems 13(2), 206–233 (1995)
21. Lunenbrug, F.C.: Organizational structure Mintzberg's framework. International Journal of Scholarly Academic Intellectual Diversity 14(1) (2012)
22. Traganos, K.: Designing a Standard Architecture for Service Management based on the BASE/X framework. Eindhoven, The Netherlands (2014)

Work-in-Progress Track

Data Movement in the Internet of Things Domain

Francesco D'Andria[1], Daniel Field[1], Aliki Kopaneli[2], George Kousiouris[2],
David Garcia-Perez[1], Barbara Pernici[3], and Pierluigi Plebani[3(✉)]

[1] Atos Spain SA, Avenida Diagonal 200, 08018 Barcelona, Spain
{francesco.dandria,daniel.field,david.garcia-perez}@atos.net
[2] Department of Electrical and Computer Engineering, National Technical University
of Athens, 9, Heroon Polytechniou Str., 15773 Athens, Greece
{alikikop,gkousiou}@mail.ntua.gr
[3] Politecnico di Milano, Piazza Leonardo da Vinci 32, 20133 Milan, Italy
{barbara.pernici,pierluigi.plebani}@polimi.it

Abstract. Managing data produced in the Internet of Things according to the traditional data-center based approach is becoming no longer appropriate. Devices are improving their computational power as the processors installed on them are more and more powerful and diverse. Moreover, devices cannot guarantee a continuous connection due their mobility and limitation of battery life.

Goal of this paper is to tackle this issue focusing on data movement to eliminate the unnecessary storage, transfer and processing of datasets by concentrating only the data subsets that are relevant. A cross-layered framework is proposed to give to both applications and developers the abstracted ability to choose which aspect to optimize, based on their goals and requirements and to data providers an environment that facilitates data provisioning according to users' needs.

Keywords: Data movement optimization · Internet of Things · Information and data quality

1 Introduction

Customised and Low Power Computing is a disruptive innovation which, while immediately of benefit to the established datacentre-centric model of the current IT world, opens the gate to many fields where datacentre-based computing is simply not appropriate. Predictions abound for the IoT, the Smart Everything Anywhere initiative and cyber-physical systems. In this scenario, applications must deal with the data deluge produced by this increasing amount of devices. To properly manage these big amounts of data, their quality needs to be certified, so the performance of mechanisms to access them must satisfy the developer requirements.

The goal of this paper is to propose a conceptual framework that tackles these issues as a basis to support the data movement optimization: how to select

© IFIP International Federation for Information Processing 2015
S. Dustdar et al. (Eds.): ESOCC 2015, LNCS 9306, pp. 243–252, 2015.
DOI: 10.1007/978-3-319-24072-5_17

what data to transfer, when and to where, in order to reduce the requirement for storage capacity and data processing capacity (reducing hardware requirements) and increasing the speed of producing meaningful output (performance), while guaranteeing data preservation where required. The approach is based on a cross-layer optimization framework enabling the data movement by introducing *data curators* as responsible for storing and managing data coming from the devices according to models able to match the data consumer requirements and the data providers capabilities. A programming abstraction is also proposed to ease the customization of devices and to hide the underlying mechanisms needed to access and to move the data in order to satisfy requirements on performances, data quality, energy, and security.

The rest of the paper is structured as follows. Section 2 motivates the need for data movement in IoT scenario. In Section 3 the envisioned cross-layer optimization framework is presented. Section 4 discusses a possible solution for managing the data movement optimization, while Section 5 introduces the metamodel supporting the programming abstraction that is at the basis of the framework. Finally, after a discussion on related work in Section 6, Section 7 concludes the paper outlining future extensions.

2   Motivation

IDC estimates that the digital universe will reach the size of 40ZettaBytes in 2020 [4] and IoT holds a significant role in this information deluge. It is now crucial to find methods and tools for making accessible these big data to the right users, at the right time, with the right quality, and easily. At the same time, customized and low-power computing devices will constitute the majority of these things, and their ever-increasing computational power opens the possibility to access to a potentially unlimited set of processors. Data movement optimization can take advantage of this situation by pushing part of the computation for optimization directly to the device in order to reduce the unnecessary storage, transfer and processing of datasets.

In a typical situation, data producers are responsible of managing and configuring devices, e.g., wearables, sensors, smartphones, single board computers, that produce data and that can be seen as data sources. Each of them has its own characteristics in terms of energy autonomy, storage size, and communication interface. On the other side, data consumers are responsible for developing and maintaining applications that need the data produced by devices. As the computational power of devices is continuously increasing, this approach does not really exploit all the potential at data sourcing layer, as the processors installed on the devices are not fully used. At the same time, due to the limitation in terms of storage and autonomy of energy, computation to be executed on the device needs to be properly balanced with respect to such limitations. Moreover, device storage limitation requires that data should move from more volatile storage systems (at device level) to more persistent ones, if data must be available for a longer period, for instance, for analysis purposes or for satisfying preservation requirements.

Data movement optimization is thus required to move data from devices that own fresh data - but limited in size - to more capable storage systems affordable only at data consumption layer, leaving the possibility for the devices to process data exploiting their computational power in order to reduce the amount of data transmitted to what is really useful for the user.

Deciding when, where, and how to move data between data sourcing layer and data consumption layer is not an easy task as it depends on several aspects. First of all, latency strictly depends on the usage: for some users, (e.g., real time applications) having timely data is crucial, for some other users (e.g., data analytics) even not so up-to-date data are considered sufficient. Data granularity depends on the user needs and the device should support the possibility of being configured to sample with different frequencies. Devices could not natively support data encryption, but users could request for an encrypted transmission, so it should be possible to install and run encryption modules on the device exploiting the processors on board. Last but not least, battery autonomy may influence the duration of the transmission and the proper amount of data to be transmitted should be calculated.

3   The Cross-Layer Optimization Framework

To be able to support data movement, taking into account the open issues discussed above, the presented approach enriches the data movement eco-system (see Figure 1) introducing data curators as key-players that mediate between the capabilities offered by the devices and the requirements posed by the consumer. Moreover, thanks to the metamodel supporting programming abstraction, the proposed approach eases the distribution of data processing among the layers to exploit the computational power now available at device layer also considering devices' limited resources.

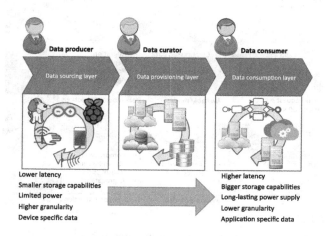

Fig. 1. Enriched data movement eco-system.

The data provisioning layer improves what the data sourcing layer offers with the possibility of additional computing power and storage, improving the quality of data provided in terms of accuracy, precision, and timeliness [11]. The higher the quality, the higher the value of the data provided and, at the same time, the higher the quality, the higher the amount of resources required, as well as costs. It is worth noting that although the role of the data curator is fundamental for having ready-to-use data with certified level of quality, with the proposed eco-system data consumers can keep accessing directly the data producers to obtain data, but without the possibility to have access to the services provided by the data curator. Moreover, the data movement can occur not only between layers, but also among peers referring to the same layer. For instance, data movement between embedded systems can be considered as a possible scenario, as well the migration of data between storage nodes living on two different platforms.

Figure 2 shows the envisioned cross-layer optimization framework supporting the enriched data movement eco-system. Each layer offers the possibility to access to the data specifying the data needed and the *goals* corresponding to the non-functional requirements (e.g., high accuracy, low energy consumption). Goals can be hard (must be satisfied) and soft (should be satisfied). To satisfy the request, each layer enables the data access according to one or more *modes*, each of them having different impacts in terms of performance, data quality, energy, and security [8]. For instance, compressed data involve more computation than uncompressed one, but it reduces the time for transmission. Secured data transmission ensures the integrity and confidentiality, but introduces an overhead before transmitting and after receiving data.

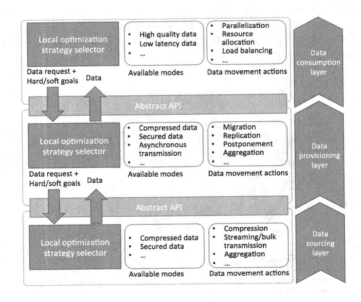

Fig. 2. Overall architecture

Data movement optimization is achieved at each layer by finding the best match between goals and modes considering that different users access the same data with different goals and according to different modes. Finding this match is the main task of the *local optimization strategy selector*, that identifies the best mode according to the user request and the current resource usage and exploiting the available *data movement actions*: layer-specific actions whose objective is to move data inside a layer or across layers to better support the data offering. For instance, at data sourcing layer, data movement actions concern the device configuration to support the transmission of compressed data or the aggregation of samples to reduce the amount of data to be transmitted.

As the data movement optimization may require some computation inside a layer to enable the execution of a mode, the proposed approach aims to exploit the full computing potential that devices installed can provide. At data sourcing layer, computing power of devices is continuously increasing and, usually, all the potential that the on-board processors can provide is not fully exploited. At data provisioning layer, servers install Advanced Processing Units (APU), such as GPUs, that can be used to execute the processing required by the data movement actions. For instance, if a device is not capable to compress data but compression is required, capabilities of the device can be extended by deploying code compliant to frameworks such as OpenACC or OpenCL, to ensure code portability. Such an extension can be directly done by the device owner when it has the skill to develop it, or even by the data curator that deploys the code to the device using the programming abstraction.

Data movement actions can also occur inside the same layer involving different peers exchanging data to better support the user request. Parameters as data proximity and data locality can be defined to move the relevant data set closer to the place in which the data will be used. For instance, at data provisioning layer, a data curator can decide to replicate a data set on different geographically distributed storage nodes to better support worldwide access. In this case, the data movement action does not have a correspondent mode, but its enactment will have an impact on the data access performance.

4   Optimizing Data Movement

To make explicit the relationship among the data movement actions, the modes and the goals are correlated through a data-movement/effects relationship map. This map defines the dependencies among the quality associated to data that a source can offer with respect to the effort required to provide those data. This map will include different types of indicators such as: (i) performance indicators that measure the efficiency of data manipulation (e.g., response time); (ii) data quality indicators that measure the effectiveness of applications (e.g., data accuracy); (iii) energy indicators that measure the resource impact of data accessing and storing (e.g., energy consumption per unit of work or per Kbyte); (iv) security indicators that define the level of trust, confidentiality, and integrity of the data. Dependencies between the goals and modes with the indicators will be defined to identify the effects on enacting a mode or requesting a goal in terms of data quality, energy, efficiency and security.

The indicators map constitutes the basis for this goal-based model, as it provides a way to specify the as-is and to-be scenarios of the system before and after the enactment of the data movement actions in terms of performance, data quality, energy, and security aspects. To pursue a data movement optimization all these variables need to be managed in a coherent way and their mutual dependencies need to be properly mapped. To this aim, goal-based models can be adopted to evaluate the impact of the data movement actions enacted [1].

Since it is difficult in the general case to design at run time all the possible relationships between indicators, learning tools, such as Bayesian Networks, can be used to derive the relations among the indicators and the goals, and to evaluate the effect of selecting a mode to provide data on these indicators [14].

A possible approach for performing dynamic correlations in service-based environments is discussed in [7]. In our case the models would be adapted as it appears in Figure 3. Available modes can be numerically encoded and introduced as inputs, along with device IDs, to indicate the used hardware. Inputs can also be considered any operation specific aspects that may affect e.g. the workload of the operation, like data size to be moved etc. The outputs should be the observed (in the case of training) or predicted effects on the defined indicators for the various goals (e.g., energy levels, performance timings etc.). Such observations may also be acquired at run-time through relevant annotations in the implemented modes, that may inject code to monitor the specific metrics. Through training with historical data the effect analysis models may be created and used a priori for optimized management and mode selection.

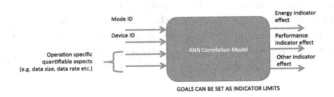

Fig. 3. Annotation correlation model

The role of the data-movement/effect relationship map is crucial in the data movement optimization at both local and global level. At local level, the map supports the data provider to identify the best mode to be proposed to satisfy the user goals and the possible effects of a data movement action on the goal satisfaction. At global level, the map provides a shared view for all the local decision-makers to understand the cross-layer effects of their local data movement actions. Furthermore, the effect of a specific mode (e.g., speed up factor following a parallelization pattern) may be quantified.

5 Metamodel Supporting the Programming Abstraction

To reduce the complexity for data curators and data consumers when accessing and manipulating data, a programming abstraction is offered. Data access provided by each layer will be offered through a single abstracted interface based on modes and goals: modes correspond to how data may be offered (e.g., compressed, aggregated), whereas goals correspond to the non-functional requirements (e.g., high accuracy, low energy consumption).

The programming abstraction is based on a metamodel to represent data sources characteristics, data consumer's requests, and related requirements. The metamodel is composed of the following elements, illustrated with some exemplifications:

- *data sources* : capabilities (for security, compression); resources (power usage, available storage, available main memory); layer (sourcing/provisioning)
- *data elements* description; characteristics:
  - data modes: compressed, aggregated (with parameters);
  - data properties: freshness/time span, update rate, locality, quality (accuracy)
- *data requests*: data elements with requested data modes and data properties; transmission mode (compressed/not compressed; secured/not secured; streamed/bulk); goals (energy efficiency, time constraints, ...)

Developers, when coding applications consuming the data, decorate with annotations the methods that access to the data with the goals (e.g., energy efficiency) to be satisfied. The local optimization strategy selector implements the logic that is able to identify the best source and the best mode to be invoked to satisfy the goal. In the example shown in Figure 4 , two possible sources could satisfy the request: one directly connected to the devices (for more recent data), another managed by a data curator that periodically collects the data (e.g., once a day, not shown in the figure) from the device and stores them into a permanent storage system to guarantee a longer persistence, but not providing up-to-date information. When the application requires for today's data, the abstract request is automatically instantiated to invoke the *getUncompressedData* offered by the data producer abstract API. If requested data are less recent, then two possibilities are open, i.e., with or without compression and the selection will be performed to satisfy the consumers goal.

To cope with additional requirements, the programming abstraction also supports the extension of capabilities provided by the devices. For instance, the developer explicitly asks for today's positions in a compressed format and with specific performance requirements in terms of data acquisition delay. As the device is the only source for this data, the possibilities for the selection are three: reading all the data uncompressed and compress them locally, deploy a standard compression module on the device to augment the available modes so that data can be sent already compressed or deploy an OpenCL implementation exploiting potential multicores (e.g. in a mobile device). Also in this case, the decision will depend on the trade-off analysis of the impact in choosing the best

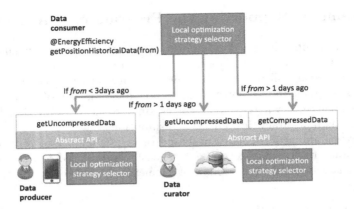

Fig. 4. Data movement strategy selection.

option considering that: initially, the more computation done at device layer, the more energy will be consumed with the risk of running out of power, secondly the use of OpenCL may guarantee performance requirements in terms of task completion or finally that the less data transmitted, the less energy consumed.

6 Related Work

The interest around the data movement topic is gaining more and more attention in the research community especially because of the diffusion of sensors and smart objects and the potentially unlimited computational power provided by Cloud solutions increased the amount of available data. As a consequence, data consumers have the possibility to access an enormous data set and proper mechanisms to optimize this access are required. Data movement techniques aim to achieve this goal especially focusing on moving data at the right time to the right place, where time and place refers to the user that needs the data. Bulk data transfer protocols [12] are usually adopted to quickly transfer massive amounts of data between storage systems geographically distributed but they do not solve the problem, as the applications that need these data are highly dynamic and data movement could be required frequently and with different properties. Live data migration aims to cover this space, and the work done in [13] goes in this direction although it focuses on an environment managed by a single entity. Data replication is another possible technique involved in the data management. Usually adopted in cloud computing domain to bring data closer to the user, data replication may have impact on the energy consumption: the more the replicas the higher the energy consumed. In this direction,[2] proposes an approach able to balance these two needs, i.e., replicas and low energy, relying on a specific power consumption model. At the same time, the gap between the I/O capacity and the computational power of the systems requires solutions for deciding which data needs to be moved and if pre-processing is required before the transmission. Data compression and data reduction mechanisms are adopted to reduce the amount of data to be transmitted without compromising the data quality, but requiring a computational effort before and after the transmission occurs. Another solution that is more focused on the device level is proposed in [3] where data collected by a sensor network are pre-processed before sending them to the storage node to reduce the energy consumption of the sensor networks without affecting the data quality requirements.

The cross-layered framework proposed in this work is based on a programming abstraction approach, to offer tools that will enable developers to limit their knowledge of the underlying layers, while achieving increased functionality levels. Especially using annotations, several work papers demonstrated the possibility to require and enforce optimization at code-level. In [5] annotations are used in software libraries as an effort for enforcing domain specific optimizations applied on them. The whole task is enabled via an annotation engine implemented as a compiler for translating the annotation semantics into code optimization. Following the same path, in [10] annotations are used for passing high-level semantic information to the compiler, in order to overcome performance issues resulting from the use of abstractions. From a slightly different point of view, [9] uses annotations via a source-to-source translation system aiming at optimizing MPI applications while [6] utilizes annotations (and an implemented annotation engine) in order to increase the speed of collaborative web applications development.

7 Concluding Remarks

The amount of smart devices is significantly increasing and, although they have an important role in causing the so called data deluge, they are also an opportunity to better manage the produced data. In this paper, we have focused on this perspective on Big Data, proposing a cross-layer framework whose main goal is to optimize the data movement.

The proposed framework enriches the usual approach by introducing the data curator as the actor in charge of mediating between the capabilities offered by the devices and the requirements posed by data consumers. Moreover, the framework supports the data movement optimization providing a programming abstraction that eases the interaction with the devices enabling the data access and their configuration to better exploit the devices' computational power.

As the proposed framework constitutes a first attempt to exploit the devices' capabilities inside the Big Data domain, future work will better investigate the impact on data movement optimization at local (inside a layer) and global (among layers) level. Validation on a real scenario is also planned to quantify the efficiency and the effectiveness of the proposed approach.

References

1. Asnar, Y., Giorgini, P., Mylopoulos, J.: Goal-driven risk assessment in requirements engineering. Requir. Eng. **16**(2), 101–116 (2011)
2. Boru, D., Kliazovich, D., Granelli, F., Bouvry, P., Zomaya, A.Y.: Energy-efficient data replication in cloud computing datacenters. Cluster Computing **18**(1), 385–402 (2015). http://dx.doi.org/10.1007/s10586-014-0404-x
3. Cappiello, C., Schreiber, F.A.: Quality- and energy-aware data compression by aggregation in wsn data streams. In: Proc. of the 2009 IEEE Int'l Conf. on Pervasive Computing and Communications, PERCOM 2009, pp. 1–6. IEEE Computer Society, Washington, DC (2009)
4. Gantz, J., Reinsel, D.: Extracting values from chaos. IDC, June 2011. http://www.emc.com/collateral/analyst-reports/idc-extracting-value-from-chaos-ar.pdf
5. Guyer, S.Z., Lin, C.: An annotation language for optimizing software libraries. In: Proc. of the 2nd Conf, on Domain-specific Languages, DSL 1999, pp. 39–52. ACM, New York (1999). http://doi.acm.org/10.1145/331960.331970
6. Heinrich, M., Grüneberger, F.J., Springer, T., Gaedke, M.: Exploiting annotations for the rapid development of collaborative web applications. In: Proc. of the 22nd Int'l Conf. on World Wide Web, WWW 2013, Rio de Janeiro, Brazil, pp. 551–560 (2013)
7. Kousiouris, G., Kyriazis, D., Gogouvitis, S., Menychtas, A., Konstanteli, K., Varvarigou, T.: Translation of application-level terms to resource-level attributes across the cloud stack layers. In: 2011 IEEE Symposium on Computers and Communications (ISCC), pp. 153–160, June 2011
8. Kousiouris, G., Menychtas, A., Kyriazis, D., Konstanteli, K., Gogouvitis, S., Katsaros, G., Varvarigou, T.: Parametric design and performance analysis of a decoupled service-oriented prediction framework based on embedded numerical software. IEEE Transactions on Services Computing **6**(4), 511–524 (2013)
9. Nguyen, T., Cicotti, P., Bylaska, E., Quinlan, D., Baden, S.B.: Bamboo: translating mpi applications to a latency-tolerant, data-driven form. In: Proceedings of the International Conference on High Performance Computing, Networking, Storage and Analysis, SC 2012, pp. 39:1–39:11. IEEE Computer Society Press, Los Alamitos (2012). http://dl.acm.org/citation.cfm?id=2388996.2389050
10. Quinlan, D., Schordan, M., Vuduc, R., Yi, Q.: Annotating user-defined abstractions for optimization. In: 20th International on Parallel and Distributed Processing Symposium, IPDPS 2006, p. 8, April 2006
11. Wang, R., Strong, D.: Beyond accuracy: What data quality means to data consumers. Journal of Management Information Systems **12**(4), 5–33 (1996)
12. Ren, Y., Li, T., Yu, D., Jin, S., Robertazzi, T., Tierney, B.L., Pouyoul, E.: Protocols for wide-area data-intensive applications: design and performance issues. In: Proceedings of the International Conference on High Performance Computing, Networking, Storage and Analysis, SC 2012, pp. 34:1–34:11. IEEE Computer Society Press, Los Alamitos (2012)
13. Tai, J., Sheng, B., Yao, Y., Mi, N.: Live data migration for reducing sla violations in multi-tiered storage systems. In: Proceedings of the 2014 IEEE International Conference on Cloud Engineering, IC2E 2014, pp. 361–366. IEEE Computer Society, Washington, DC (2014). http://dx.doi.org/10.1109/IC2E.2014.8
14. Vitali, M., Pernici, B., OReilly, U.M.: Learning a goal-oriented model for energy efficient adaptive applications in data centers. Information Sciences (2015)

Formal Verification of Virtual Network Function Graphs in an SP-DevOps Context

Serena Spinoso[1], Matteo Virgilio[1]([✉]), Wolfgang John[2], Antonio Manzalini[3], Guido Marchetto[1], and Riccardo Sisto[1]

[1] DAUIN - Politecnico di Torino, Turin, Italy
{serena.spinoso,matteo.virgilio,guido.marchetto,Riccardo.sisto}@polito.it
[2] Ericsson AB, Stockholm, Sweden
wolfgang.john@ericsson.com
[3] Strategy and Innovation - Future Centre, Turin, Italy
antonio.manzalini@telecomitalia.com

Abstract. The role of software and its flexibility is becoming more and more important in todays networks. New emerging paradigms, such as Software Defined Networking (SDN) and Network Function Virtualization (NFV), are changing the rules of the game, shifting the focus on dynamicity and programmability. Perfectly aligned with this new spirit, the FP7 UNIFY European project aims at realizing this appealing vision by applying DevOps concepts to telecom operator networks and supporting the idea of fast network reconfiguration. However, the increased range of possibilities offered by the DevOps approach comes at the cost of designing new processes and toolkits to make SDN and NFV a concrete opportunity. In this paper we specifically focus on the verification process as part of the challenging tasks that must be addressed in this scenario and its fundamental role of automatically checking some desired network properties before deploying a particular configuration. Our preliminary results confirm the feasibility of the approach and encourage future efforts in this direction.

Keywords: DevOps · Formal verification · Service graphs · Network function forwarding graph

1 Introduction

Ultra broadband diffusion, progresses in Information Technologies (IT), tumbling hardware costs and a wider and wider availability of open source software are shaping the evolution of Telecommunications and ICT infrastructures. In this context, paradigms such as Software Defined Network (SDN) and Network Function Virtualization (NFV) can be seen as expressions of a systemic trend called "Softwarization". Other expressions of the same trend are Cloud, Edge, and Fog Computing, Cloud Networking, etc. In essence, the disruptive innovation of "Softwarization" stands in the techno-economic feasibility of virtualizing most (if not all) network and service functions of Telecommunications and ICT

© IFIP International Federation for Information Processing 2015
S. Dustdar et al. (Eds.): ESOCC 2015, LNCS 9306, pp. 253–262, 2015.
DOI: 10.1007/978-3-319-24072-5_18

infrastructures. In this directions, it is argued that future Telecommunications infrastructures are likely to become highly dynamic, flexible and programmable production environments of ICT services. A first evaluation of this idea is carried out by the EU FP7 UNIFY[1] consortium, which sets out to integrate modern cloud computing and networking technologies by considering the entire network as a unified service production environment, spanning the vast networking assets and data centers of telecom providers. In order to reach a high level of agility for service innovation, UNIFY has one focus on providing dynamic service programming and orchestration, deploying logical service components, namely Virtual Network Functions (VNFs), across multiple network nodes. In particular, UNIFY architecture follows SDN principles with a logically centralized control and orchestration plane. Additionally, compute, storage and network abstractions are combined into a joint programmatic interface referred to as Network Function Forwarding Graph (NF-FG). An NF-FG defines a selected mapping of VNFs and their forwarding overlay definition into the virtualized resources presented by the underlying layer. Current OSS/BSS do not seem to cope with the requirements posed by this evolution: in fact, the operations of future Telecommunications infrastructures will involve the management and control of a myriad of software processes, rather than closed physical nodes. Thus, another important goal of UNIFY is the design and development of integrated operations and development capabilities under the name of Service Provider-DevOps (SP-DevOps). In fact, DevOps paradigm, formerly developed for Data Centers (DCs), is getting momentum as a source of inspiration regarding how to simplify and automate management processes for future Telecommunications infrastructures.

Among the above challenges, this paper focuses on the UNIFY verification process (i.e., the definition of methods and techniques to validate a particular network configuration before deploying it), which can be seen as an essential task in environments where reconfiguration of services is expected to be triggered very frequently, both in response to user requests and also in case of management events. Misconfiguration of dynamic network middleboxes[2], violation of specified network policies, or artificial insertion of malicious network functions are just examples of cases that a complete solution must properly handle in order to preserve network integrity and reliability. For this reason, the work presented in this paper goes in the direction of verifying complex graph of services through an intense modeling activity, targeted at the specific middleboxes and the network as a whole. We are motivated by the observation that most existing tools are "Openflow oriented", i.e. they mostly consider networks with a controller which installs <match, action> rules on the switches. Alternatively (and more generically but with the same fundamental limitations), they consider networks with devices that only perform forwarding decisions according to the packet header, i.e. without taking into account any additional traffic history information. Works as [5,6,9,11] fall in this category and represent a valuable efforts in this research area. Our contribution is intended to move a step forward and overcome the

---

[1] www.fp7-unify.eu

[2] In this paper we use the terms VNF and middlebox interchangeably.

above mentioned limitations by extending these works. In this sense, one important reference is [8], which tackles exactly the same problem and provides a scalable solution based on an off-the-shelf SMT solver. We experiment with this approach and further develop it to meet our specific requirements, also enriching the available VNF models catalog in order to satisfy the demands for more and more complex service graphs and to validate the approach with different kinds of VNFs. We specifically consider the UNIFY use cases, but it is worth noticing how our work is much general and easily applicable to other scenarios since it involves very common network functions.

The rest of the paper is organized as follows. First, we introduce and clarify how and to which extent the DevOps approach can be applied in a network operator infrastructure (Section 2). After defining the processes needed to implement this vision, we move on our current approach to formally verify complex and rapid deployments of network function chains including a variety of middleboxes, deployed to augment the set of in-network services the operator is able to offer to its final customers (Section 3). In order to show our approach is feasible, we provide some preliminary performance evaluation results based on the extension of the above mentioned tool (Section 4). Section 5 finally concludes this work by summarizing our contribution and drawing up some possible near future directions.

2   The SP-DevOps Concept

In order to cope with the high service velocity and increased dynamicity enabled by UNIFY and comparable SDN/NFV based environments, we consider a novel management and operation paradigm for Service Providers, called Service Provider DevOps - SP-DevOps. SP-DevOps is based on the same major underlying principles as identified for DevOps [10]: i) Monitor and validate operational quality; ii) Develop and test against production-like systems; iii) Deploy with repeatable, reliable processes; and iv) Amplify feedback loops. While we acknowledge that DevOps has also a crucial cultural dimension (reflected barely by the feedback loop principle), our work focuses on technical aspects associated to these principles, which reflect on processes and associated capabilities for integrated monitoring, verification, and testing software and programmable infrastructure. Even if significant parts of the telecommunication networks are foreseen to be virtualized in the future, we in [3] identified important characteristics of telecommunication networks that differ from traditional data centers, i.e.: (i) higher spatial distribution, as telecom resources are spread over wide areas due to coverage requirements; (ii) lower levels of redundancy in access and aggregation networks compared to the massive data centers of typical cloud computing companies; (iii) stronger requirements on high availability and latency in according to standards and customer expectations. These characteristics pose new challenges for applying DevOps principles in telecommunications environments [4]. SP-DevOps addresses them with a set of technical processes supporting developer and operator roles in a virtualized telecom network. Figure 1 illustrates the

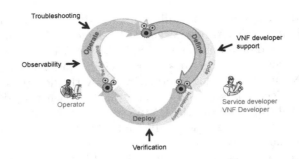

Fig. 1. SP-DevOps cycle for UNIFY service creation.

relation between the four SP-DevOps processes and the developer/operator roles by means of a service creation lifecycle. The four SP-DevOps processes follow the DevOps principles to meet specific challenges regarding Observability and Troubleshooting (Principle: Monitor and validate operation quality); Verification (Principle: Deploy with repeatable, reliable processes); and Development (Principle: Develop and test against production-like systems). We also identified three main roles involved in the processes: two Developer roles, where one is associated to a classical operator role assembling the service graph for a particular category of services (the Service Developer), and a second associated to the classical equipment vendor role in actually programming a VNF (the VNF Developer). The role of the Operator is to ensure that a set of performance indicators associated to a service are met when the service is deployed on virtual infrastructure within the domain of a telecom provider. SP-DevOps might not be a new form of DevOps as such, but it must include solutions that are uniquely tailored for the characteristics of its environment. Consequently, we propose the SP-DevOps Toolkit as an instantiation of the SP-DevOps concept [7]. The SP-DevOps Toolkit consists of a set of DevOps solutions that are developed targeting specific research challenges identified in the UNIFY production environment [3,4]. Besides scalable and programmable infrastructure monitoring functions, the toolkit will also provide modules for deploy-time functional verification of various abstraction levels of service definition, supporting the three SP-DevOps roles. As in any development process, identification of problems early in the service or product livecycle can significantly reduce times and costs spent on complicated debugging and troubleshooting processes. In this paper, we focus on verification with respect to the service definitions and configurations initiated by the Service Developer. Automated verification functions operating during deploy-time on each layer of the orchestration and control architecture, facilitate verification as part of each step in the deployment process, allowing identification of problems early in the service lifecycle.

3   The Verification Process

The SP-DevOps paradigm represents a significant opportunity for service providers to implement more complex services in their networks and increase the agility by which a new function (or a chain of) can be automatically configured and deployed in their infrastructure. However, while the process of inserting and/or modifying functions throughout the network can be automated with technologies similar to the ones used for the Cloud Computing scenario [2], great importance has also to be placed on the design and implementation of automatic tools that can verify a network configuration on the fly, *before* it is deployed. For example, an operator may want to ensure that a given traffic flow is permitted (or not permitted, due to a policy constraint) from one node to another. Concerning this last aspect, our verification process is currently based on a verification approach recently proposed in [8]. In order to achieve high performance, this verification approach exploits Z3 [1], a state of the art SMT solver, and translates network scenarios with multiple middleboxes into sets of First Order Logic (FOL) formulas that are then analyzed by Z3. This choice is motivated by the overall verification tool performance and scalability, which would be hard to achieve with standard model checking based techniques. In fact, the latter requires time and memory that usually increase exponentially with the system complexity, while the SAT-based approach proposed in [8] seems to be less prone to this problem. The FOL formulas given to Z3 represent the network operating principles along with the functional behavior of all the VNFs involved in the scenario being considered. While [8] presents the general ideas of the proposed approach, not all the details are fully developed, and not all the different situations that may arise when considering different kinds of VNFs are considered. Here, we present our preliminary work towards integrating the approach presented in [8] into a SP-DevOps context like the one of UNIFY. A considerable part of this work has been about developing models for new VNFs that were not explicitly considered in [8], and making some first experiments with them.

In our design, the formal verification task is split into multiple sub-tasks, so that the whole process is simpler and faster. More precisely, at NF-FG deploy time, or when the graphs undergo modifications in response to higher level events (e.g., administration events or user requests), the VNF chains composing the graph are computed and then, for each of them, a formal model is generated, including the model of all the involved VNFs. Finally, the verification engine processes the whole VNF chain model to check the satisfiability of a given property. In particular, this paper focuses on reachability problems in service graphs, leaving the verification of other network properties as possible future work. Furthermore, since we are using abstract models of the real middleboxes, we assume that these models are correctly defined. This means that we verify abstract models of the real middleboxes, considering them as faithful representations of the real VNFs. Verification of possible mismatch between a VNF model and its implementation is out of scope for the current prototype. For further details about the adopted formal verification theory and other background concepts, please refer to [8].

$$(send(cache, n_0, p_0, t_0) \land \neg isInternal(n_0)) \implies \neg isInCache(p_0.url, t_0)$$
$$\land \; p_0.proto = HTTP\_REQ \land \exists(t_1, n_1) \mid (t_1 < t_0 \land isInternalNode(n_1) \tag{1a}$$
$$\land \; recv(n_1, cache, p_0, t_1)), \forall n_0, p_0, t_0$$

$$(send(cache, n_0, p_0, t_0) \land isInternal(n_0)) \implies \; isInCache(p_0.url, t_0)$$
$$\land \; p_0.proto = HTTP\_RESP \land p_0.ip\_src = p_1.ip\_dest \land p_0.ip\_dest = p_1.ip\_src \land$$
$$\land \; \exists(p_1, t_1) \mid (t_1 < t_0 \land p_1.protocol = HTTP\_REQ \land p_1.url = p_0.url \tag{1b}$$
$$\land \; recv(n_0, cache, p_1, t_1)), \forall n_0, p_0, t_0$$

$$isInCache(u_0, t_0) \implies \exists(t_1, t_2, p_1, p_2, n_1, n_1) \mid (t_1 < t_2 \land t_1 < t_0 \land t_2 < t_0$$
$$\land \; recv(n_1, cache, p_1, t_1) \land recv(n_2, cache, p_2, t_2) \land p_1.proto = HTTP\_REQ \tag{1c}$$
$$\land \; p_1.url = u_0 \land p_2.proto = HTTP\_RESP \land p_2.url = u_0 \land isInternal(n_2))$$
$$\forall u_0, t_0$$

Fig. 2. Web cache model.

3.1   VNFs Models

The approach for modeling network function chains proposed in [8] has been experimented by the authors of [8] with some middlebox types, such as stateless and stateful firewalls. When modelling scenarios that include VNFs that may alter packets (e.g. a NAT), it is necessary to also consider the possibility for a target VNF to receive a packet different from the one originally transmitted. This kind of situation regards a significant set of middleboxes that is currently deployed in SP networks and that is envisioned to be included in the NF-FG within the UNIFY project, e.g. NAT, VPN gateway and so on. We revisited the network constraints developed by the authors of [8], by introducing the possibility of verifying reachability properties between two network nodes and intermediate VNFs that do modify forwarded packet headers. Finally, we checked that verification works as expected with these revisited constraints, by experimenting with the new middlebox models that we developed.

The first VNF we consider is a simple web cache (reported in Figure 2). The functional model consists of two interfaces connected respectively to the private network, i.e., the one which contains the clients issuing HTTP requests, and the external network. Formula 1a states that a packet sent from the cache to a node belonging to the external network, implies a previous packet, containing a HTTP request and received from an internal node, which cannot be served by the cache (otherwise the request would have not been forwarded towards the external network). Formula 1b states that a packet sent from the cache to the internal network contains a HTTP RESPONSE for an URL which was in cache when the request has been received. We also state that the packet received from the internal network is a HTTP REQUEST and the target URL is the same as the response. The final formula expresses a constraint that the *isInCache()* function must respect. In particular, we state that a given URL (u_0) is in cache at time t_0 if (and only if) a request packet was received at time t_1 (where $t_1 < t_0$) for that URL and a subsequent packet was received at time t_2 (where $t_2 < t_0 \land t_2 > t_1$) carrying the corresponding HTTP RESPONSE.

$$(send(nat, n_0, p_0, t_0) \land \neg isPrivateAddress(p_0.ip\_dest)) \implies p_0.ip\_src = ip\_nat$$
$$\land \exists(n_1, p_1, t_1) \mid (t_1 < t_0 \land recv(n_1, nat, p_1, t_1) \land isPrivateAddress(p_1.ip\_src)$$
$$\land p_1.origin = p_0.origin \land p_1.ip\_dest = p_0.ip\_dest \land p_1.seq\_no = p_0.seq\_no \tag{2a}$$
$$\land p_1.proto = p_0.proto \land p_1.email\_from = p_0.email\_from \land p_1.url = p_0.url)$$
$$\forall n_0, p_0, t_0$$

$$(send(nat, n_0, p_0, t_0) \land isPrivateAddress(p_0.ip_dest)) \implies \neg isPrivateAddress(p_0.ip\_src)$$
$$\land \exists(n_1, p_1, t_1) \mid (t_1 < t_0 \land recv(n_1, nat, p_1, t_1) \land \neg isPrivateAddress(p_1.ip\_src)$$
$$\land p_1.ip\_dest = ip\_nat \land p_1.ip\_src = p_0.ip\_src \land p_1.origin = p_0.origin$$
$$\land p_1.seq\_no = p_0.seq\_no \land p_1.proto = p_0.proto \land p_1.email\_from = p_0.email\_from \tag{2b}$$
$$\land p_1.url = p_0.url) \land \exists(n_2, p_2, t_2) \mid (t_2 < t_1 \land recv(n_2, nat, p_2, t_2)$$
$$\land isPrivateAddress(p_2.ip\_src) \land p_2.ip\_dest = p_1.ip\_src \land p_2.ip\_dest = p_0.ip\_src$$
$$\land p_2.ip\_src = p_0.ip\_dest), \forall n_0, p_0, t_0$$

Fig. 3. NAT model.

The second middlebox we modeled is the NAT function. The corresponding model is reported in Figure 3. In order to model the NAT behaviour, a distinction between the private and external network is needed. This separation is modeled by using a boolean function ($isPrivateAddress()$) that returns true if a given IP address belongs to the set of internal node addresses. Analyzing the reported formulas, we start by considering an internal node which initiates a communication with an external node (Formula 2a). In this case, the NAT sends a packet (p_0) to an external IP address, if and only if it has previously received a packet (p_1) from an internal node. The received and sent packets must be equal for all fields, except for the ip_src, which must be equal to the NAT public IP address.

On the other hand, the traffic in the opposite direction (from the external network to the private) is modeled by the Formula 2b. In this case, we state that if the NAT is sending a packet to an internal address, this packet (p_0) must have an external IP address as its source. Moreover, p_0 must be preceded by another packet (p_1 in the formula), which is, in turn, received by the NAT and it is equal to p_0 for all the other fields. It is worth noting that, generally, a communication between internal and external nodes cannot be started by the external node in presence of a NAT. As a consequence, this condition is expressed in the Formula 2b by imposing that p_1 must be preceded by another packet p_2, sent to the NAT from an internal node.

4   Preliminary Results

In order to evaluate the new developed models and the overall approach, we consider the NF-FG[3] shown in Figure 4 as a use case. In our reference graph, four end-hosts (two clients and two servers) can generate either HTTP or POP3 and also SMTP traffic, which is processed by different middleboxes when traversing the graph. Moreover, some of those network functions may require a different

---

[3] We do not provide the firewall VNF model as it was presented as use case in [8].

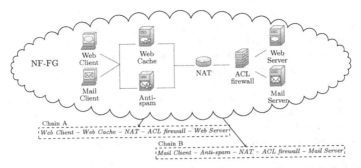

Fig. 4. An example of Network Function-Forwarding Graph.

configuration. Specifically, the NAT must be configured in order to know which hosts belong to the private network (as the web cache) and which IP address must be used as masquerading address; the firewall must be provided with a set of ACL entries that specify which couples of nodes are authorized to exchange traffic. Additionally, the forwarding is configured such that the web traffic is forwarded to the web cache, while the email traffic (both POP3 and SMTP) is routed to an anti-spam function. A first step towards the NF-FG verification is the VNF chains extraction. In our use case, two chains are extracted from the NF-FG (Figure 4): the *Chain A* processes the web traffic, while the *Chain B* is traversed by POP3 and SMTP packets.

We perform multiple tests on the two chains to cover different cases and configuration options: *(i)* anti-spam and firewall configurations and *(ii)* traffic directions (from client to server and vice-versa). Concerning the Chain A, only the ACL firewall can be configured, hence we setup two tests: one with the firewall configured to allow all the traffic (test A.1) and the other one with the firewall configured to drop all packets exchanged between the web client and server (test A.2).

Instead the Chain B is tested in three scenarios, obtained by changing the firewall and anti-spam configurations as follows: *(i)* test B.1, similarly to test A.1, is performed without any function configured to drop the received traffic; *(ii)* in test B.2, the firewall drops the traffic between the mail client and server (Figure 5); *(iii)* test B.3 is such that the anti-spam is configured to drop all the emails sent by the mail client, while the traffic originated by the server is allowed (Figure 5). Our evaluation is executed on a workstation with 32GB of RAM and an Intel i7-3770 CPU running an Ubuntu 14.04.01 with kernel 3.13.0-24-generic. The results are shown in Figure 5, where the verification time is reported for each presented scenario.

In test A.1 the reachability problem from the client to the server (the light grey colored bar in Figure 5) is satisfied as expected. It is worth noting that the unsatisfiability of the problem in the opposite direction (the dark grey colored bar in Figure 5) is due to the fact that client and server can exchange traffic only if the connection is initiated by the client. In test A.2, in both cases the reachability problems are not satisfied because of the firewall VNF configuration.

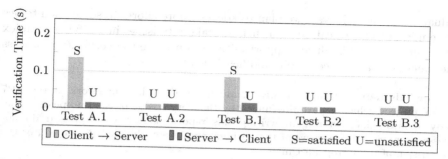

Fig. 5. Test {A, B}.1: firewall and anti-spam configured to accept packets; **Test {A, B}.2**: firewall configured to drop server/client packets; **Test B.3**: anti-spam configured to drop server/client packets.

In test B.1, the verification problem is satisfiable in case of traffic sent by the mail client, while the reachability property is not verified for the traffic sent by the mail server for the above-mentioned reasons.

As it can be seen from the achieved results, performance is promising also in the worst case scenario, since we are able to solve the reachability problem in less than 200ms, while the verification time is less than 50ms in most cases. This is reasonably in line with the UNIFY requirements, especially in terms of time required by the verification process to authorize a newly asked network reconfiguration.

5   Conclusion

It is argued that in the future Telecommunications infrastructures are likely to become highly dynamic, flexible and programmable production environments capable of providing any ICT services. Future operations will involve the management and control of a myriad of software processes, rather than closed physical nodes.

In fact, today most SPs still have rather complicated and static operational processes. DevOps, formerly developed for managing Data Centers (DCs), is attracting a growing interests as a paradigm to be extended to future Telecommunications infrastructures. Nevertheless, it is argued that the DevOps will jump ahead current ossification only if it will be sustainable from a business viewpoint (CAPEX, OPEX saving are not enough): importantly DevOps criteria of success depend on how closely the related future infrastructures (e.g. UNIFY) will be capable of enabling new service paradigms for SP's (e.g., Immersive Communications, Anything as a Service, etc). Motivated by these considerations, in this paper we presented our initial contribution related to the verification process on service graphs, which is one of the most important pillars in the SP-DevOps feedback cycle. After generalizing the applicability of a state of the art approach to the verification of complex network graph, we presented and discussed a couple of models we developed to validate our key ideas. Given the promising evaluation results achieved, we plan to address more efforts to some open topics in the middlebox verification area such as scalability issues in verifying complex service graphs and significant opportunities to optimize the verification process when incremental service graph modifications come into play.

Acknowledgments. This work was conducted within the framework of the FP7 UNIFY project, which is partially funded by the Commission of the European Union. Study sponsors had no role in writing this report. The views expressed do not necessarily represent the views of the authors' employers, the UNIFY project, or the Commission of the European Union.

References

1. de Moura, L., Bjørner, N.S.: Z3: An efficient smt solver. In: Ramakrishnan, C.R., Rehof, J. (eds.) TACAS 2008. LNCS, vol. 4963, pp. 337–340. Springer, Heidelberg (2008)
2. Jain, R., Paul, S.: Network virtualization and software defined networking for cloud computing: A survey. IEEE Communications Magazine **51**(11), November 2013
3. John, W., Meirosu, C.: Unify d4.1: Initial requirements for the sp-devops concept, universal node capabilities and proposed tools (2014). https://www.fp7-unify.eu/index.php/results.html#Deliverables
4. John, W., Pentikousis, K., Agapiou, G., Jacob, E., Kind, M., Manzalini, A., Risso, F., Staessens, D., Steinert, R., Meirosu, C.: Research directions in network service chaining. In: 2013 IEEE SDN for SDN4FNS, November 2013
5. Kazemian, P., Varghese, G., McKeown, N.: Header space analysis: Static checking for networks. In: NSDI 2012. USENIX, San Jose (2012)
6. Khurshid, A., Zou, X., Zhou, W., Caesar, M., Godfrey, P.B.: Veriflow: Verifying network-wide invariants in real time. In: NSDI 2013. USENIX, Lombard (2013)
7. Meirosu, C.: m4.1: Sp-devops concept evolution and initial plans for prototyping (2014). https://www.fp7-unify.eu/index.php/results.html#Deliverables
8. Panda, A., Lahav, O., Argyraki, K.J., Sagiv, M., Shenker, S.: Verifying isolation properties in the presence of middleboxes. CoRR abs/1409.7687 (2014)
9. Porras, P., Shin, S., Yegneswaran, V., Fong, M., Tyson, M., Gu, G.: A security enforcement kernel for openflow networks. In: HotSDN 2012. ACM, New York (2012)
10. Sharma, S., Coyne, B.: DevOps For Dummies. Limited IBM Edition' book, October 2013
11. Son, S., Shin, S., Yegneswaran, V., Porras, P.A., Gu, G.: Model checking invariant security properties in openflow. In: ICC, pp. 1974–1979. IEEE (2013)

Author Index

Printed in the United States
By Bookmasters